S/4 P

PRACTICAL SKILLS IN

BOBBIN LACE

PRACTICAL SKILLS IN

BOBBIN LACE

Bridget M. Cook

B.T. BATSFORD LTD · LONDON

ISBN 0 7134 4366 9

Typeset by Tek-Art Ltd, Kent
and printed in Great Britain
by Courier International Ltd
Tiptree, Essex
for the publishers
B.T. Batsford Ltd
4 Fitzhardinge Street
London W1H 0AH

CONTENTS

GLOSSARY

Arrow Markings
On diagrams these indicate the hanging on of new pairs (fig. 1).

Cross
Cross left-hand thread over right-hand thread (fig. 2).

Footside
This term usually indicates a straight edge.

Halfstitch
Figures on diagram refer to positions of threads only and not to the bobbins. They must therefore be recounted before each move. Cross 2 over 3, twist 2 over 1 and 4 over 3 (fig. 3).

Headside
Usually a curved edge on the opposite side of a footside.

Leaf
Woven in a way resembling a leaf (fig. 4).

Numbering
When the threads are numbered, start counting on the left-hand side and count to the right-hand side. The threads need to be renumbered after each movement of the bobbins (fig. 5).

Passive
Inactive pairs through which the worker passes.

Picot
There are several types of picot, but, basically, these are twisted loops.

Pin
Illustrated in this book as a black spot or alternatively drawn or pictured (fig. 6).

Sewing
Joining one section to another, by use of a hook or needlepin to pull a loop through the pin hole of the worked side, and then threading the bobbin of the worker through this loop (fig. 7).

Tallies
Woven shapes.

Thread
Drawn in this book either as two parallel lines, or, as a single black line (fig. 8).

Twist
Twist right-hand thread over left-hand thread (fig. 9).

Whole stitch
Figures on the diagram refer to the position only and not to the bobbins. Cross 2 over 3, then twist 2 over 1 and 4 over 3, then cross 2 over 3 (fig. 10)

Windmill
Whole stitch, carried out with two threads at all times but treated as one (fig. 11).

Worker
The active pair, also called weavers or travellers by some lacemakers.

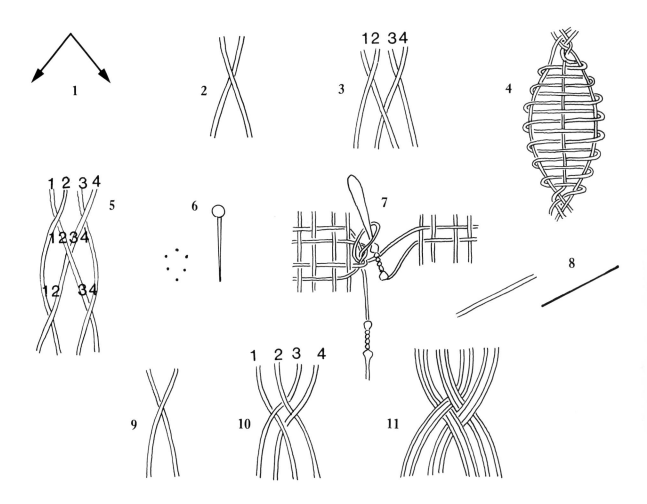

INTRODUCTION TO EQUIPMENT

1

EQUIPMENT PILLOWS

Lace is constructed on a pillow, and these pillows can be of various shapes and sizes. Essentially they must be firm enough to hold the lace well, yet at the same time allowing pins to be inserted without too much difficulty and be capable of standing firmly in the cushion to hold the work. Nowadays, with many lace suppliers, these pillows can be easily purchased and the advanced lacemaker will possess pillows of several designs (see fig. 1).

COVER CLOTHS

These cloths are normally firm, dark pieces of material used for covering the lace and for placing beneath the bobbins. The cloths can be frequently laundered in order to keep the lace clean during the progress of the work.

BOBBINS

The type of bobbin in common use today in the U.K. is a slim, straight bobbin with a head to hold the thread and a ring of spangled beads to weight the shaft. They are normally wood or bone, but plastic is also in fairly common use for the cheaper bobbin. For Honiton Lace the bobbin normally has no double head and is a simple shaft, tapered towards the bottom end with no spangled beads. Other than these two types of bobbins there are an infinite variety of others used throughout the world, with which local lacemakers will be familiar. (See fig. 2 for a selection of varieties.)

THREADS

Any type of thread is currently used in lacemaking. Normally one would expect to find natural fibre threads such as cotton, linen or silk. For exotic work silver or gold thread can be used and nowadays a mixture with man-made fibres is in frequent use. It is important that the threads should not be capable of stretching as, after the lace has been made, the tension will affect the stability of the lace.

PINS

Place pins are made of brass. Other kinds would rust in the pillow – and cause iron mould on the lace being constructed, if left for some time. The pins should be suitable in size for the lace being worked.

PATTERNS

Patterns are normally drawn or photocopied on pricking card, which should be fairly stiff and in a muted colour so that the work, when in position, can be easily seen and is restful to the eyes.

BOBBIN WINDER

There are numerous varieties of bobbin winders on the market to assist the lacemaker in winding the thread on to the bobbin. Many lacemakers still prefer to wind by hand.

PRICKER

This tool is used for pricking the pattern and needs to be no taller than the pin. Perhaps a steel needle held in a pin vice, and of similar thickness but firmer, is ideal.

SEWING TOOLS

A fine crochet hook, wig maker's needle or needle pin – which is a fine needle with a handle – will be necessary in order to make the sewings in lace. A needle pin is a very fine needle with the eye inserted in a handle and the tip then used in the same manner as a hook.

STARTS AND EDGES

1 Winding the bobbin.
Hold an end of the thread against the neck of the bobbin. Wind the thread in a clockwise direction around the bobbin neck, securing the loose end (see fig. 1a). The neck should be completely (but not over) filled and a single half-hitch is tied to secure it.

Make a loop in the thread (see fig. 1b) and slip the head of the bobbin into this loop and pull tight (see fig. 1c). As bobbins are usually wound in pairs, wind off sufficient thread from the supply to fill equally another bobbin in the same manner, leaving about 15cm of thread between the two bobbins thus wound (see fig. 1d).

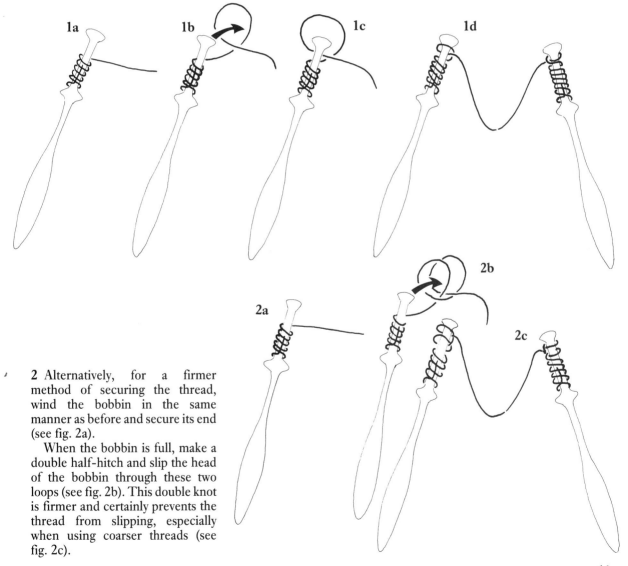

2 Alternatively, for a firmer method of securing the thread, wind the bobbin in the same manner as before and secure its end (see fig. 2a).

When the bobbin is full, make a double half-hitch and slip the head of the bobbin through these two loops (see fig. 2b). This double knot is firmer and certainly prevents the thread from slipping, especially when using coarser threads (see fig. 2c).

11

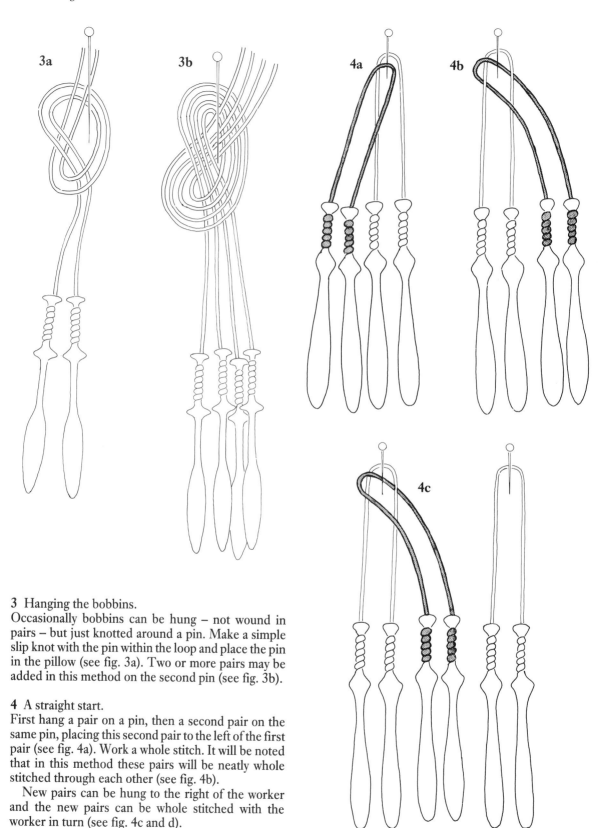

3 Hanging the bobbins.

Occasionally bobbins can be hung – not wound in pairs – but just knotted around a pin. Make a simple slip knot with the pin within the loop and place the pin in the pillow (see fig. 3a). Two or more pairs may be added in this method on the second pin (see fig. 3b).

4 A straight start.

First hang a pair on a pin, then a second pair on the same pin, placing this second pair to the left of the first pair (see fig. 4a). Work a whole stitch. It will be noted that in this method these pairs will be neatly whole stitched through each other (see fig. 4b).

New pairs can be hung to the right of the worker and the new pairs can be whole stitched with the worker in turn (see fig. 4c and d).

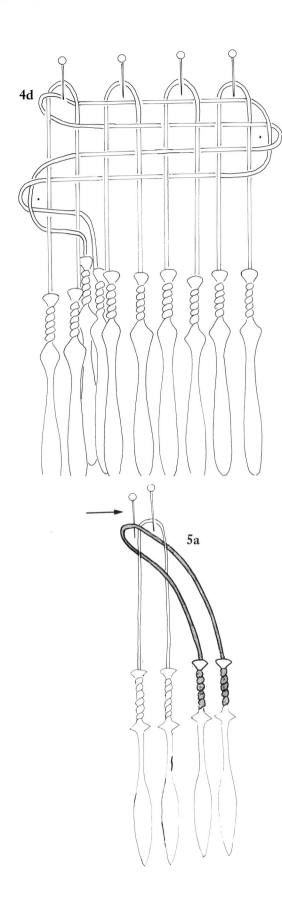

4d

5 Another way of starting is to place two pairs on two pins close together. These pairs will then whole stitch through each other (see fig. 5a).

New pairs can then be hung to the right of the worker and the work whole stitched through them in turn. It will be noted that there are small loops at the end of the row still left at the top where the pairs were hung around the pin (see fig. 5b).

Occasionally these loops are not required and they can be removed by working two rows, then pulling out the pin. Place the pin under the first whole stitched row and then pull each pair evenly to eliminate the loops (see fig. 5c).

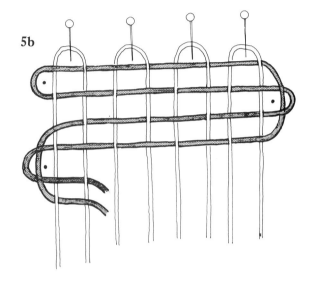

5b

5a

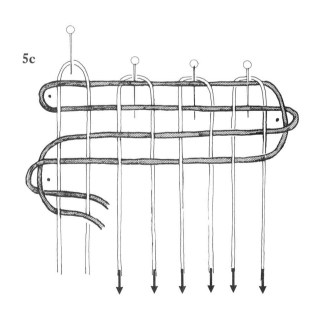

5c

6 Alternatively, in order to remove the loops, whole stitch the first two pairs together.

Hang a new pair to the right of the worker and place the right thread of the worker over the pin and down between the new pair (see fig. 6a). By this action the first stage of the whole stitch has been worked – bobbin 2 over 3, or a cross, has been made. Complete the whole stitch (see fig. 6b). Another pair may be

hung on the right and the process repeated (see fig. 6c).

At the end of the row the workers will be twisted right-over-left around the turning pin (see fig. 6d). Similarly, when working from right to left, the bobbins are hung in the same manner with the first pair on the right and the second pair on the left (see figs 6d and 6e, with the whole row shown at 6f).

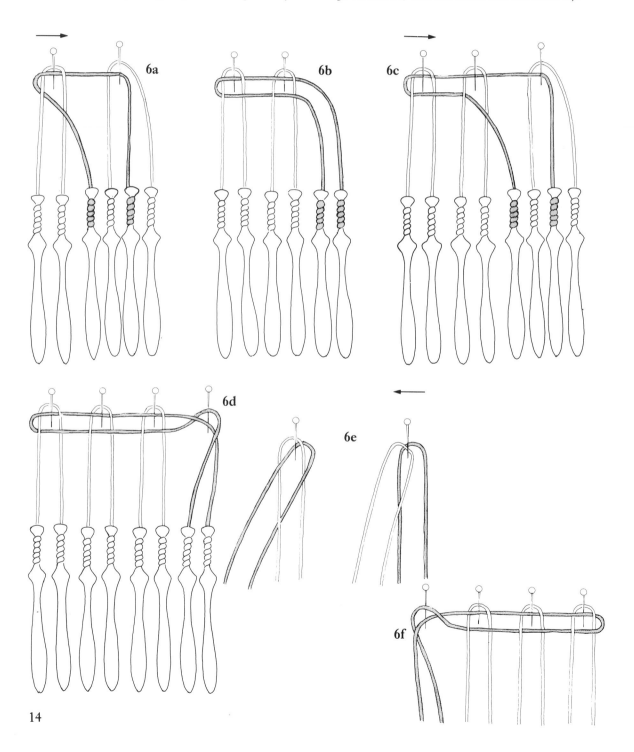

7 A Selvege.

To make a selvege (a hem) at the beginning of a piece of lace, hang as many bobbins as are required to work the lace in a straight row. Work four rows in whole stitch across all these pairs, making a footside on each side. Twist all pairs once and work another four rows in whole stitch, keeping the footside edge.

Twist all passives once and repeat again, working four rows and twisting the passives once. The pattern can then be worked as designed. When the lace is completed this selvege start can be folded like a hem on itself on the twisted rows and sewn along the final edge to produce a firm selvege (see fig. 7a).

7a

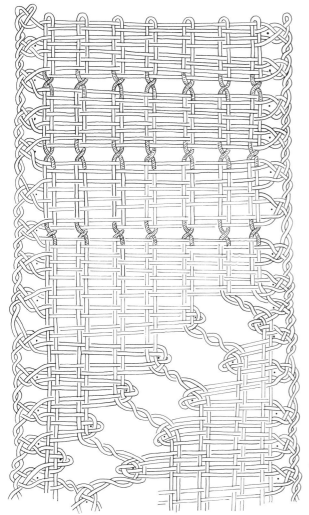

8 To start many pairs when massed together – as in a tape or heading.

Support a slightly longer pin between two upright pins and hang the pairs needed on to the longer pin. At the end of the work, if this is to be joined, it is quite easy slowly to slip loop by loop off this pin as the join progresses; the bobbins will remain in the correct order (see fig. 8a).

8a

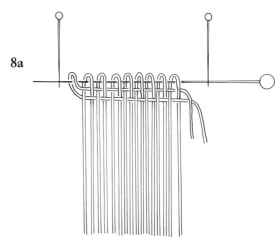

9 Starting diagonally in net.

When starting on the diagonal the footside and the passives are worked first. Then each new pair can be hung diagonally above where it is required on a pin. These pins can then either be left in and the loops formed around them be used for joining the end of the work, or, if preferred, these pins can be treated as temporary and, after working a row, be removed and the threads gently pulled down to provide a diagonally straight start (see fig. 9a).

9a

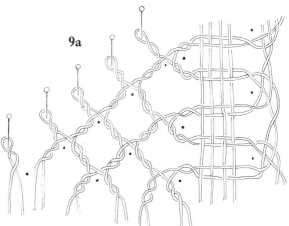

10 Starting a straight net ground. The footside and the passives are started first. Temporary pins are placed above the work and the first row of the lace is worked. The temporary pins will be removed and the threads gently pulled to give a straight start (see fig. 10a).

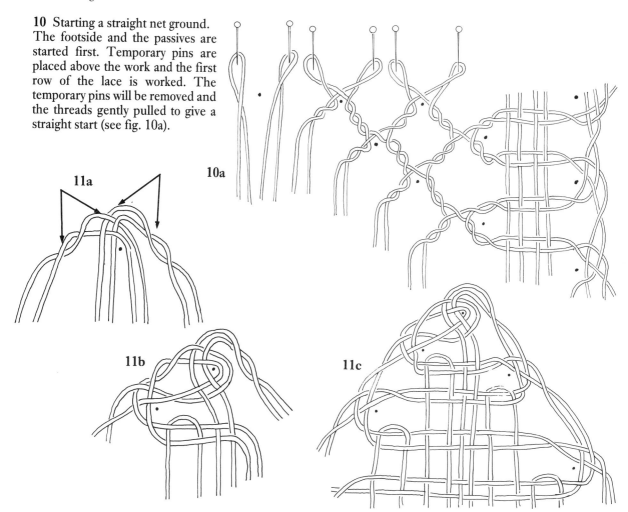

11a

10a

11b

11c

11. Starting at a point.

Insert two temporary pins with two pairs on either side above the work. Whole stitch the centre two pairs and place a pin supporting this whole stitch (fig. 11a). Whole stitch these two pairs again. Twist the two left hand pairs of bobbins and whole stitch these together. Support on a pin and twist them both. The right-hand bobbin is now the worker.

Pairs can be added on to the worker as it travels across the work (see fig. 11b). Complete the footside on the right-hand side and work back, adding pairs as required (see fig. 11c).

12 Starting at a point without a footside.

Hang two pairs around the pin and twist them twice – (see fig. 12a).

Whole stitch these two pairs together – (see fig. 12b). Hang two pairs on the first pin on the right-hand side and twist these twice.

With the right-hand bobbin from the first pair, whole stitch through these two pairs and twist the worker (see fig. 12c). The two pairs just worked should then be whole stitched through each other and left. Add two new pairs on the first pin on the left-hand side; the worker from the top pair whole stitches through them (see fig. 12d). The third pair from the right now whole stitches through the last two pairs just added. These two pairs are then whole stitched through each other and the right-hand pair becomes the worker and progresses to the right (see fig. 12e).

Add pairs in the same way until the desired width of the piece is reached (see fig. 12f).

13 Starting at a point but adding pairs on the inside of the passive trail.

Hang two pairs on two temporary pins above the work. Whole stitch the centre two pairs together and pin (see fig. 13a). Whole stitch them again. Hang two more pairs to the right on a temporary pin above the edge, twist the right-hand pair at the top and whole stitch this pair through the left-hand pair of those hung on the temporary pin. Place a pin between them

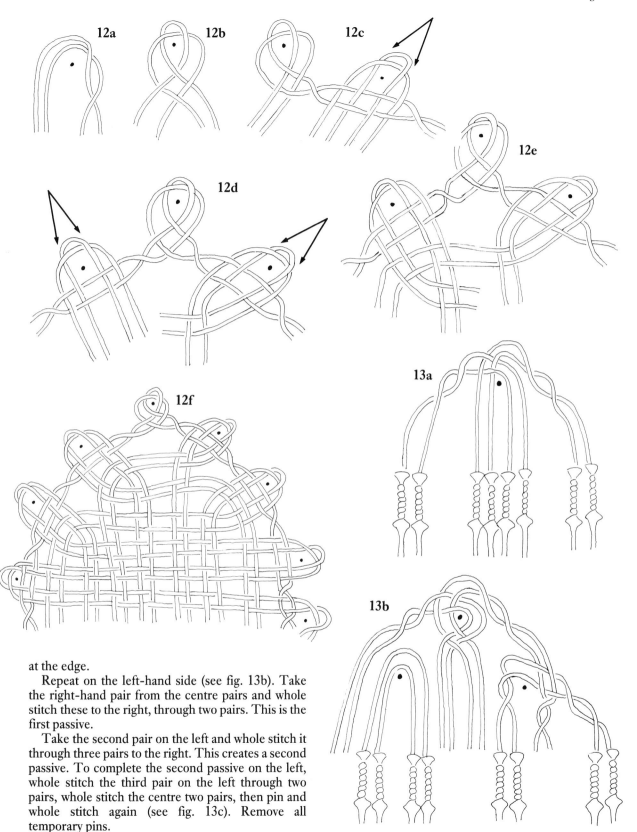

at the edge.

Repeat on the left-hand side (see fig. 13b). Take the right-hand pair from the centre pairs and whole stitch these to the right, through two pairs. This is the first passive.

Take the second pair on the left and whole stitch it through three pairs to the right. This creates a second passive. To complete the second passive on the left, whole stitch the third pair on the left through two pairs, whole stitch the centre two pairs, then pin and whole stitch again (see fig. 13c). Remove all temporary pins.

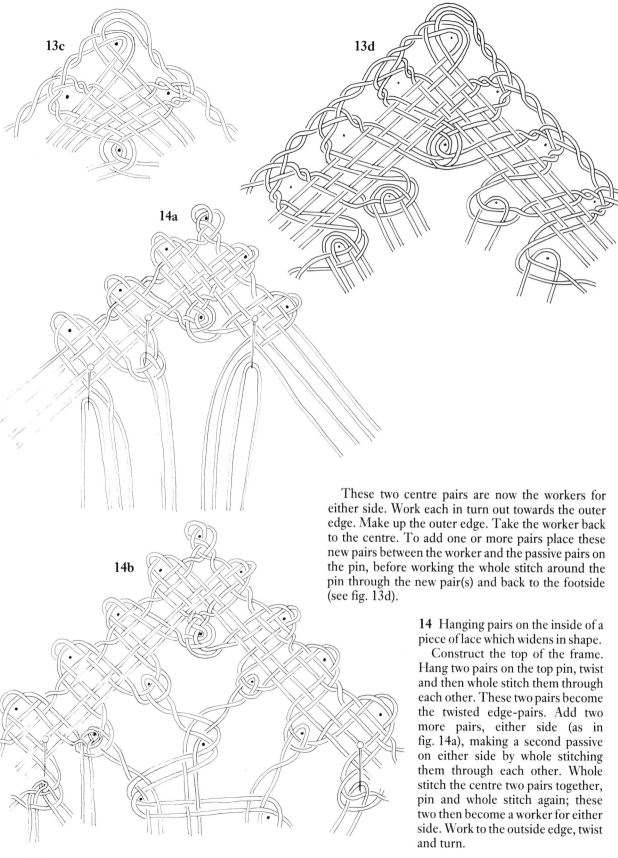

13c

13d

14a

14b

These two centre pairs are now the workers for either side. Work each in turn out towards the outer edge. Make up the outer edge. Take the worker back to the centre. To add one or more pairs place these new pairs between the worker and the passive pairs on the pin, before working the whole stitch around the pin through the new pair(s) and back to the footside (see fig. 13d).

14 Hanging pairs on the inside of a piece of lace which widens in shape.

Construct the top of the frame. Hang two pairs on the top pin, twist and then whole stitch them through each other. These two pairs become the twisted edge-pairs. Add two more pairs, either side (as in fig. 14a), making a second passive on either side by whole stitching them through each other. Whole stitch the centre two pairs together, pin and whole stitch again; these two then become a worker for either side. Work to the outside edge, twist and turn.

Insert a pin and hang a new pair between the worker and the passives. Whole stitch the worker through the new pair and work to the outer edge, and return to the centre where another pair can be added if required.

If more pairs are required at any pin hole these may be added at each pin, but for the best results four pairs should be the maximum or there is the danger of a lump being formed. (Fig. 14b shows two pairs added on the right-hand side.)

15 Hanging pairs on the inside of a piece of lace which widens in shape in a different manner.

Work frame as for Method 14. To add the pairs, simply slip the new pair over the worker before the worker returns after having worked the inner pin (see fig. 15a).

It will be noted that adding pairs in this way will take up less room. Therefore, if more pairs are needed at a pin hole, either two, three or four can be introduced and will lie flat when the work is completed (see fig. 15b).

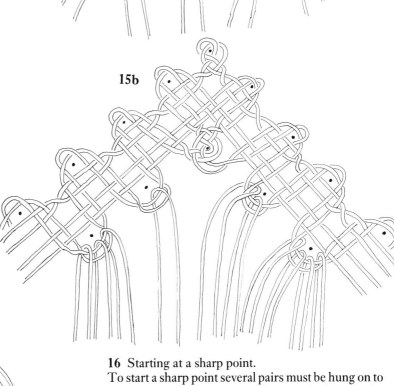

16 Starting at a sharp point.

To start a sharp point several pairs must be hung on to the top pin at the same time. These can be hung in the form of a horseshoe, starting with the first pair being hung on the pin and the second pair flanking it on either side. Continue adding pairs until the required number are achieved, usually an average of about six pairs (see fig. 16a).

Starting on the left, twist each pair of threads twice. It will be noted that these are not the original pairs but the threads adjacent to each other. Then, with the extreme left-hand pair of bobbins, work across to the right-hand side. These can be either treated as a footside or can go around the pin (see fig. 16b). As the

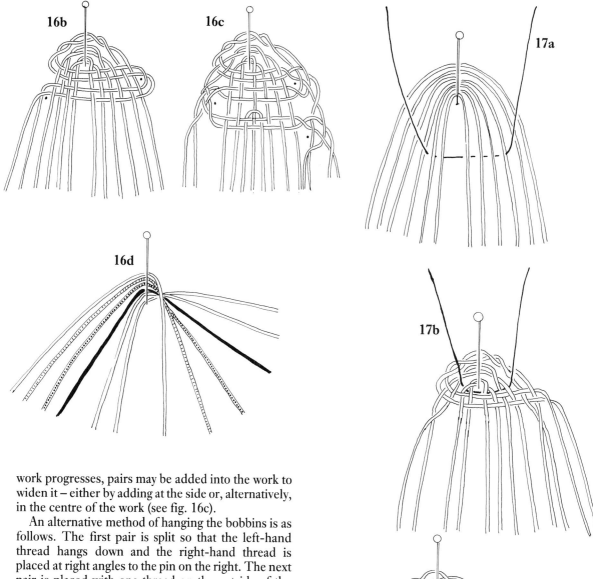

16b 16c 16d 17a 17b 17c

work progresses, pairs may be added into the work to widen it – either by adding at the side or, alternatively, in the centre of the work (see fig. 16c).

An alternative method of hanging the bobbins is as follows. The first pair is split so that the left-hand thread hangs down and the right-hand thread is placed at right angles to the pin on the right. The next pair is placed with one thread on the outside of the left-hand thread and inside the right-hand thread (see fig. 16d). This forms a tight loop at the top which is often needed if the piece of work is to be joined, as a single loop assists this joining process.

17 Starting at a sharp point but adding a gimp cordonnet.

Place a pin in the top hole of the pattern. Pairs are hung on the pin in sequence (as in fig. 16d). To add in the gimp, set aside two pairs of workers on one side and one pair on the other.

Slide the gimp pair up under all the centre bobbins and put over the work and to the back of the pillow (see fig. 17a). If there are fewer pin holes on one side than on the other, set aside the two pairs of workers on that side ready to commence work. Work across to the

other side and make up the edge (see fig. 17b). Lay down the gimp thread and work across, using this gimp thread as the outside thread on either side (see fig. 17c).

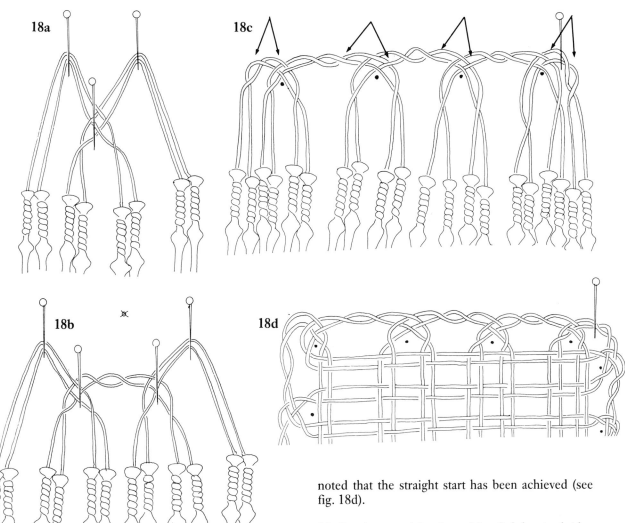

noted that the straight start has been achieved (see
fig. 18d).

19 Starting a straight piece with a slightly raised ridge
effect

Hang two pairs on each of two temporary pins
above the work – whole stitch the centre two pairs and
place a pin between them at the inner junction of the
corner. A cordonnet and a spare pair are whole
stitched through the two centre pairs (see fig. 19a).
The two centre pairs are then whole stitched through
each other and the pair which now lies on the right is
whole stitched through the cordonnet and thread.

Hang a new pair on this whole stitch pair and make
up the edge with the outside right-hand pair from the
start (see fig. 19b). Whole stitch the spare pair and the
edge-pair through the cordonnet and thread. Whole
stitch these together. Whole stitch the pair sitting
inside the cordonnet and single thread through the
two pairs just whole stitched, and through the
cordonnet and single thread. Add a new pair on to this
pair and make up the edge with it (see fig. 19c).
Continue, adding and making up the edge along the
top, until the desired width is obtained. Then work as

18 Starting a straight piece of work with a footside at
the top as well as the edges.

Hang two pairs on each of two temporary pins
above the work and whole stitch the centre two pairs.
Place a pin between them (fig. 18a). Twist these pairs
and leave. Twist the right-hand pair and hang the two
new pairs on a temporary pin above them.

Whole stitch the twisted pair and the nearest new
pair to it. Place a pin supporting this whole stitch and
twist both pairs. Remove the temporary centre pin and
pull gently (see fig. 18b).

Continue adding pairs across the work and
removing the temporary pins until the desired width is
achieved. A temporary pin can be placed supporting
the outside bobbins at the apex of the corners to give
a sharper corner (see fig. 18c).

Take the second pair from the left as workers.
Work across the work and make up the edge. It will be

21

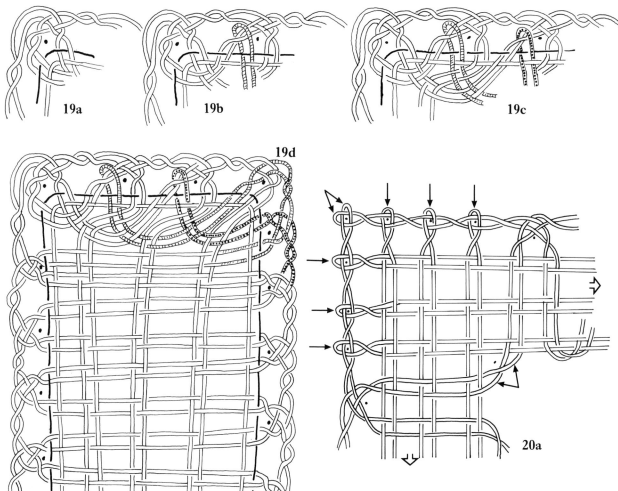

19a

19b

19c

19d

20a

normal (see fig. 19d). This forms a raised bar under the cordonnet.

20 Starting at the corner going both ways, such as at the corner of a collar or a frame.

Hang two pairs on one pin and whole stitch them through each other at the outside point on the corner. Twist them the appropriate number of times as required to form the footside. Add pairs along the top of the line as required, twisting in between each pair as for a footside. All these pairs now worked need twisting before the other side can be started.

Turn the pillow and add pairs down the work. Proceed to work each of these pairs across the work in turn, twisting as for a footside in between each stitch until they are all worked. Twist all the side pairs, as for a footside, before whole stitching them through those pairs hanging from the top. To obtain the other two workers, add two pairs on the inside of the apex of the corner and work one pair in each direction. Make up

edge on either side and work each as desired (see fig. 20a).

21 Shape one: curve developing from a straight edge. Hang two pairs on each of two temporary pins above the work, whole stitch the centre two pairs and place a pin between them (as fig. 18a). Twist these pairs and leave.

Twist the right-hand pair and hang two more pairs on a temporary pin above them. Whole stitch the twisted pair and the nearest new pair to it. Place a pin supporting this whole stitch and twist both pairs. Remove the temporary centre pin and pull gently (as fig. 18b).

Continue adding pairs across the work, removing the temporary pins until the desired width of the top of the curve is achieved.

Starting at the left, take the second pair and whole stitch through all the pairs to the right. Leave this pair as a passive when it has worked across the work. As the curve bends, two new pairs need to be added. Add in the same manner as before.

Whole stitch the left-hand pair from these. This whole stitches the left-hand pair through the pair that was the worker but now has been left as a passive. Both pairs now remain as passives. Take the right-hand pair from the edge; this is the worker which works to the left and makes up the edge. The other edge-pair is then worked across to within the last pair and is left as a passive. Add two more pairs on the edge. The first left-hand pair whole stitches through two pairs and is left as a passive. The right-hand pair works across the work and exchanges for a footside. Continue in this way until the desired shape is achieved. When this is reached, work the footside as normal on both sides (see fig. 21a).

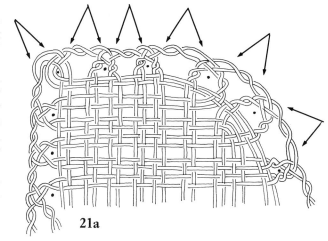

21a

22a

22 Shape two: D End 'curve'.
This can be worked with a footside or a twisted footside, as in this instruction. From four pins in a row across the top, hang eight pairs – two from each. With another two pairs starting at the left-hand side, work the right-hand threads across the eight pairs, twisting in between each whole stitch, then leave.

On the left-hand side add two pairs on a pin and work the right-hand pair through the twisted footside and leave. Take the left-hand pair and work this straight across the work to within the twisted footside pair.

Two more pairs may be added on the right. The first left-hand pair whole stitches through the twisted footside and through the pair that has just worked across the work. These two pairs are now left as passives. The right-hand pair then works across the work to within the twisted footside on the left-hand side. Two more pairs are added. The right-hand pair

of the newly added pairs is whole stitched through the twisted footside and the pair just worked across, and left. The left-hand pair of those newly added is then taken as the worker across the work. The worker can then be used to make the twisted footside and can be worked back, unless more pairs need to be added, in which case add as described above (see fig. 22a).

If the shape is to resemble a 'crescent' the work can be carried through as for fig. 22a, but adding only on one side. If the inner curve is very tight, pin holes may be used twice to achieve this effect (see fig. 22b). A tighter curve can also be achieved by adding pairs at every pin hole on one side and using every pin hole on the inner curve twice (see fig. 22c).

An alternative method of adding pairs in the shape of a curve can be obtained by adding pairs within the actual work, by whole stitching through the new pairs and letting them into the work (see fig. 22d).

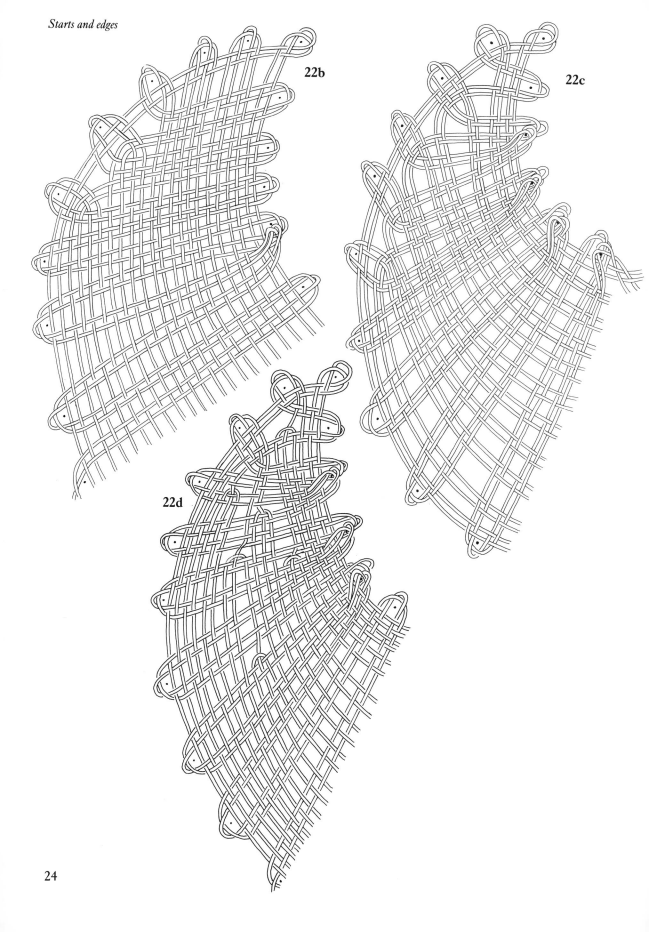

22b

22c

22d

23 Starting with picots.

A false picot is achieved by hanging two pairs on a pin and twisting these several times. Then whole stitch them through each other (see fig. 23a). To start a straight piece of work with picots it is necessary to make false picots along the top line. Two pairs are then needed to become the footside pairs.

Hang two pairs on a pin and work the right-hand threads through all the picot pairs to the right. The second pair from the left can then be worked through the footside pair to the outside edge. Make a picot and work back across the work to make another picot on the other side (see fig. 23b).

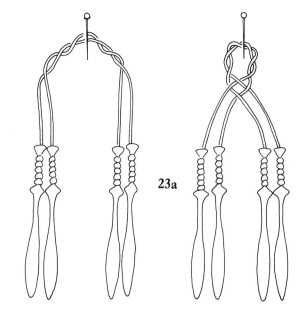

23a

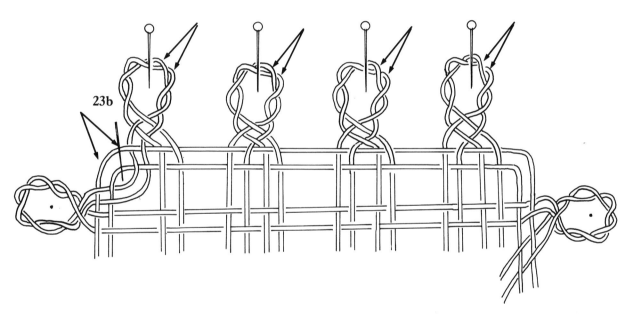

23b

24 Working out from the centre of a frame in both directions.

Lay as many pairs across the work as are needed for the passives. There must be an even number. Lay two more pairs at the top of the work and support these with a pin, and work the right-hand pair through all the passive pairs (see fig. 24a). These can then be turned around the pin and worked out again towards the outer edge, so producing a worker in either direction (see fig. 24b).

The lacemaker may find it easier to attach one side of each bobbin with a slip knot around the pin to

secure one side whilst starting, especially if half stitch is to be used, as this secures the work in place (see fig. 24c). If a footside is required, four pairs must be laid down above the passive pairs. These are whole stitched through each other and twisted. Support on a pin before the inner pair of the right-hand two pairs is worked through the work (see fig. 24d).

The pair from the inner side that has just worked across the passives can be twisted on a pin and worked out again. Twist before making up the edge. It will be seen that the footside pairs are working in either direction (see fig. 24e).

24a

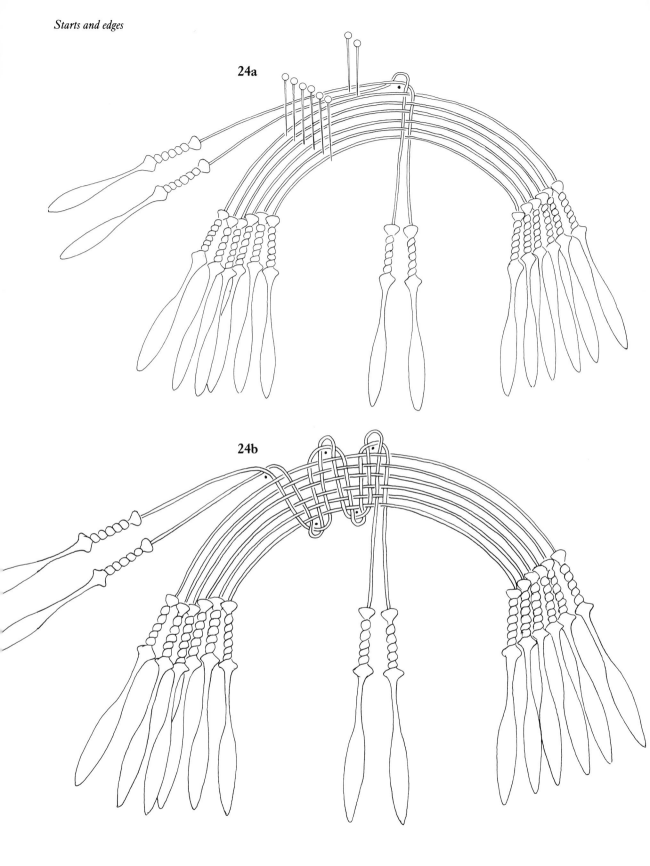

24b

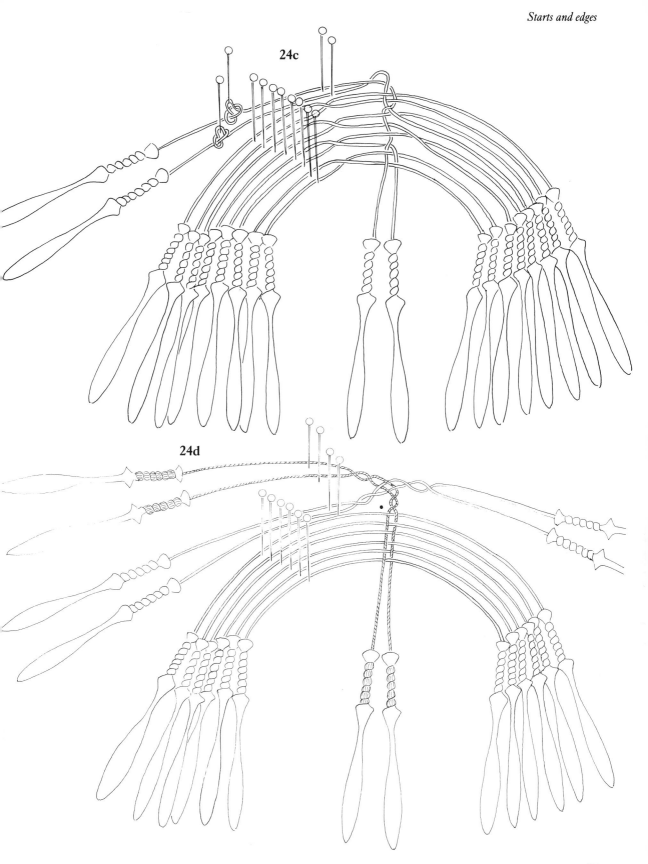

24c

24d

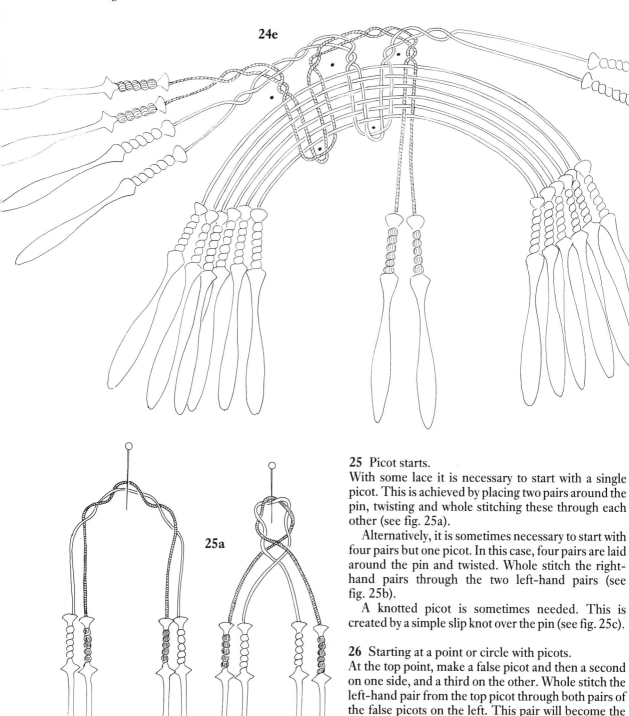

24e

25a

25 Picot starts.

With some lace it is necessary to start with a single picot. This is achieved by placing two pairs around the pin, twisting and whole stitching these through each other (see fig. 25a).

Alternatively, it is sometimes necessary to start with four pairs but one picot. In this case, four pairs are laid around the pin and twisted. Whole stitch the right-hand pairs through the two left-hand pairs (see fig. 25b).

A knotted picot is sometimes needed. This is created by a simple slip knot over the pin (see fig. 25c).

26 Starting at a point or circle with picots.

At the top point, make a false picot and then a second on one side, and a third on the other. Whole stitch the left-hand pair from the top picot through both pairs of the false picots on the left. This pair will become the outside passive pair. Then repeat on the right-hand side.

Whole stitch the two centre pairs together. These now become the second passives, one pair going to the right and one to the left. Work the left side first. Whole stitch the second passive through the second pair from the false picot. This pair can now be used in the pattern.

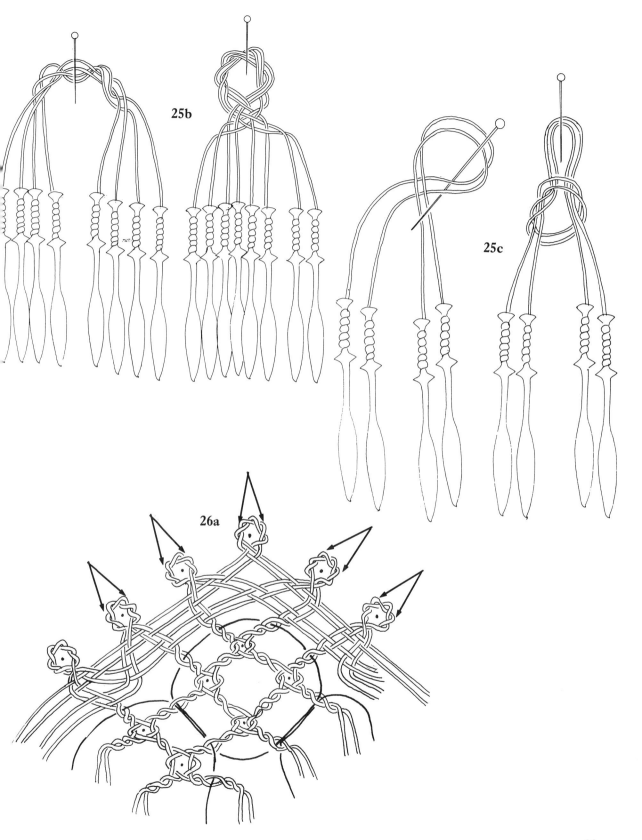

25b

25c

26a

26b

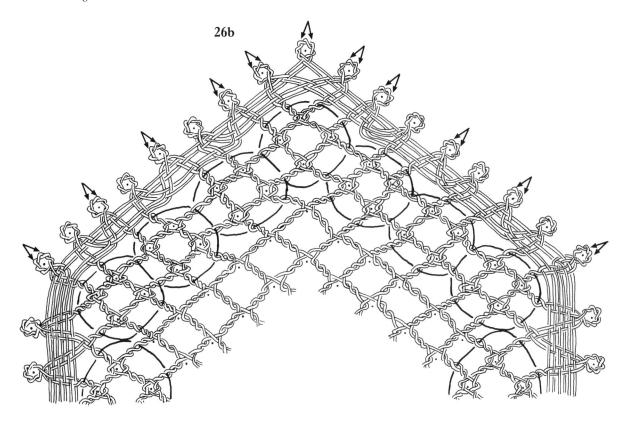

Make another false picot on its left and whole stitch the right-hand pair through the two passives. This pair can be used in the pattern. Then whole stitch the left-hand pair through the two passives and exchange with the inner passive at this stage. The pair that was the inner passive now works out to the outer edge and makes a picot. This is worked back to be used in the pattern (see fig. 26a).

This method of making one false picot from which one pair enters the work and the other exchanges with

the inner passive – before that pair works out to the outer edge – makes a picot and then works back in to make the pattern. Pairs are added alternatively along the outer edge, until the required number is achieved. This is repeated on the right-hand side (see fig. 26b).

27 A picot start as a point or a circular motif.
This method produces a more even appearance to the passives and edge. This alternative start is where only one false picot is made.

At the centre of the top make a false picot. Then, on a temporary pin, lay two pairs across the work inside the split pairs from the false picot. These pairs laid on the temporary pin – one each from the false picot and one pair from the two pairs – are the two pairs of passives on either side. Lay another two pairs under the temporary pin and – working the left-hand side first – whole stitch that new pair out through the two passive pairs to the outer edge. Then make a picot and work back.

This pair will then be ready to work the pattern, but before using it in the pattern it is necessary to loop over a new pair, which will then be worked out towards the outer edge. Here it will make a picot and then again work back through the passives before it is taken into the pattern.

The next new pair is hung on it in the same manner, ready to work out for the next picot (see fig. 27a).

27a

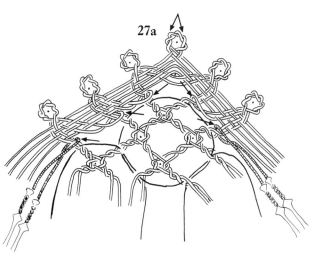

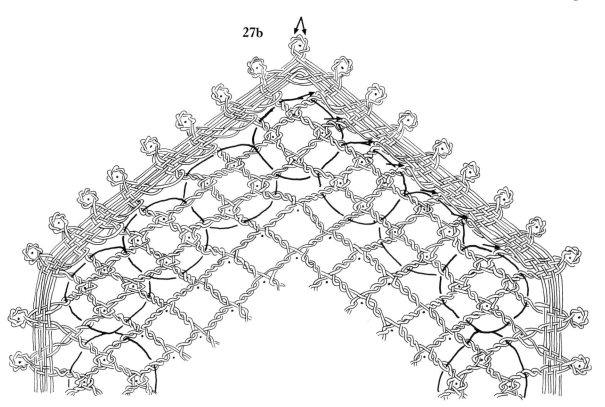

27b

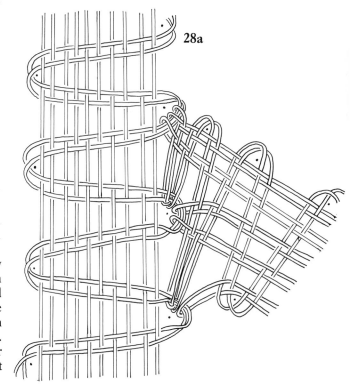

28a

This method is useful not only to provide an even symmetrical shape but for uneven shapes where two pairs have to be added at the same place. This presents no difficulty. It is merely a case of sliding two pairs up the pair to be worked in the pattern, instead of just one. Firmness and evenness is achieved by this method of adding pairs and usually also matches the casting off at the end.

28 Starting an angled branch to an existing braid. This is started by hanging three pairs at the top pin hole of the braid with a sewing and taking the outside pair as the worker. Work this pair through the other two pairs and at the next pin hole join with a sewing. Work back to the top outside edge pin – add two or more pairs at the pin hole where the sewing was made and then, from the outside edge, whole stitch through all the pairs. Make a sewing at the next pin hole down the braid.

Work back around the next pin on the next new branch. Add more pairs on to the pin hole into which the worker was last sewn and work down through all the pairs. Work around the pin on the lower side of the branch. The branch is now joined and work can proceed in accordance with the pattern (see fig. 28a). If footsides are required, it only needs one extra pair to be added at the first and last pin holes of the first braid.

31

29 Starting on a frame, a bar for wall hanging, picture frame or bar in a buckle.

This is a loop start and is quite simple. Take a pair of bobbins. With the hook, pull a loop through under the bar (see fig. 29a). Put both bobbins through its own loop (see fig. 29b). Pull tight (see fig. 29c).

As many pairs of bobbins can be added in this way across the bar as are required for the work. If it is to be a belt, then tight work is needed in order to hold the shape when worn.

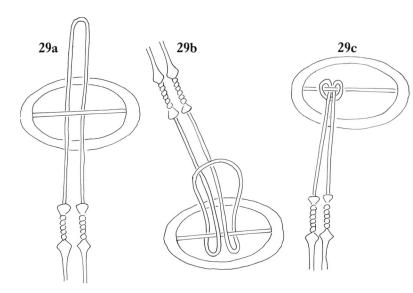

30 Centre starting to make four braids, each in an outward direction as in a cross.

Secure the required number of passives on two sides and, in the correct sequence, whole stitch these through each other. The centre is thus made. Then, in order to add the workers for each braid – and the footside pairs – start at the right-hand corner of the centre already created.

Place two pairs above a pin and two further pairs below the same pin. Whole stitch the under and upper pairs together on either side of the pin.

Take the inner pairs and work one across the top braid and the other across the side braid, after first twisting the workers for each braid. Repeat in the diagonal corner. Place two pairs across the corner not yet used and take one pair – making up a footside with the right-hand pair – and work this across the top braid, where there will be a footside pair waiting. Then repeat with the side braid. Again, repeat the process from the point where the two pairs were added in the unused corner.

The work is now ready for the four braids to work outwards, each with a footside on either side of each braid (see fig. 30a).

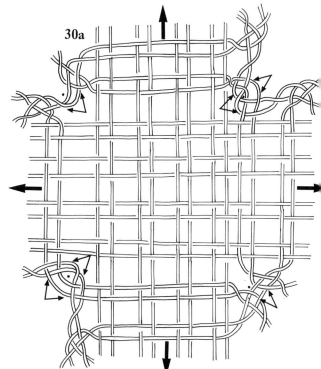

31 To make a small centre for a flower.
Place four pins in a square. If the centre is to be large then six or eight pins in a circle would be needed. Take a pair of bobbins and, holding one bobbin, wrap the other end about three times around the four pins in a clockwise direction (see fig. 31a).

Take a hook under the wrapped around thread (see fig. 31b). Make a sewing with the two threads (see fig. 31c). This merely holds the threads together.

This pair now becomes the worker and other threads, as required for working, are placed in a straight line beside the centre (see fig. 31d). The worker can then be worked after making up the edge and worked back again to the centre – a sewing made into the large hole made by the wrapped-around thread.

Many sewings can be made into this hole as the pairs can be squashed close together forming a neat, smooth centre of any circle (see fig. 31e).

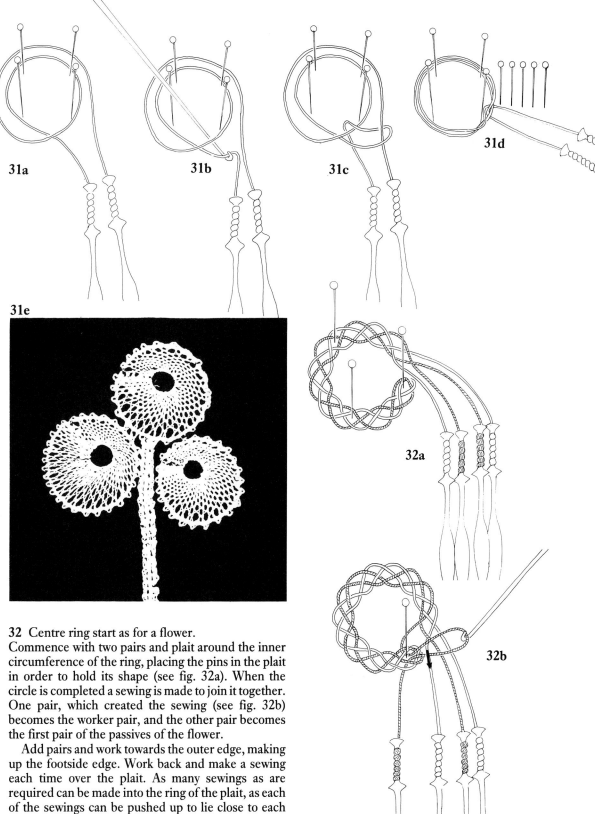

31a   **31b**   **31c**   **31d**

31e

32a

32b

32 Centre ring start as for a flower.

Commence with two pairs and plait around the inner circumference of the ring, placing the pins in the plait in order to hold its shape (see fig. 32a). When the circle is completed a sewing is made to join it together. One pair, which created the sewing (see fig. 32b) becomes the worker pair, and the other pair becomes the first pair of the passives of the flower.

Add pairs and work towards the outer edge, making up the footside edge. Work back and make a sewing each time over the plait. As many sewings as are required can be made into the ring of the plait, as each of the sewings can be pushed up to lie close to each other.

33 The starting of a central cobweb filling.
Place a pin and a loop of the first pair in the centre of
the pillow. Wrap the next pair around the first pair.
Leave the first pair out in the same way as a spoke of
a wheel. Wrap a new pair around the second pair.

Leave that pair pointing out from the centre, the
second spoke, and keep adding pairs as required. The
last pair will then pass both its bobbins through the
loop held by the pin at the commencement, so that
each pair now lies looped into its neighbour and faces
out in the same way as wheel spokes (see fig. 33a). The
lacemaker may find that everything seems just a little
loose and wobbly, so pins can be left in each loop until
the next stage is worked, in order to firm the work up.

The second stage of working the cobweb is started
by taking a pair and bending it around a pin. This pair
becomes the worker. Add sufficient twists to reach the
next pair which has been left out. With the worker,
make a sewing around that pair and twist the workers
again and repeat – making a sewing at each pair in turn
(see fig. 33b). On completion of the circle, make a
sewing into the bend. This pair is now left out in order
to be joined to the place where it is making the filling
at the braid edge (see fig. 33c). If a fuller filling is
required, the worker can go around the spokes as
many times as are required before being sewn out.

34 Scroll start.
Place two pairs of bobbins over the first pin to the right
of the centre pin. Whole stitch them together. Then
around those pairs and the pin, place another two
pairs (see fig. 34a). From the centre whole stitched
pairs, take the pair lying on the right and the next pair
to the right. Whole stitch them together and make up
the edge; pin and work towards the centre, whole
stitching through two pairs. Then place the centre pin
of the scroll in the centre pin hole, to the left of the last
pair not yet worked. Insert a larger pin than the others
for easier identification. Then take the worker over
the last pair around the pin – this may or may not be
twisted according to requirements – and then on the
return journey, outwards under the first pair, whole
stitching across to the outer edge.

Pairs can now be added in each row, in order to fill
the scroll and to have enough pairs for the following
braid (see fig. 34b). Work back through all pairs
towards the centre pin, except for the last pair. Take
the worker over that last pair – around the pin – then
under the pair, before working back to the outer edge.

The central pin can be raised and the loops
released, every two rows giving a more even
placement of the loops at the completion of the scroll
(see fig. 34c).

On completion of the scroll, remove the central pin,
pull up and sew the pair that the worker has been

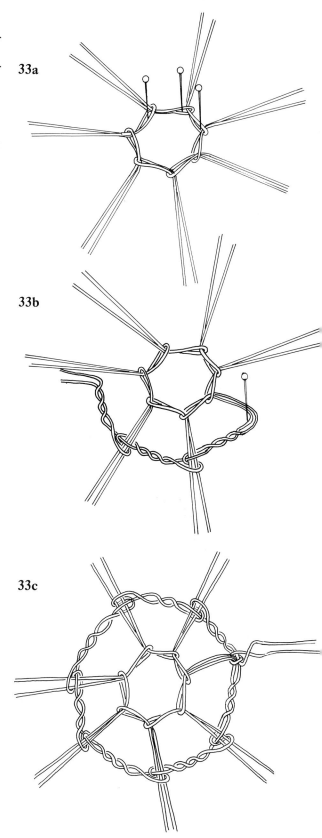

33a

33b

33c

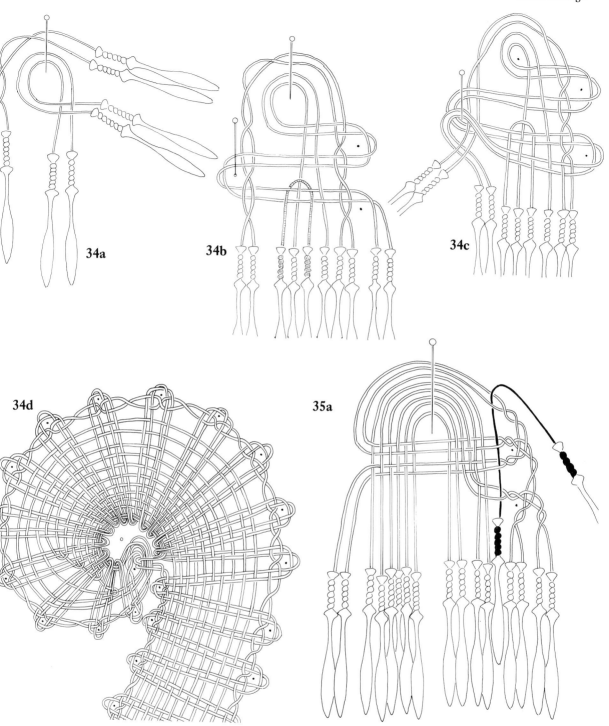

34a

34b

34c

34d

35a

travelling over and under. This completes the scroll, and the pair that made the sewing can now become the other twisted footside pair (see fig. 34d).

35 A wide scroll start.
A fuller scroll can be obtained by working passive pairs as alternate workers and passives. To start, hang eight pairs around the central pin in a 'U' shape, each pair around the next.

Starting with the outside left-hand pair, whole stitch across the next six pairs. Then place in a cordonnet between the outside right-hand pair.

35b

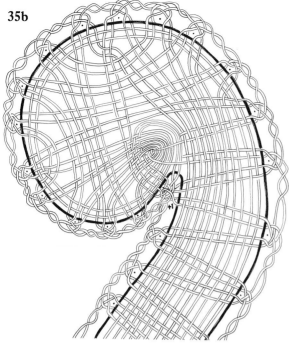

After all the pairs have been used the process can be repeated by working the fifth pair across all the pairs to the centre, and then starting again with the second pair working to the outer edge. This whole process can be repeated once more in order to fill out the wider shape. After the curve has been completed a sewing with the worker can be made into the starting loops before the straight part of the work is made.

The cordonnet which was left can now be used. A single new pair is added at the first pin hole of the scroll. This becomes a second edge-pair of the left-hand side of the braid. The braid can then be made (see fig. 35b).

Edges
The worker pair must be turned and worked back through the work. There are several ways of achieving this – some are very simple and others can make a decorative edge on their own.

36 Simplest edge.
The simplest way of turning the worker is to place a pin at the edge. Turn the worker around that pin and continue back across the work (see fig. 36a). This form of turning will leave two loose threads, which is sometimes not entirely desirable. The lacemaker may therefore prefer to twist the pairs around the pin. Normally, in a section of work, the number of twists can be either one or two but usually at the outer edge three or more are used in order to make a firmer edge (see fig. 36b).

When making a block or braid in half stitch the edge-pair on either side must be made in whole stitch. If the pins are taken out of half stitch work without an edge, the entire piece would collapse.

The edge-pair can be either a straight pair or a twisted pair and the worker can be twisted around the pin as many times as the lacemaker requires, according to the firmness needed and the thickness of the thread used (see fig. 36c).

Leave the right-hand thread of the cordonnet to work later down the braid.

Pass the left-hand thread of the cordonnet between the pair worked across the six whole stitches. Twist both this pair and the outside pair, then make up the edge. Take the inner pair back across the work to the centre of the scroll and leave.

To make the filled-out part of the scroll, take the second pair from the cordonnet. Work this pair to the right. Pass the cordonnet through it and make up the edge (see fig. 35a). Take the inner edge-pair back right across the work but excluding the first pair worked across. Leave this pair as well. Repeat the movement and, on each occasion, take the second pair to the right and then, after the edge has been completed, work the inner pair to the centre.

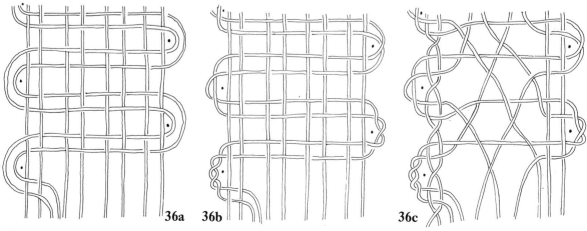

36a   **36b**   **36c**

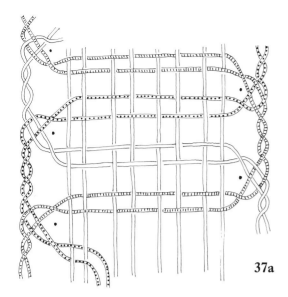

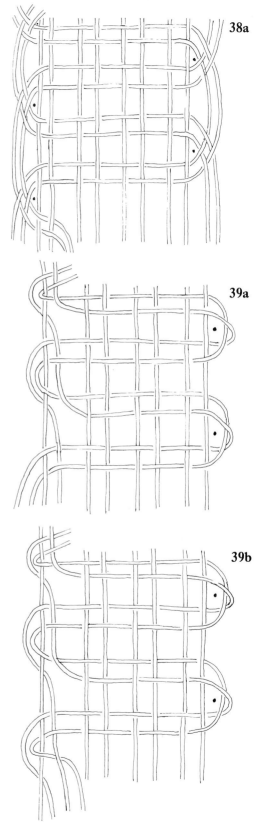

37a

37 Straight foot side edge.
This is achieved by twisting the two edge-pairs. Place a pin on the inside of both pairs. Whole stitch the two pairs and twist both, then take the inner pair back across the work. The number of twists used is dependent on the firmness required. This footside edge can be made on either side of the work (see fig. 37a).

38 Footside on a braid with no separation.
Creating a footside on a braid without separation from the work can be carried out by constructing without twists when exchanging the pairs, as in Method 37. The pin, on the inside of both edge pairs, is placed as close to the work as possible (see fig. 38a).

39 In this method a single thread retains the shape. It is often used when making a curved inner edge, where the pins would have been too close together.
Work to the last pair on the side that has no pins. Whole stitch the last pair and the worker together. Then, with the same two pairs, make a half stitch, and then work back to the pin side. It will be noted that the outside thread of the inner pair remains on the inside, and it is this thread that retains the shape.
There is less bulk when using this method, as the pairs sit closer together around an inner curve. It can also be used to retain a straight unpinned edge (see fig. 39a and 39b).
This stitch, whole stitch followed by a half stitch, is also called a 'turning stitch', and can be used not only at the edge but also in the middle of a row. If the row is to be only worked half way, this turning stitch can be used before working out again to the outer edge, thus gaining on the row.

38a

39a

39b

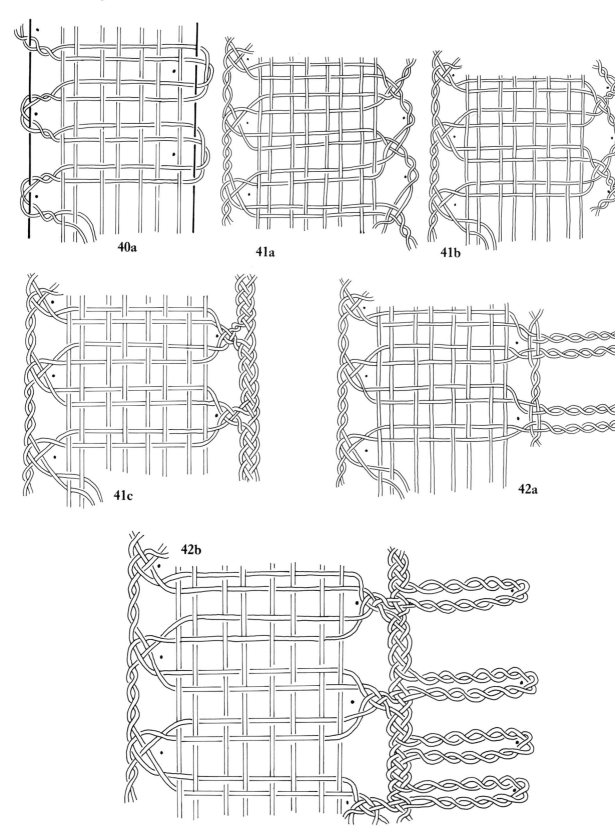

40a

41a

41b

41c

42a

42b

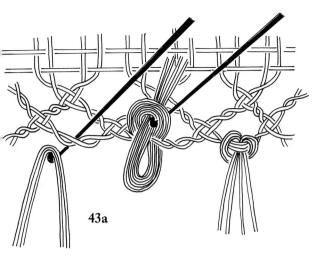

43a

40 Cordonnet/gimp edge.

A strong gimp can be used to hold an edge in two different ways. On the left-hand side of fig. 40a the gimp has been used slightly separated from the work, by working all the pairs of the braid, then twisting the workers once or twice; passing the gimp through the workers and giving the worker another twist before passing the gimp through the workers again.

To continue, pin on the inside of the gimp. Twist the worker and work back. The gimp needs to be pulled firmly to remain smooth and straight (see fig. 40a on the left-hand side).

An alternative method is to include the gimp into the outside edge-pair as its outside thread. Work to the edge, thread and gimp pair. Whole stitch through that pair, twist the workers, pin on the inside of the pair and whole stitch back through the thread and gimp the first pair. Then work back across the work.

The gimp and thread pair needs to be pulled firmly into its correct position when making up the opposite edge. If the worker is pulled too tight it distorts the straightness of the edge (see fig. 40, on right-hand side).

41 Decorative edge.

A slight scalloped edge can be produced by working to the edge, twisting, and then whole stitching the edge-pairs together. Twist both pairs and then exchange the workers. Pin the outside pair only – half way along between the whole stitch just worked and the next whole stitch edge-pair (see fig. 41a).

The scallop edge can be extended by working another pair at the edge. Work across the pair to the first edge-pair, twist, whole stitch and twist these. Take the inner pair back as the worker and whole stitch the outer pair with the other twisted edge-pair. Twist them both – as in Method 41a. The pin will support the scallop. As there are two edge-pairs this pin is above the whole stitch of the exchange of the worker pairs and not between them (see fig. 41b).

A plaited edge produces a firm and almost raised edge. Three pairs are needed for the footside. Plait two pairs together until they reach the edge-pin hole. Take the worker from the braid and twist. Then whole stitch the worker with the inner pair from the plait; twist both. This completes the changing of the pairs. The inner pair goes into the work and the outer plaits to the next pin hole, with the pair that has been left on the extreme outside edge. Repeat (see fig. 41c).

42 Frills.

A simple frill can be introduced by taking the worker from the braid to the edge, twisting and whole stitching with the outside pair. The pair that is now the outside pair is twisted sufficiently to reach the pin hole at the outer pin edge of the frill. Place the pin again and twist on the return passage, whole stitch again with the edge-pair, twist both, and then take the inner pair across the work again. It will be noted that the edge-pair stays constant and it is the worker which makes the frill (see fig. 42a).

A firmer and fuller frill can be produced by working two pairs on the outside edge. Plait the outer edge pairs to the first edge-pin hole. From the plaited pair, twist the outside pair sufficiently firmly to work this pair around the frill pin. Twist back again and whole stitch with the other plaited pair. Twist both and make up the edge with the inner pair of the plait and the twisted worker from the lace. Twist them both. The inner pair from these pairs works the lace and the outer pair plaits with the second edge-pair to the next pin hole, where the processs is repeated (see fig. 42b).

If a denser frill is desired then an extra frill can be worked, between making the edge-pin holes. To achieve this plait to half-way between the edge-pin holes, take the outer pair of the plait and make a frill. Plait again to the pin hole where another frill is made before making up the edge (see lower section of fig. 42b).

43 Frills can also be added subsequently.

Work the piece with a decorative edge, as in fig. 41b. Then, in order to make the frill, take a pair of threads (or more if desired) and working with a hook pull up a loop through the edge pair, tuck the ends of the threads through the loop and pull tight.

The loose ends can then be cut off to a uniform length (see fig. 43a).

KNOTS, REPLACING THREADS AND ADDING PAIRS

1 The slip knot is used in many ways, in order temporarily to anchor threads – as a knot for joining, or for hanging on – if threads are to be started individually.

First make a loop by winding the thread anti-clockwise over itself (see fig. 1a). Insert a pin in the loop and pull up a loop from the right-hand thread (see fig. 1b). Pull this loop above the first loop and insert a pin into the pillow (see fig. 1c). Then pull tight (see fig. 1d). This will hold the thread firm, and when the pin is removed will easily undo.

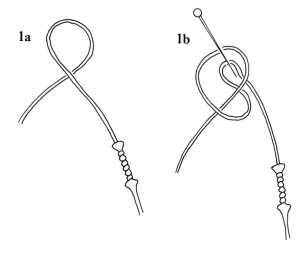

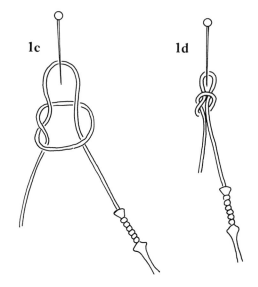

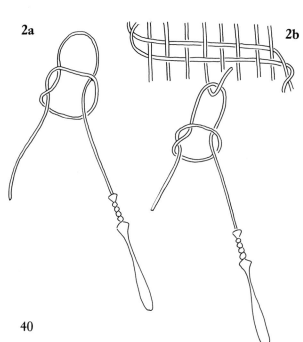

2 The weavers knot is used when an end unfortunately breaks and a new thread needs to be joined on to a small tuft.

First make a slip knot, leaving long ends both on the bobbin side and on the loose end side (see fig. 2a). Place this slip knot over the tuft end, ensuring that this slip knot has not turned over. It is of the utmost importance that the knot is the correct way round (see fig. 2b). Then, holding the loose end of the knot and the tuft end, gently pull up.

Let go of the tuft end as it is pulled up (see fig. 2c). When pulled tight the knot will automatically turn over and trap the tuft end tightly (see fig. 2d).

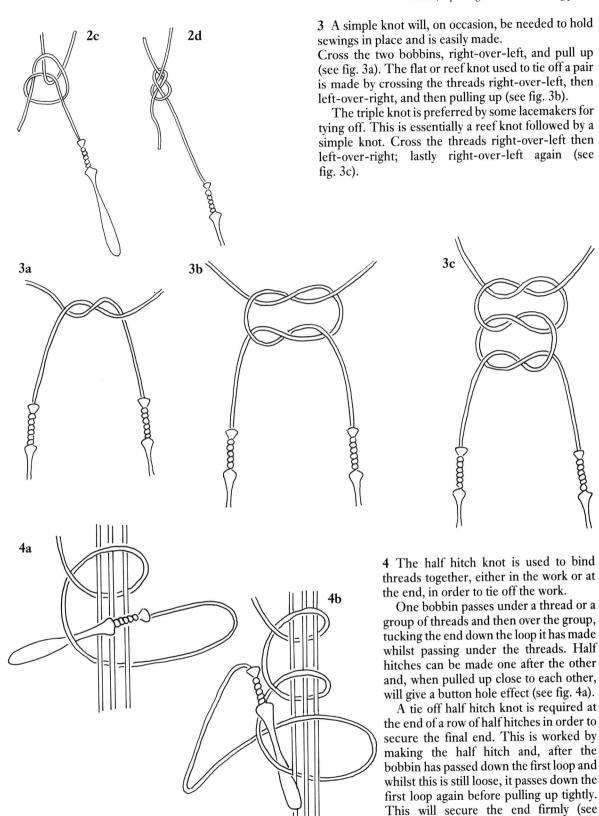

2c

2d

3a

3b

3c

4a

4b

3 A simple knot will, on occasion, be needed to hold sewings in place and is easily made.
Cross the two bobbins, right-over-left, and pull up (see fig. 3a). The flat or reef knot used to tie off a pair is made by crossing the threads right-over-left, then left-over-right, and then pulling up (see fig. 3b).

The triple knot is preferred by some lacemakers for tying off. This is essentially a reef knot followed by a simple knot. Cross the threads right-over-left then left-over-right; lastly right-over-left again (see fig. 3c).

4 The half hitch knot is used to bind threads together, either in the work or at the end, in order to tie off the work.

One bobbin passes under a thread or a group of threads and then over the group, tucking the end down the loop it has made whilst passing under the threads. Half hitches can be made one after the other and, when pulled up close to each other, will give a button hole effect (see fig. 4a).

A tie off half hitch knot is required at the end of a row of half hitches in order to secure the final end. This is worked by making the half hitch and, after the bobbin has passed down the first loop and whilst this is still loose, it passes down the first loop again before pulling up tightly. This will secure the end firmly (see fig. 4b).

5 Bowing off.

Pairs cut off from the work can be cut and knotted together in pairs in the same movement. In order to do this, take a rather blunt pair of scissors and with the unopened scissor-point place the scissors under the threads and wind the loose ends in a clockwise direction around them (see fig. 5a).

Open the scissors and gently hold the threads between the points (see fig. 5b). Then pull the scissors through the loop, holding the threads gently. When pulled tight the scissors cut the threads that were held between the points; it will be seen that the threads are cut off from the work but that the bobbins are joined with a knot (see fig. 5c).

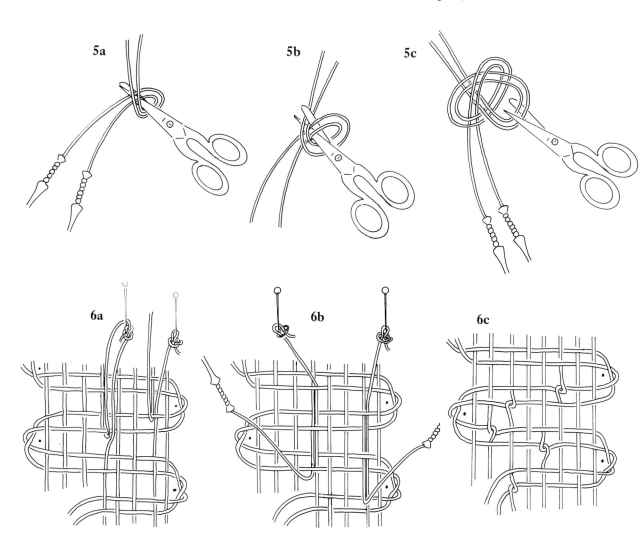

6 Replacing the threads.

Threads can be replaced in several ways. If a thread runs out a new thread can be directly knotted on and the knot pinned back over the pillow. The work can then be continued with the new thread; when a section has been completed the two ends can be simply cut off (see the left-hand side of fig. 6a).

Alternatively, a new thread can be secured with a slip knot pinned at the back of the pillow; the old thread laid back and the new one worked. Later, when a section of work has been completed, the two loose

ends can be cut off (see the right-hand side of fig. 6a).

Both these ways are workable if the lace is fairly dense, but tend to leave a small hole if the work is a loose weave.

A further method is where two threads can be worked together for two or three rows. Where a thread can be seen to be running out, lay a new one beside it. Working the two threads as one continue for two or three rows before throwing back the short end. At the completion of a further section of work, the two spaced-out ends can be cut off closely. The overlapping will hardly show and it is certainly a secure way of adding a new thread (see fig. 6b).

If the worker is running out of thread it is advisable to exchange it first of all with a passive, so that the strain of pulling up the worker does not pull out the new thread. It is a simple matter to make the stitch and then give the thread running out and the passive an extra twist. By doing this the threads are exchanged. Threads can be exchanged after a whole stitch has been completed or in the middle of a whole stitch. After three or four more rows the thread can then be exchanged with a new thread, as there will be little strain on a passive (see fig. 6c).

7 Using two threads as one.
In order to assist with the handling of two threads, it is easier if they are joined together as one. Undo the new thread slightly, just sufficiently to tuck the end of the old thread into two or three turns. Pull both the loose ends and the new bobbin knot tight. These two threads will run together for the two or three rows required to work out the old thread (see fig. 7a).

As an alternative, the old and new bobbin can just be tied together (one of the plastic covered metal ties will do well for this) and then work together for the number of rows required (see fig. 7b).

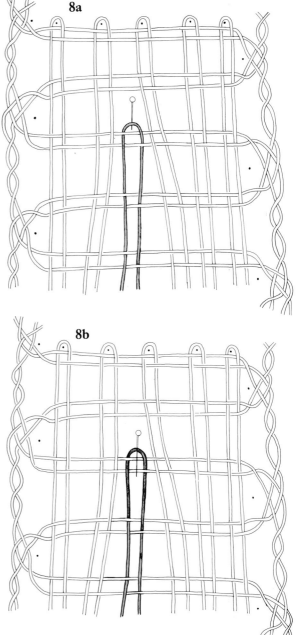

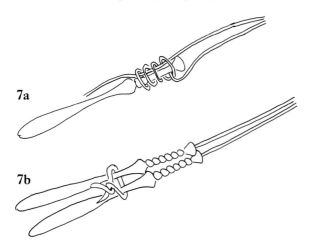

8 Adding pairs.
Pairs can be added to widen the work in many ways.

(a) To add in at the centre of the work, place a pin in the spot where the new pair is to be started. Work through the new pair (see fig. 8a). This method leaves a slight hole and a small loop where the new pair is hung on to the pin.

(b) The same method may be used, but after having worked the first row the pin is removed and placed under the workers in a supporting role. This does remove the slight loop, but still leaves a small hole in the work (see fig. 8b).

(c) Place the new pair on a pin at the side of the work. Place one thread of this new pair on the left of a pair of passives, and the other new thread between the pair of passives. Work through both split pairs and, after completing the row, remove the holding pin. Gently pull down the new pair. The new pair will sit on the top thread of the worker and, as the work is distorted only by the width of one thread, the joining will not show (see fig. 8c).

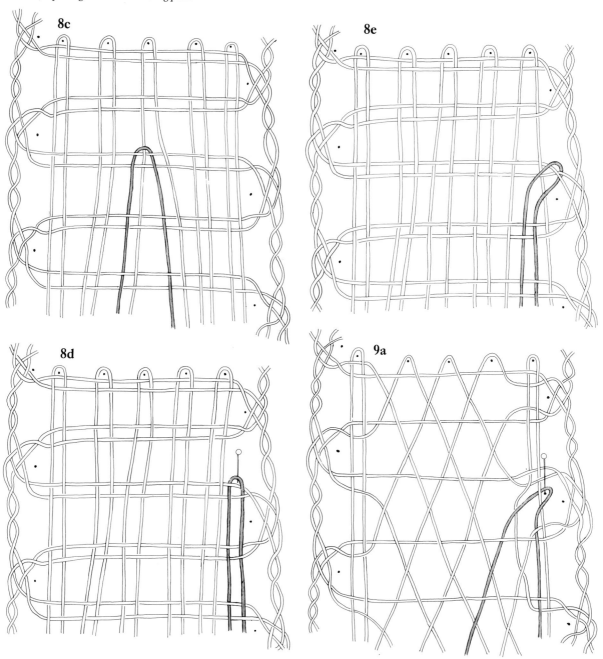

8c

8e

8d

9a

(d) For joining at the side, a pin can be placed at the side with a new pair on it. The worker simply works through the new pair, and this method leaves a stepped shaped edge which is not always desirable (see fig. 8d).

(e) The most satisfactory way of adding at the edge is to slip the new pair over the worker and then to lay this new pair over the outside thread, between its partner. When the worker travels back, the outside edge makes an even retaining thread and a smooth overall effect is given (see fig. 8e).

9 Adding in half stitch.
Work to the edge and, with the worker and edge-pair twist, pin, whole stitch and twist these edge-pairs. Place a pin close to the work, next to the edge-pin which was just worked. Hang a new pair on this and cross the right-hand thread of the whole stitch pair over the first thread and under the second thread of the new pair. Then twist the left-hand pair and the next thread to its left.

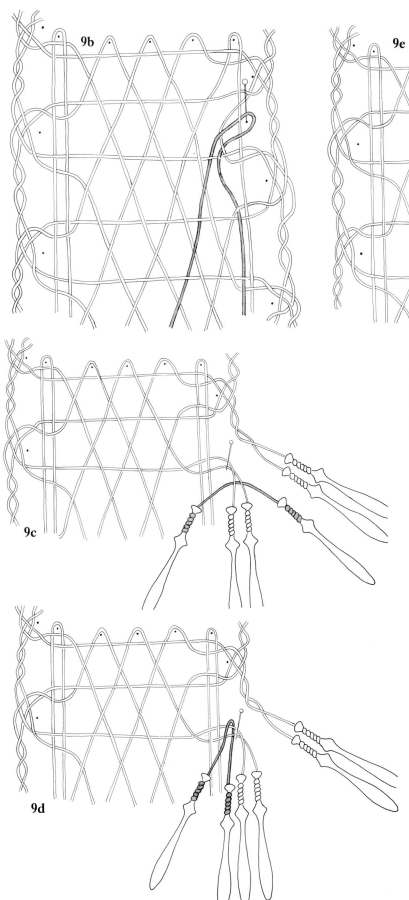

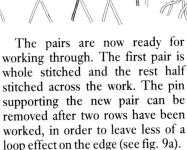

The pairs are now ready for working through. The first pair is whole stitched and the rest half stitched across the work. The pin supporting the new pair can be removed after two rows have been worked, in order to leave less of a loop effect on the edge (see fig. 9a).

Alternatively, a pair can be hung between the rows worked. Work to the right, make up the edge, then half stitch the first pair instead of whole stitching, and work to the end of the row before working back. Whole stitch the new pair with the two edge-threads. Then work back to the right-hand side in half stitch until the last pair which is whole stitched. The pin supporting the new pair can be removed after two or three rows and all can be adjusted evenly (see fig. 9b).

Perhaps the easiest method of adding in half stitch is to work the row to the edge, twist the workers and pin these up. Then slide the new pair up the workers (see fig. 9c). Slide them around the pin (see fig. 9d). Then lay them between the first pair. Half stitch them with the first pair before working back with the workers. Then work the first whole stitch, and across the work in half stitch (see fig. 9e).

45

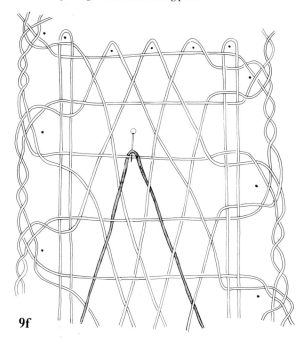

9f

Although rarely used, a pair can be added within the work. Place a pin above the line of the single worker thread, hang the new pair on that pin and work across, including the new pair in half stitch. It will show, as the other pairs are then placed closer together, which distorts the overall shape of the piece but, with careful arranging of the bobbins, it can be successfully used (see fig. 9f).

10 Adding two pairs at once to increase the width evenly.

Work the worker across the lace and let this worker pair turn and become a passive. Support the turn with a temporary pin. Lay two new pairs on a pin on the opposite edge to the hanging workers/passives and work the right-hand threads of the new pairs as a pair across the work (see fig. 10a).

These pairs are now the new workers and are worked around the edge pin and back, working in the two new threads as a pair at the left-hand side.

More pairs can be added in this manner, but if not required the work can be continued with these two new pairs included in the piece (see fig. 10b).

11 Adding two pairs to a plait.

Work the plait to a point where the new pairs are to be added. Part the plait pairs and lay two new pairs, supported on a pin, between them (see fig. 11a). Work the right-hand pairs together to form the new plait, and then the left-hand pairs. The join of the new pairs is barely discernable (see fig. 11b).

Alternatively, when adding two new pairs to a plait, the two new pairs may be hung around the pin to the side of the plait (see fig. 11c). The pairs are all windmilled together, then the two pairs now on the right-hand side are plaited together.

The old plait continues on the left. The support pin of the new pairs should be removed as soon as possible. This method tends to leave a slight distortion of the braids (see fig. 11d).

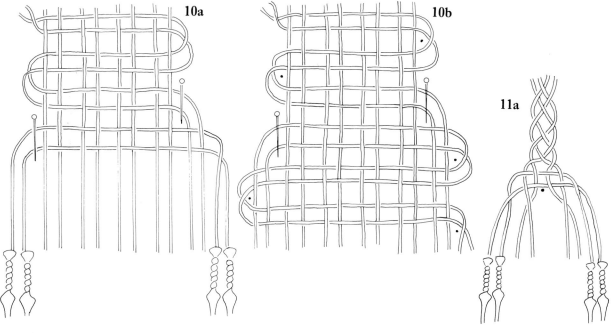

10a

10b

11a

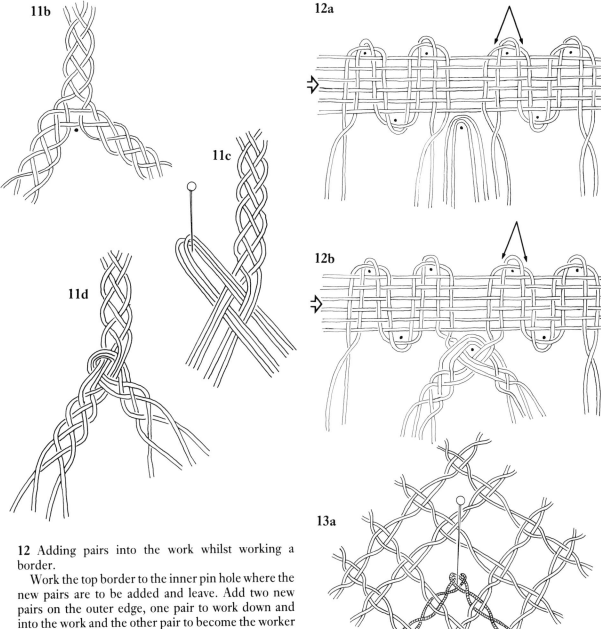

11b

11c

11d

12a

12b

13a

12 Adding pairs into the work whilst working a border.

Work the top border to the inner pin hole where the new pairs are to be added and leave. Add two new pairs on the outer edge, one pair to work down and into the work and the other pair to become the worker for the border.

The two pairs hanging into the work can be whole stitched around the pin on the inner edge of the braid not yet used, and become the two new pairs in the work.

If four pairs are needed at this point, before whole stitching the edge pairs together, hang two pairs on the inner edge-pin (see fig. 12a).

Windmill or whole stitch the left- and right-hand pairs together, then windmill or whole stitch the centre pairs together before working these new pairs into the work. In this method there is little bulk and it is therefore a neat way to add pairs (see fig. 12b).

13 Adding two pairs into a net of any type.

Find the centre point of the shape of the net and place the pin in at this point. Hang two new pairs in the stitch of the net. Then work the net, incorporating these two new pairs (see fig. 13a).

A single pair can also be added into the net. Divide the old pair and, on a pin between the old pair add the new pair, twist the two pairs together (see black-headed pin in fig. 13b).

To remove a pair in the same style of net requires a pair to be turned so that it flows out of the work. In this case a pin is placed in the centre of the normal fall of the net and the pair to be removed is bent around this pin and so worked down into the next row, and on until it can be removed – either at the edge or against a gimp (see fig. 13b).

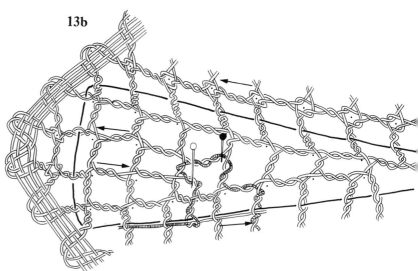

13b

14 Adding a branch and keeping the footside for both braids.

Where the branch is to be added, slip a pair over the worker of the braid before making up the footside edge. Lay this new pair between the first inner edge-pair and, with the worker from the edge, work one whole stitch – then twist the workers.

Work to the left-hand side of the work and make up the edge, then work back to the last pair before the edge; twist the workers. Work the last pair, twist the workers, pin and make up the edge. Twist both edge-pairs.

Add the new pair within the first pair and then work the inner pair from the edge through the first and new pairs. Working whole stitches, twist the workers and work to the left. After making up the left side, work back to the last two pairs, twist the workers and continue through these pairs, twist, and work the edge as normal. Before working back add the new pair within the first pair working through the three whole stitches, twist, and then continue across the work.

The twist between the braid and the branch is worked in each row, and pairs added into the branch to its required shape. More pairs may be added in the row if the increase is to be more marked. At the point where the branch leaves the main braid, work across the branch and the main braid. Add a new pair which will become the worker for the branch on to that worker, make up the edge and leave both edge-pairs.

Take the new pair across the main braid and branch, make up the edge and work the inner pair back only across the branch to within the last pair of the branch. Whole stitch the last pair of the branch and the first pair of the main braid together; twist both. The right-hand pair now makes up the edge with the worker from the branch. This branch is now independent from the braid, with its own edge-pairs and worker.

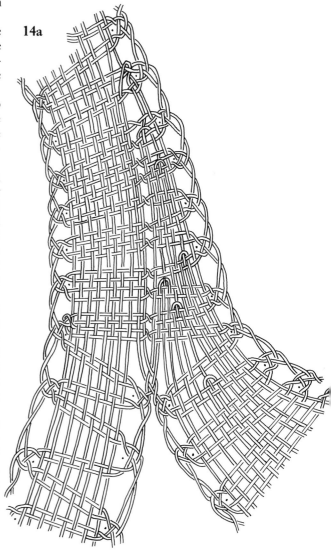

14a

Return to the two edge-pairs left on the main braid left-hand side, work the inner pair across the work and make up the edge with the waiting pair. The appearance of a footside throughout will have been achieved (see fig. 14a).

15 To make an upward Y-shaped branch on to a piece of lace, such as a segmented leaf which is started at the top and then has to be expanded upwards to produce a side segment (see fig. 15a).

Work from the top down to where the first branch is to be formed and work the edge, but place the pin between the pairs instead of inside both pairs. Hang two new pairs on to this pin, laying them between the edge-pairs.

Whole stitch the inner edge-pair through the new pairs and through the outer edge-pair. These new pairs fill the hole that occurs in the apex of the corner. Then whole stitch through the first gimp and thread pair and leave pairs Y and Z. Whole stitch the edge-pairs together.

The outside pair now continues up the branch, whilst the other pair works through the gimp and thread pair and pair Y of the new pairs just added (see fig. 15b). Pair Y then whole stitches up through the gimp and thread pair (see fig. 15b). Hang two new pairs on pair Y before twisting and making up the footside edge with the pair from the original footside pair. Whole stitch both new pairs through the gimp and thread pair.

The inner footside pair whole stitches through the gimp and thread pair, and the two new pairs: W and X. Then, whole stitch pair W through pair X and the gimp and thread pair (see fig. 15c). Make up the edge, hanging on two new pairs before so doing. The first new pair – pair U – lays back over the pillow for later use.

Work pair V through the gimp and thread pair (see fig. 15d). The inner edge-pair then works through the gimp, the thread pair and pair V, and is left as a passive. Pair X is worked up to the outer edge with two new pairs hung on it, before it makes up the edge.

One pair is then laid back on the pillow and the other is then worked back into the work, and the process repeated until all the pairs are added and the corner pin is reached. Before the corner pin is worked only add one pair and whole stitch it through the gimp and thread pair. Make up the corner and work the inner pair through the gimp and thread pair and the last new pair added. This new pair now makes up the side edge and works back across the work to the first laid-back pair, T (see fig. 15e).

Whole stitch the worker with the laid-back pair. This pair may have a simple knot tied now, in order to hold the worker firmly before it hangs down as a passive. The knotted pair is now worked to the outer edge. Make up the edge and return, working through all the pairs to the next laid-out pair, where the process is then repeated. Continue until the pin hole,

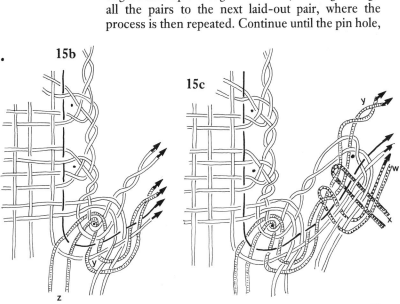

15a

15b

15c

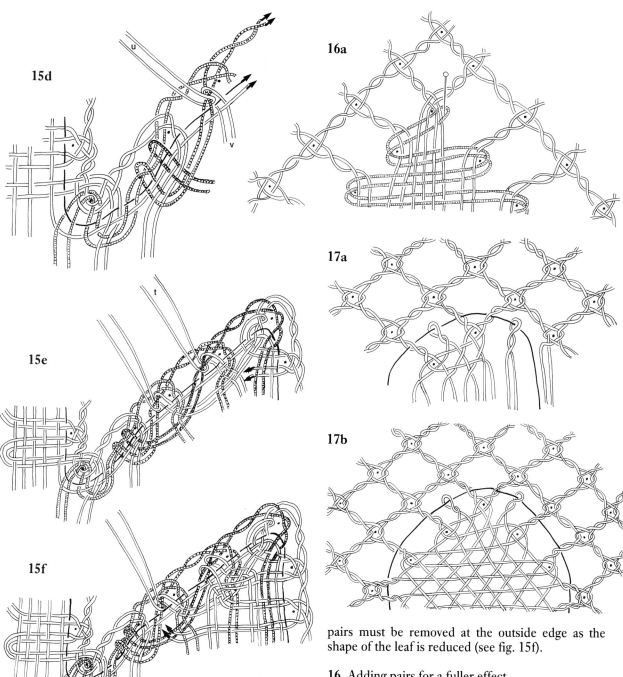

15d

15e

15f

16a

17a

17b

pairs must be removed at the outside edge as the shape of the leaf is reduced (see fig. 15f).

16 Adding pairs for a fuller effect.
Pairs may be added in the net in order to give an even and full effect to the shape worked. Join the two net pairs: in this diagram these are whole stitched. Place a temporary pin close to the right-hand pair of the join and hang a new pair on that pin.

This pair is used as the worker and the shape can be worked as required. After having worked two rows, remove the temporary pin and pull up. The loop will slide up close to the outside pair and will not be noticed (see fig. 16a).

where there were no laid-back pairs, and here complete a sewing with the worker pair to keep the work level.

Another sewing will be needed on the next row at the apex of the branch. This depends on the angle of the branch – and no two pieces are exactly alike. The work can now continue to the next branch, but the

17 Adding pairs for a fuller effect on a gimp. Pass the gimp between the new pair to be added (see fig. 17a). It may temporarily be supported by a pin, but will hold itself on the gimp after one or two stitches have been worked (see fig. 17b).

18 Adding with sewings on to a completed piece of work.

Remove the pin from the hole at the edge of the completed braid. Insert a hook, needle pin or a threaded needle under the bar made by the change of workers on the footside, then draw up a loop from the pair to be added (see fig. 18a).

Remove the hook and place one of the bobbins from the new pair through the loop that has just been made (see fig. 18b). Pull both new bobbins gently and it will be noted that a small neat join has been achieved (see fig. 18c).

19 Joining two or more pairs on to a completed piece at the same time.

Remove the pin from the pin hole in the edge of the completed piece. Draw up a loop from one of the pairs to be added (see fig. 19a). Then, through that loop, slide the other pairs to be added (see fig. 19b). It may be found that there is undue movement in the bobbins; adding a single knot tied with the pair of the bobbins from which the loop was made does assist in securing all the threads.

Alternatively, pairs can be added by making a loop with one pair. Then lay the other pairs to be added across this looped pair (see fig. 19c). A bobbin from the top pair can be taken over those pairs which have been laid across and into the loop. When pulled tight all the pairs will be held firmly, but again, if more rigidity is required, a single knot with the loop pair might be preferable (see fig. 19d).

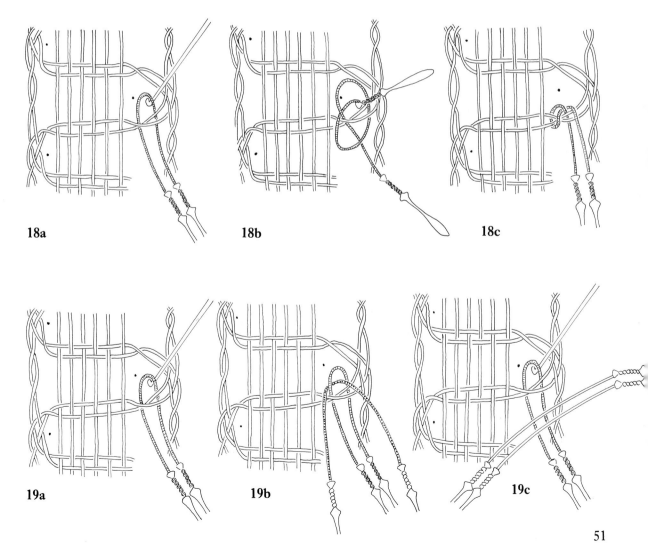

18a

18b

18c

19a

19b

19c

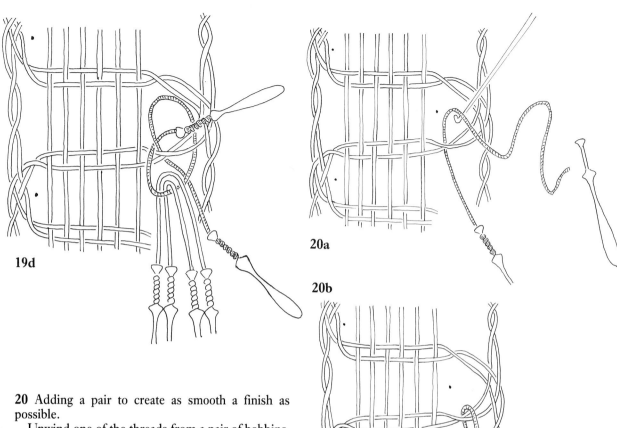

19d

20a

20b

20 Adding a pair to create as smooth a finish as possible.

Unwind one of the threads from a pair of bobbins. Pull this single thread right through the bar of the edge of the complete piece (see fig. 20a). Rewind the bobbin. This gives a very clean, uncluttered appearance to the join (see fig. 20b).

JOINING AND SEWINGS

1 TOOLS FOR SEWINGS

A crochet hook is very suitable when the thread is not too fine. The hook can pass into the pin hole of the completed lace without distorting the shape (see fig. 1a).

A needle pin is a fine needle with the eye of the needle pushed into a small handle. The handle can be either of wood, cork or bone. This needle must, necessarily, be as fine as the pin hole that it has to work with, as otherwise it would distort the whole shape by stretching. A needle pin is used like a crochet hook, but as there is no hook on the end, the thread must be trapped around the needle pin and then drawn back under the bar and out to make a loop. With some practice this becomes quite straightforward (see fig. 1b).

A fine beading needle with the point of the needle embedded into a wooden handle can also be used for making some sewings. Thread the needle with fine thread (a different colour to the work is a help). Put the eye of the needle under the bar, as far as is necessary in order to catch the loop from the coloured thread in the eye of the needle. Into this, place one of the bobbins from the pair to be sewn (see fig. 1c).

Pull out the needle and thread, and the thread of the bobbin. Hold this new loop and remove the needle/thread, then make a sewing by placing the other bobbin of the pair through this loop (see fig. 1d).

2 AID TO SEWINGS

If it is known at the start of a piece of lace that a sewing is to be made through several pairs, the lacemaker can use a lazy loop in order to assist the sewing.

Place a knotted loop under half the pairs and then back over the pairs when they have been hung on at the commencement of the lace. Pin this loop out of the way (see fig. 2a). Work around the lace and when the sewing is to be made into the multi-loop commencement, place one bobbin into the spare loop. Pull the other knotted end (see fig. 2b).

It will be found that the loop will draw out of the starting pin hole, taking with it a loop from the bobbin of the pair to be sewn. Hold the loop from the bobbin and cut off the extra aid loop. Then make a normal sewing with the other bobbin from the sewing pair (see fig. 2c).

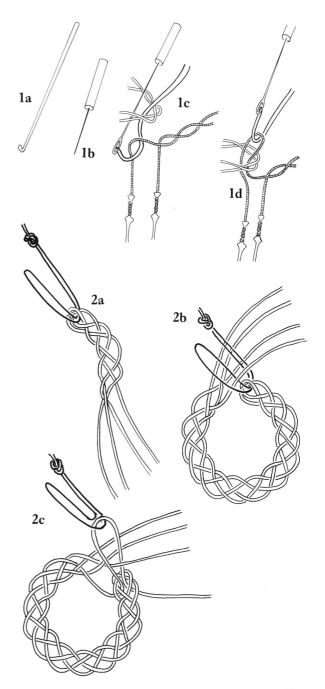

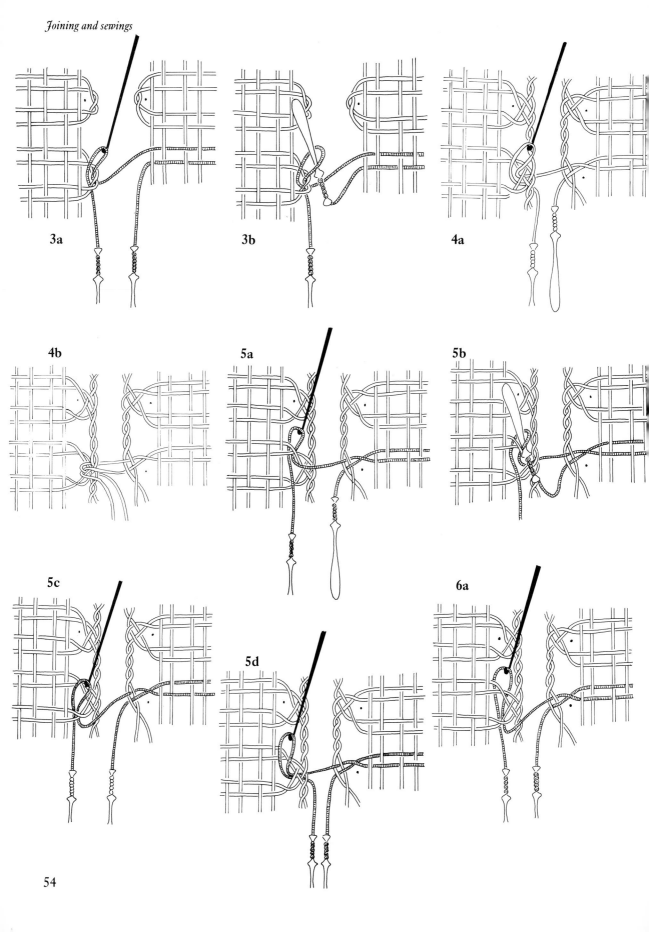

3a

3b

4a

4b

5a

5b

5c

5d

6a

3 A sewing to join two pieces together whilst the work is still proceeding.

Place the two pieces of lace close together and, depending on whether there is to be a definition between the work, or the two pieces are to be joined up tightly against each other; twist the pairs that are to make the sewing, or leave them untwisted for a close join.

Place a hook in the loop made by the pin on the completed piece and take up a loop through this top bobbin from the side being worked (see fig. 3a). Into this loop, place the other bobbin from the pair; pull both bobbins and then work back across the work. The join will have been made (see fig. 3b).

4 Sewing into a footside edge.
There are several places where a sewing can be made into a footside edge. It really depends on the finished effect that is required.

The pin is removed from the hole, then a hook is placed into the hole and under the edge-threads. A thread is then drawn up from the pair to be sewn in order to form a loop (see fig. 4a). Place the other bobbin from the drawn-up pair through this loop, and pull both bobbins gently. Replace the pin and the work can be continued (see fig. 4b).

5 A raised effect is achieved by making a top or bottom sewing.

In order to make a top sewing, place the hook in the pin hole under the bar only. Draw a loop from one of the pairs of bobbins to be sewn (see fig. 5a). Pass the other bobbin from the sewn pair through the loop and pull up (see fig. 5b). This sewing raises the footside edge so that when the work is turned over it achieves a raised edge.

A bottom sewing is worked in the same way, except that the lower bar of the pin hole is used. Insert the hook in the pin hole and then under the bar, then draw up a loop from the sewing pair (see fig. 5c). Into this loop, place the other sewing pair and pull up. Sometimes a sewing will be made at the top and bottom of the same pin hole (see fig. 5d).

6 A double sewing.
Remove the pin from the hole and place the hook under the two bars of the pin hole the pin has just been removed from. Draw one of the sewn threads up into a loop and pass the other sewn thread through this loop. Draw up gently.

This gives a raised effect on the reverse side of the lace, but also draws up the pin hole and thus alters the shape which can, in itself, be an attractive feature.

7 Self sewing for a single bar.
Take the thread from one bobbin up through the pin

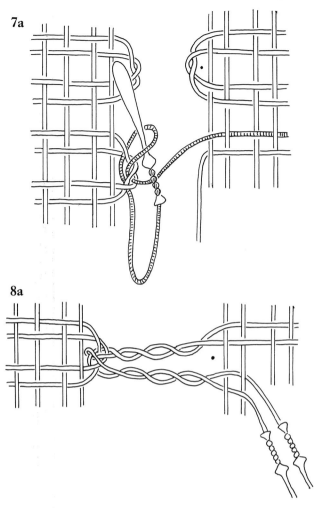

7a

8a

hole with a hook to form a loop, then – in this loop – put the same bobbin and gently draw it up. The single thread can then be worked with its partner across the piece. This is a very light sewing, not particularly strong if there is going to be much pull (see fig. 7a).

8 To create a double twist bar.
Twist the worker from the side being worked and make a sewing into the finished lace. Twist back and continue working. This produces two twisted bars spaced out to one side – but narrow where the sewing took place (see fig. 8a).

To space the bars out evenly, make a sewing with the twisted sewn pair, then twist once and make a sewing in the same hole. This widens the sewn side and so the two bars to continue the lace will be parallel (see fig. 8b).

If the lace is a footside edge and the bars are to be kept parallel, make a sewing on the top bar, twist, make a side sewing, twist and make another bottom sewing before working back. This keeps the bars parallel (see fig. 8c).

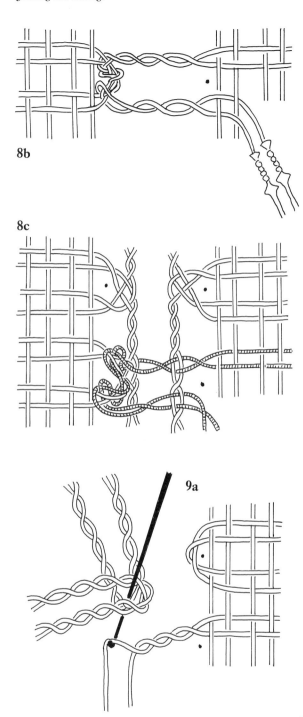

8b

8c

9a

9 Multi sewing.

A sewing can be used to join several sections of lace together, such as a decorative centre. Place the hook through all the loops of the lace to be joined. Draw up a loop from the sewn pair and place the other sewn pair bobbin through the loop. Pull up gently (see fig. 9a).

10 A single twist bar.

If a single twist bar is required, the first piece of lace must be worked with the bars first. Work to the edge of the lace. Twist the pair of workers (see fig. 10a). Then twist the lower thread of the worker to make a twisted loop. Pin this loop at the pin hole of the second section (see fig. 10b). Twist back and twist with the thread that was left from the original workers (see fig. 10c). Work back across the piece. The loop-twisted bar is now made and waits for the second piece of lace to join to it (see fig. 10d).

Work the adjoining piece of lace; when level with the bar, twist the workers. With a hook, pull up a loop of the nearest thread which was the lower worker thread (see fig. 10e). Place the other sewn bobbin through it (see fig. 10f). Gently pull both pairs (see fig. 10g). Twist these pairs before working back across the second piece.

It will be noted that the appearance of both edges will be completely smooth, as if no sewing had taken place (see fig. 10h).

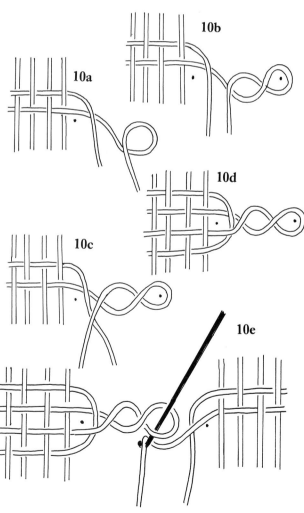

10b

10a

10d

10c

10e

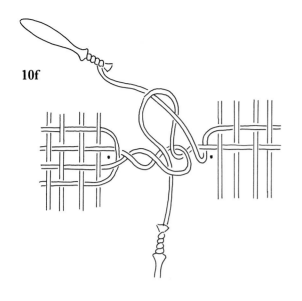

10f

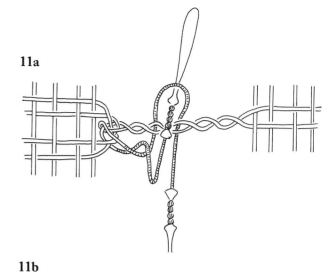

11a

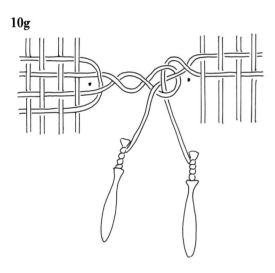

10g

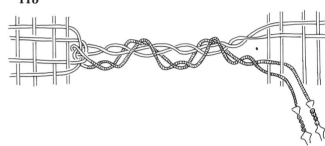

11b

11 A false plait.
A false plait is often needed to join two sections together with a strong join. Also, a false plait is often used to make a decorative filling, using a single pair only from the work.

The worker from one piece of work is twisted sufficiently to form a reasonably tight twist, before making a sewing into the opposite edge. The number of twists should be noted, as, for every two twists on the outward journey, a sewing will be made over the twisted bar on the return.

After the sewing has been made, to join the twisted bar to the completed lace, twist this sewn pair twice and insert the hook under the twisted bar and draw up a loop from one of the bobbins. Place the other bobbin through this loop and pull gently (see fig. 11a). Make two more twists with this pair and make another sewing around the bar. Continue in this way until two twists and a sewing have been made for every two twists on the outward journey. The pair can then be returned to the work to continue (see fig. 11b). This will give a finish which is almost indistinguishable from the real plait.

10h

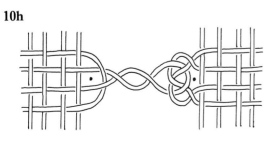

12 Using a knot to secure a sewing. When making a sewing where there is considerable pull to the side after the sewing, make a single knot with the sewn pair. This draws up and holds the lace together (see fig. 12a).

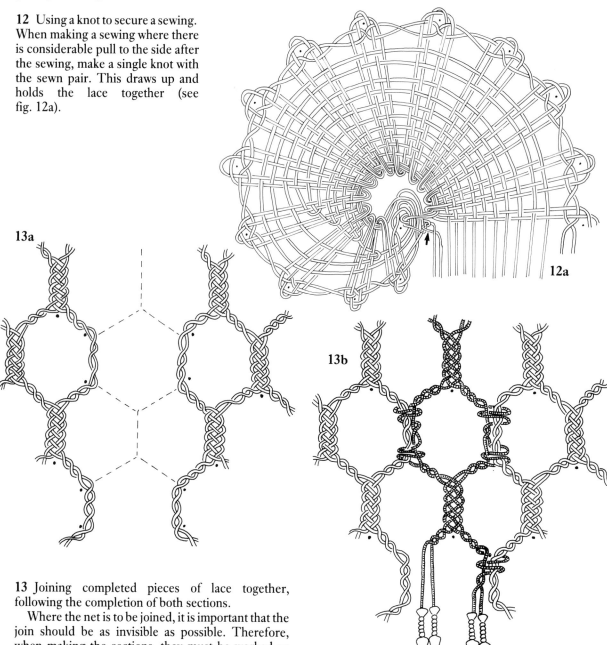

13a

13b

12a

13 Joining completed pieces of lace together, following the completion of both sections.

Where the net is to be joined, it is important that the join should be as invisible as possible. Therefore, when making the sections, they must be worked so that the edge will join neatly. For any of the plaited grounds, work the outer edge with just the pair that would have joined with a partner pair to make a plait – but as there is no partner pair, just twist this pair around pins so that the correct shape is held (see fig. 13a).

Work the other side in the same manner and then pin the two sections back on to the pillow, leaving a centre section for the joining. Start a new plait with two pairs at the centre top of the join and plait the equal number of plaits to match the lace. Then, working the right-hand side, first twist the right-hand

pair to reach the twisted pinned edge. Make a sewing around this twisted bar, twist the sewn pair twice and sew around the bar again. This makes a false plait. On the completion of the false plait, twist the sewn pair back to the centre and leave. While the process is repeated on the other side, join the two pairs together in a plait and plait down the next section. This join will not be seen if it has been worked smoothly (see fig. 13b).

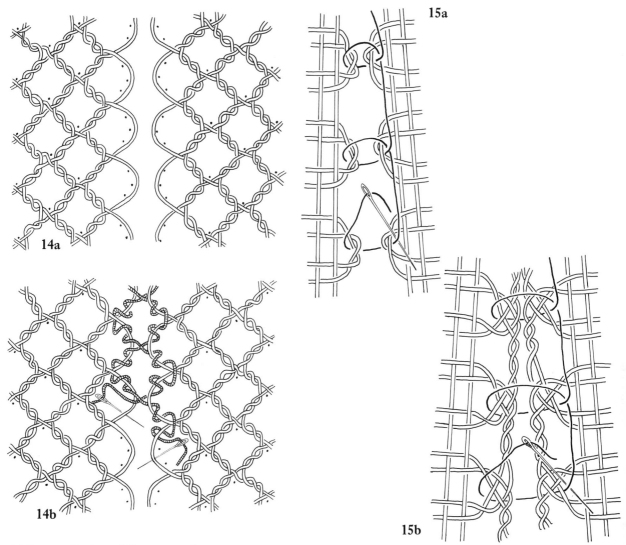

14a

14b

15a

15b

14 Joining Bucks or Lille net together.

When making the sections it is essential that these be worked so that the edges will join neatly.

A single thread is taken around the shape, supported by pins on every row of the net (see fig. 14a). To join, first lay the two pieces of net together on the pillow and pin, leaving an equal gap in the centre which needs to be worked. Take two threaded needles of the same thread and cross these threads in the centre, then, working the right-hand side, take the right-hand needle over and under the single thread that was supported on a pin. Take the needle over the next two threads and into the lower section. Make a loop over and under the next bar. Repeat on the other side and then cross the two needles in the centre. Then repeat the whole process for the length of the work. This join will barely show when the two pieces have been joined together (see fig. 14b).

15 Sewing two pieces of lace together with a needle after each piece has been completed.

Place a threaded needle into the pin hole of one side of the lace and under the edge, then up through the pin hole on the opposite piece of lace. Place the needle down through the loop made by the thread of the needle at the start of the movement (see fig. 15a). Repeat this sewing at each pin hole. The single sewing thread will sit close to the work, very neatly sewing the two pieces together. When each piece of lace has a footside edge, sewing together is carried out in the same way – with the exception that the needle passes down the first pin hole under both edge-threads, and then up through the other pin hole before going down its own loop (see fig. 15b).

This sewing may be worked on, or off, the pillow.

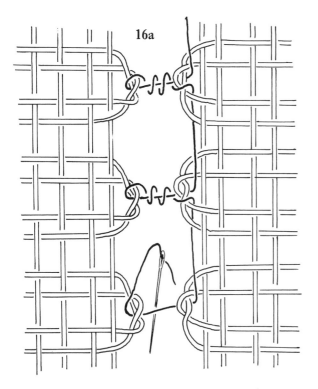

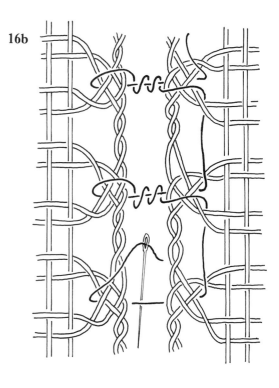

16 Sewing two pieces of lace together but making a separating decorative bar between them.

Place a threaded needle down the hole in the first side of lace and then up through the adjacent lace, leaving the thread loose. Oversew the single crossover thread as many times as required, in order to give a neat bar between the two pieces of lace. Then sew down into the first pin hole; it may pass down its own loop as in Method 15, or may pass down the hole and then down to the next pin hole, where the process is repeated (see fig. 16a).

When a footside edge is on the two pieces of lace to be joined together, the threaded needle passes down the holes and under the two edges, then up the other side of the lace before it oversews the bar in the centre. It may be found that joining on the pillow tends to give a more even join; with the two pieces of lace being pinned along the edges, the shape cannot be distorted by pulling the sewing thread too tightly (see fig. 16b).

CONNECTIONS AND CROSSINGS

This section deals with the passing/crossing/ transferring of pairs from one section of the work to another. For example: passing the worker pair from the footside edge into the work and back, or carrying a group of pairs between sections of work, or crossing a pair of plaits, or carrying a considerable number of threads across the work.

1 The first diagram (fig. 1a) shows six ways of changing the worker from one section with another.

Z join. A simple exchange is achieved by whole stitching the two workers together. The worker which had been on the right-hand side then works the left-hand side, while the left-hand worker works the right-hand side. Pins can be placed on the inside of the returning workers in order to support a good, well shaped piece.

Y join. This is the same as the Z join, but the pairs are held slightly apart by the inclusion of a twist before and after the whole stitch. A pin can be placed in the centre of the whole stitch, or as in the diagram at either side to support the overall shape.

X join. This makes a feature of the crossing by twisting the pairs before whole stitching, and then twisting and pinning under the whole stitch before a second whole stitch is made. The pairs are then twisted again before working back.

W join. This is similar to Method X but without the twist in the actual join. The method of working is to twist the pairs, then whole stitch, pin, whole stitch and twist both the pairs. This is sometimes called a single spider.

V join. In this the pairs are twisted, half stitched, supporting pin added, and then worked back.

U join. In this connection the pairs are twisted, followed by a half stitch, pinned and half stitched prior to working back. This produces the same effect as join Y, but is worked in a different manner. It is sometimes called 'Torchon Ground'.

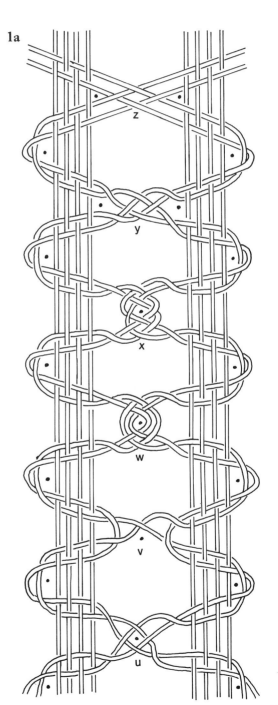

1a

2 A straight crossover with two threads. In order to make a very straight crossover bar: if two threads are to give the appearance of a bar or plait (see fig. 2a).

Work the two workers to the crossover point and then take the outer thread from both workers and cross them (see fig. 2b). Then, taking one of the bobbins, wrap it over and under the other bobbin thread (see fig. 2c). For a firmer crossing, repeat the wrapping process; this may be done three or four times. The two single threads are then gently drawn up and the threads join a partner in order to work back over their appropriate sides (see fig. 2d).

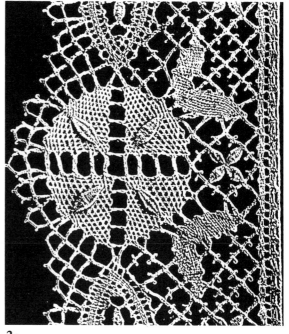

2a

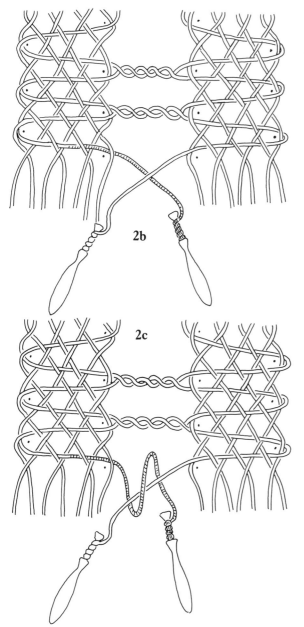

2b

2c

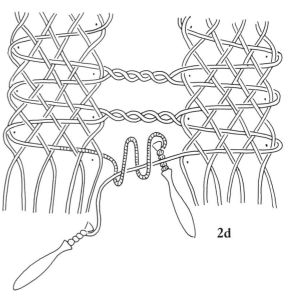

2d

3 Connecting a plait or leaf to a section of lace and then releasing it at the same point.

There are several methods of working this. Some pull the work closer together, whereas other methods are merely decorative. This whole section is easier to follow if one counts the position of the bobbins in relation to each other. Always count from the left before each new movement.

Whole stitch pairs 1 and 2, then 2 and 3. Pin on inside of pairs 2 and 3 (see fig. 3a). Whole stitch pairs

3a

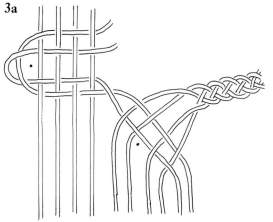

3b

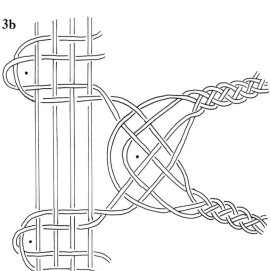

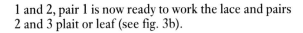

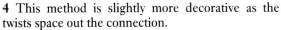

4a

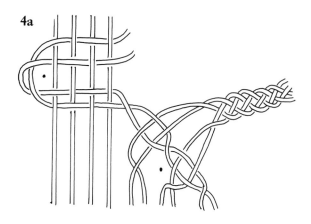

4b

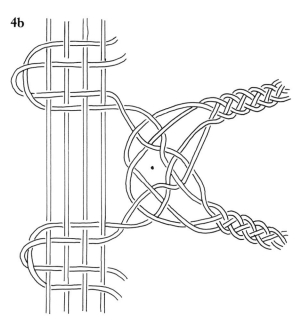

5a

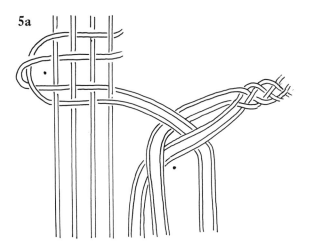

1 and 2, pair 1 is now ready to work the lace and pairs 2 and 3 plait or leaf (see fig. 3b).

4 This method is slightly more decorative as the twists space out the connection.

Twist pair 1 and whole stitch pairs 1 and 2. Then twist both. Whole stitch pairs 2 and 3 and twist both; pin on the inside of pairs 2 and 3 (see fig. 4a).

Whole stitch pairs 1 and 2 and twist both before pair 1 works back through the lace and then pairs 2 and 3; plait (see fig. 4b).

5 Windmill Connection.

Treat and count each pair of threads as a single unit.

Cross 1 over 2 and twist pairs 3 over 2, and then cross 1 and 2. Pin under pairs 2 and 3 (see fig. 5a). Twist 3 over 2 and cross 1 over 3. The connection is completed; pair 1 works the lace and 2 and 3 the plait (see fig. 5b).

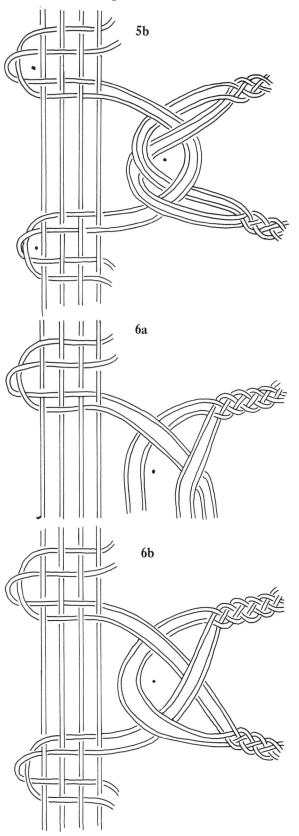

5b

6a

6b

6 A second windmill connection. Treat and count each pair as a single unit.

Cross 1 over 2 and twist 3 over 2. Pin under 1 and 2 (see fig. 6a). To complete the join, cross 1 and 2; pair 1 works the lace and 2 and 3 make the plait (see fig. 6b).

7 Treat the pairs from the plait as a single unit, but the pair from the lace as two threads.

Cross thread 2 over pair 3, twist pair 4 over thread 3. Pin in centre (see fig. 7a). Twist thread 2 over pair 1, twist thread 4 over pair 3. Lastly, cross pair 2 over thread 3 (see fig. 7b).

8 Twist pairs 1 and 2 and then whole stitch them together. Twist both, and pin under whole stitch (see fig. 8a).

Whole stitch pairs 1 and 2 together again and twist both. Pair 1 works the lace; twist pair 3 before making the plait with pair 2 (see fig. 8b).

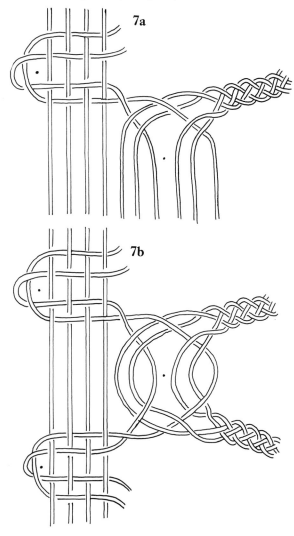

7a

7b

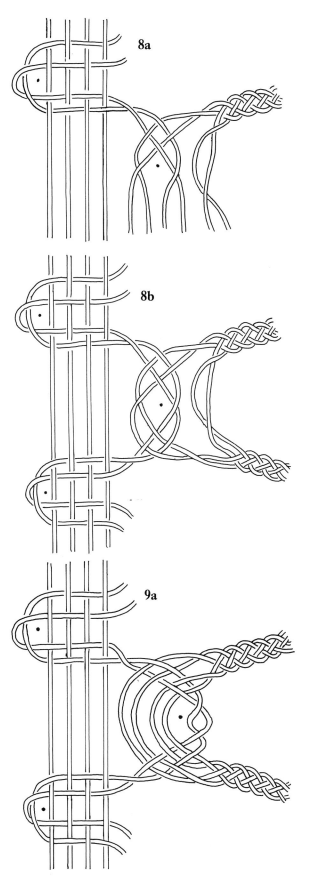

8a

8b

9a

9 Twist pair 1 and pass the top thread of pair 1 over pair 2 and under pair 3. The lower thread of pair 1 goes under pair 2 and over pair 3. Twist pair 3 twice and pin between 3 and 2. Pass the top thread of pair 3 under pair 2 and over pair 1 and the lower thread of pair 3 over pair 2 and under pair 1. Pair 1 is now ready for the lace and pairs 2 and 3 for the plait (see fig. 9a).

10 Treat each pair of threads as a single unit. Cross pairs 1 and 2, then twist pairs 3 and 2. Twist all three pairs and pin between pairs 1 and 2. Twist pairs 3 and 2, cross pairs 1 and 2. Lastly, twist all pairs once. Pair 1 is now ready for the lace and pairs 2 and 3 for the plait (see fig. 10a).

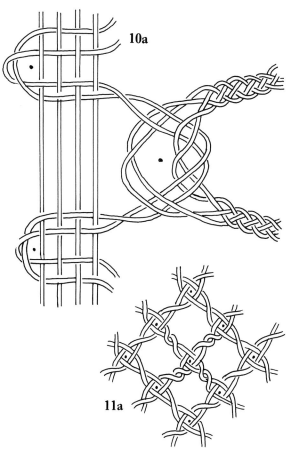

10a

11a

11 Pairs can be joined decoratively: this is sometimes used in net ground.

A two pair crossing. The two pairs within the frame are joined in the most simple form. Twist pairs from either side to separate them from the net, half stitch, pin, half stitch and then twist the pairs again to match the number of twists before the half stitch join (see fig. 11a).

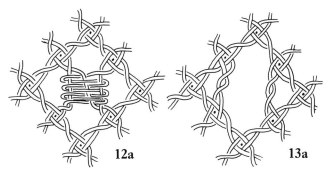

12a **13a**

12 The two pairs can be joined with a tally (see fig. 12a).

13 Pairs can just be left twisted and not crossed at all for an alternative decorative movement (see fig. 13a).

14 For a three pair crossing, whole stitch the left-hand pairs 1 and 2, then the right-hand pairs 2 and 3. Lastly, whole stitch pairs 1 and 2. The three pair crossing is completed (see fig. 14a).

15 For a tighter three pair crossing, half stitch pairs 1 and 2.

Whole stitch pairs 3 and 2 and then pairs 2 and 1. Twist pairs 2 and 3. Cross the centre threads 4 over 5. The crossing is complete (see fig. 15a).

16 Crossing two pairs through a third pair.
Treat pairs 1 and 2 as a single unit but pair 3 as single threads. Half stitch pairs 1 and 2 with pair 3, pin, then cross pair 2 over thread 3. This is rather like a windmill crossing (see fig. 16a).

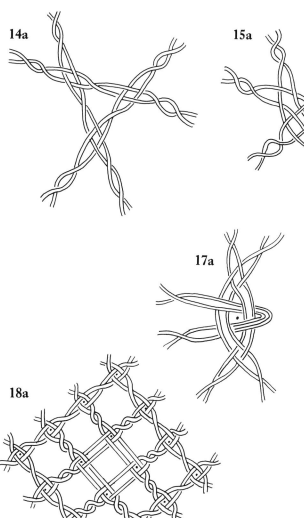

14a **15a** **16a**

17a

18a

17 Passing a pair through two pairs and back out again before the two pairs continue into the work.

Whole stitch the two pairs. Then, treating each pair of threads as a single unit, cross the passing through pair 1 over pair 2 and then under pair 3. Use this to make the type of stitch that is needed in the lace or, alternatively, simply take this pair around a pin.

To return this pair through the two pairs, take the crossing pair over pair 2 and under pair 1. Pairs 2 and 3 then whole stitch together to secure the crossing (see fig. 17a).

18 A plain crossing of four pairs.
The pairs to be crossed are twisted twice. Whole stitch centre pairs 2 and 3, whole stitch pairs 1 and 2, then 3 and 4. Lastly, whole stitch the centre pairs 2 and 3. To complete, twist all pairs twice (see fig. 18a).

19 A spider with a cross over centre.
All pairs to be crossed must be twisted twice.

Whole stitch centre pairs 2 and 3, whole stitch pairs 1 and 2 and pairs 3 and 4. Whole stitch centre pairs 2

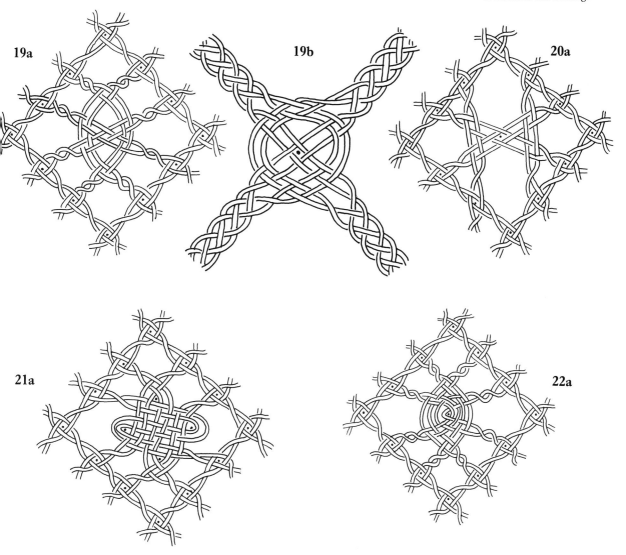

19a **19b** **20a**

21a **22a**

and 3, whole stitch pairs 1 and 2, and pairs 3 and 4. Lastly, whole stitch pairs 2 and 3. To complete the spider, twist all the pairs twice (see fig. 19a). This spider is sometimes used to cross two plaits (see fig. 19b).

20 A four pair open spider crossing.
Twist all pairs to be crossed once or twice.

Whole stitch pairs 1 and 2 then pairs 3 and 4. Whole stitch the centre pairs 2 and 3; a pin can be placed in the centre of this crossing. Whole stitch pairs 1 and 2 and pairs 3 and 4. Lastly, twist all the pairs to correspond with the number of twists at the start (see fig. 20a).

21 A four pair whole stitch block crossing.
Twist all the pairs to be crossed.

Whole stitch pairs 2 and 3; pin in order to support

the whole stitch. Whole stitch pair 1 through pairs 2, 3 and 4 and around the pin. Whole stitch back through pairs 4, 3 and 2 and around the pin on the left-hand side. Whole stitch again through pairs 2, 3 and 4. Leave. Whole stitch pairs 2 and 3. Twist all pairs (see fig. 21a).

22 A four pair two-legged spider.
Twist all pairs two or three times.

Whole stitch pairs 2 and 3 and then pairs 3 and 4. Whole stitch pairs 1 and 2 and then pairs 2 and 3. Pin in the centre under the last whole stitch made. Pull all the pairs up gently, and then repeat by whole stitching pairs 2 and 3, and then pairs 3 and 4.

Whole stitch pairs 1 and 2, then pairs 2 and 3. Gently pull up again. Twist all the pairs to correspond with the start (see fig. 22a). This spider can be used to join and cross two plaits (see fig. 22b).

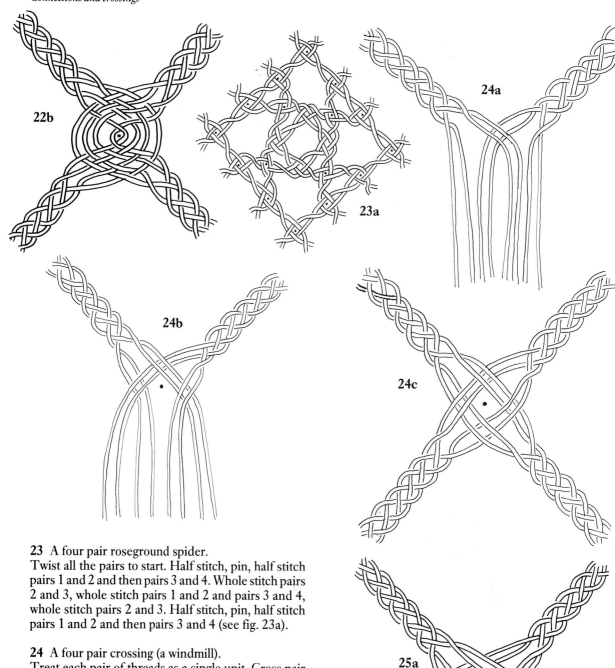

23 A four pair roseground spider.
Twist all the pairs to start. Half stitch, pin, half stitch pairs 1 and 2 and then pairs 3 and 4. Whole stitch pairs 2 and 3, whole stitch pairs 1 and 2 and pairs 3 and 4, whole stitch pairs 2 and 3. Half stitch, pin, half stitch pairs 1 and 2 and then pairs 3 and 4 (see fig. 23a).

24 A four pair crossing (a windmill).
Treat each pair of threads as a single unit. Cross pair 2 over pair 3 (see fig. 24a). Twist pairs 4 over 3 and 2 over 1. Pin in the centre (see fig. 24b).

Lastly cross pair 2 over 3. The windmill crossing makes a neat, tight crossing (see fig. 24c).

25 A four pair twisted windmill crossing.
Treat each pair of threads as a single unit. Cross pair 2 over 3. Twist pairs 4 over 3 and 2 over 1, pin in centre. Twist pairs 4 over 3 and 2 over 1.

Lastly, cross pair 2 over 3. This leaves a decorative centre hole (see fig. 25a).

68

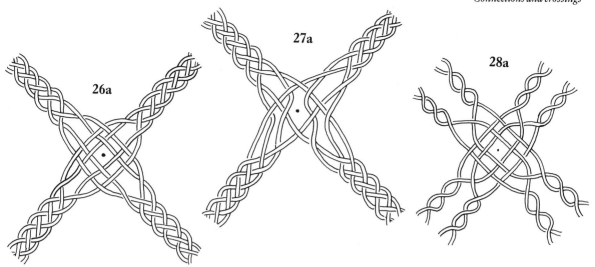

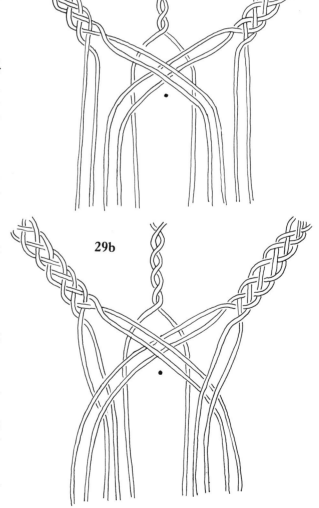

26 A four pair whole stitch crossing.
Whole stitch pairs 2 and 3. Whole stitch pairs 4 and 3, then 2 and 1. Pin in the centre. Whole stitch pairs 2 and 3. This crossing is very firm and takes up slightly more space than a windmill (see fig. 26a).

27 A four pair half stitch crossing.
Half stitch centre pairs 2 and 3. Half stitch side pairs 4 and 3, then 2 and 1. Pin in the centre. Lastly, half stitch pairs 2 and 3. This light crossing is used for its decorative effect and should not be used where considerable strain is to be placed on the lace (see fig. 27a)

28 A four pair starburst spider.
Twist all pairs to be crossed two or three times. Cross the two inside threads of pairs 1 and 2. Repeat with pairs 3 and 4. Whole stitch pair 2 through pairs 3 and 4; pin in the centre. Whole stitch pair 1 through pairs 2 and 3.

Cross the two inside threads of pair 1 and 2, repeat with pairs 3 and 4.

All the pairs can then be twisted to correspond with the start (see fig. 28a).

29 A five pair crossing: windmill variety.
Count all the pairs of threads as a single unit, except for the single pair where each thread is counted singly.

Cross pair 2 over single thread 3 and twist pair 5 over single thread 4.

Cross pair 3 over 4 and single thread 5. Twist pair 3 over single thread 2; pin in the centre (see fig. 29a).

Twist pair 6 over 5 and 2 over 1 (see fig. 29b). Twist single thread 3 over pair 2 and cross single thread 4 over pair 5. Cross pairs 3 and 4. Lastly, cross single thread 2 over pair 3 and twist single thread 5 over 4. Each pair is now crossed in the exact opposite position to its starting point on the crossing (see fig. 29c).

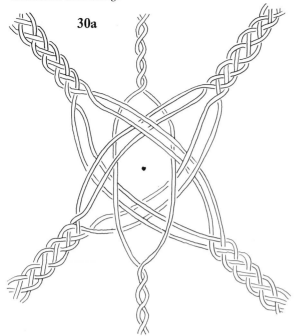

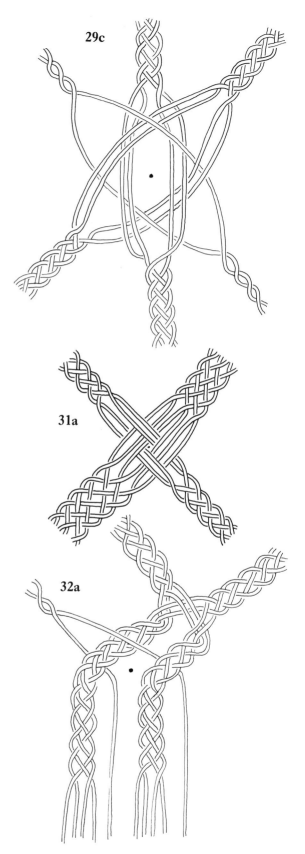

30 A five pair crossing where the single pair is on the left-hand side for the start.

Work exactly in the same manner as Method 29; the single pair now lies to the left of the two plaits rather than between them.

Cross single thread 2 over pair 3 and twist pair 5 over pair 4.

Cross single thread 3 over 4 and 5. Twist pair 3 over pair 2 and single thread 1. Pin in the centre.

Twist pair 6 over single thread 5, twist pair 3 over single thread 2. Cross single thread 3 over pair 4.

Lastly cross pair 2 over 3 and twist pair 5 over the single thread 4. Each pair crossed is in the exact opposite position to its starting point (see fig. 30a).

31 Crossing three pairs through two pairs.
A large windmill can achieve this crossing. Cross pair 2 over the first three threads of pairs 3, 4 and 5 and then under the last three threads. Pin in the centre. Pair 1 then travels under the first three threads of pairs 3, 4 and 5, and the over the next three threads (see fig. 31a).

32 Taking a single pair through two plaits and returning that pair to the same side.

Count each plait (four threads) as a single unit and count the single pair as two single threads.

Cross thread 2 over group 3; twist group 4 over thread 3 and group 2 over thread 1. Pin in the centre (see fig. 32a).

Twist thread 4 over group 3 and thread 2 over group 1 (see fig. 32b). Cross group 2 over thread 3. This draws the crossing of two plaits and a worker pair close together (see fig. 32c).

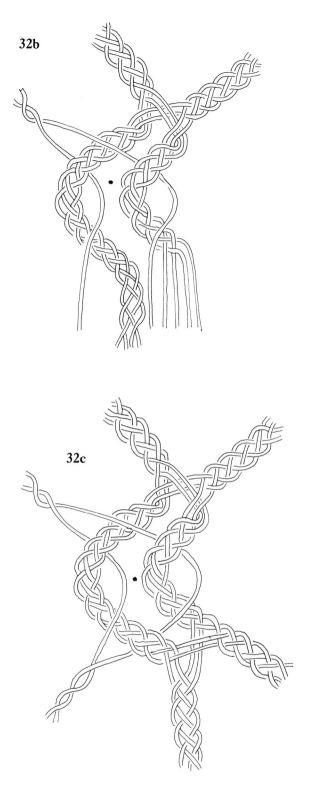

32b

32c

Cross pair 2 over 3. Twist pair 2 over 1 and pair 4 over 3. The left-hand thread of pair 5 passes under pairs 4 and 3 and over pairs 2 and 1. The right-hand thread of pair 5 passes over pairs 4 and 3 and under pairs 2 and 1. Pin in the centre of the pairs and the split pair.

Cross pairs 3 over 4, twist pair 3 over 2. Split pairs 4 and 5 and twist the centre two threads of these pairs (see fig. 33a).

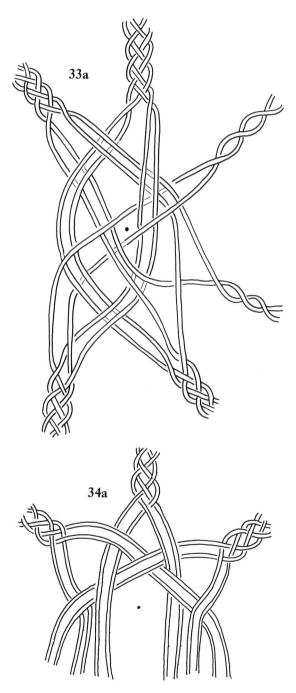

33a

34a

33 An alternative to Method 32.
Count each pair of threads as a single unit (except the single pair where each thread is counted singly).

34b

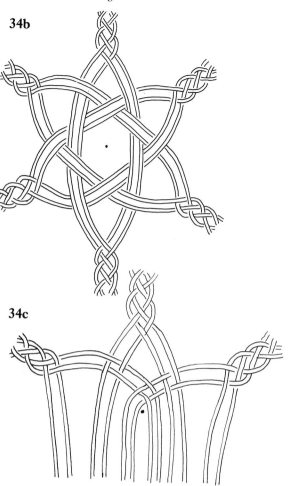

34d

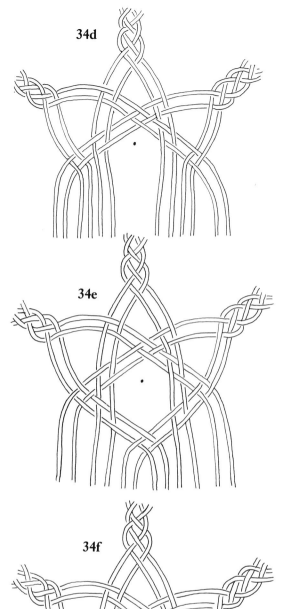

34c

34e

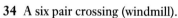

34 A six pair crossing (windmill).
Treat each pair of threads as a single unit.
  Cross pair 2 over 3 and pair 4 over 5.
  Twist pair 4 over 3.
  Cross pair 4 over 5, and twist 3 over 2.
  Twist pair 2 over 1 and pair 6 over 5.
  Pin in centre (see fig. 34a).
  Cross pair 2 over 3 and pair 4 over 5.
  Twist pair 4 over 3.
  Cross pair 2 over 3 and pair 4 over 5.
  Pull all pairs up gently (see fig. 34b).

  This method can also be worked in whole stitch.
  Whole stitch pairs 2 and 3, pairs 4 and 5.
  Whole stitch pairs 3 and 4, pin in centre (see fig. 34c).
  Whole stitch pairs 2 and 3, pairs 4 and 5.
  Whole stitch pairs 1 and 2, pairs 5 and 6 (see fig. 34d).
  Whole stitch pairs 2 and 3, pairs 4 and 5.
  Whole stitch pairs 3 and 4 (see fig. 34e).
  Finally, whole stitch pairs 2 and 3, pairs 4 and 5.
  Pull up all pairs (see fig. 34f).

← 2 over 3

34f

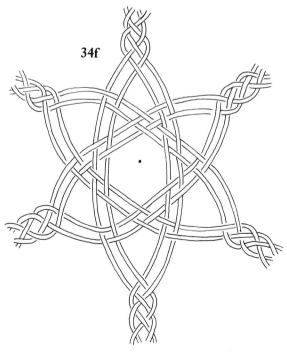

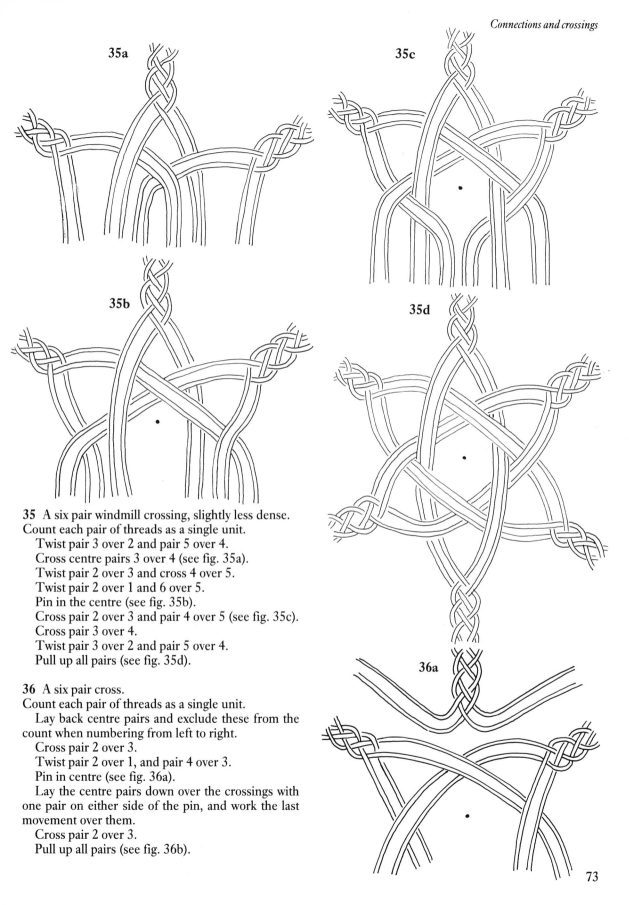

35 A six pair windmill crossing, slightly less dense.
Count each pair of threads as a single unit.
  Twist pair 3 over 2 and pair 5 over 4.
  Cross centre pairs 3 over 4 (see fig. 35a).
  Twist pair 2 over 3 and cross 4 over 5.
  Twist pair 2 over 1 and 6 over 5.
  Pin in the centre (see fig. 35b).
  Cross pair 2 over 3 and pair 4 over 5 (see fig. 35c).
  Cross pair 3 over 4.
  Twist pair 3 over 2 and pair 5 over 4.
  Pull up all pairs (see fig. 35d).

36 A six pair cross.
Count each pair of threads as a single unit.
  Lay back centre pairs and exclude these from the
count when numbering from left to right.
  Cross pair 2 over 3.
  Twist pair 2 over 1, and pair 4 over 3.
  Pin in centre (see fig. 36a).
  Lay the centre pairs down over the crossings with
one pair on either side of the pin, and work the last
movement over them.
  Cross pair 2 over 3.
  Pull up all pairs (see fig. 36b).

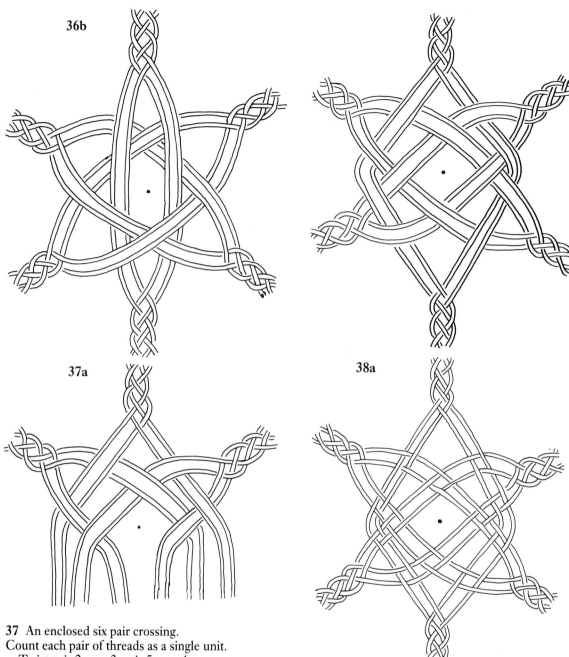

36b

37a

38a

37 An enclosed six pair crossing.
Count each pair of threads as a single unit.
  Twist pair 2 over 3, pair 5 over 4.
  Cross pair 3 over 4.
  Cross pair 1 over 2, pair 5 over 6.
  Twist pair 3 over 2, pair 4 over 5.
  Pin in centre (see fig. 37a).
  Cross pair 1 over 2, pair 3 over 4, pair 5 over 6.
  Twist pair 3 over 2, pair 5 over 4
  Pull up all pairs (see fig. 37b).

38 An enclosed whole stitch six pair crossing.
Worked as Method 37, except that each pair is whole stitched through each other.

  Whole stitch pair 2 and 3, pair 5 and 4.
  Whole stitch pair 3 and 4.
  Whole stitch pair 1 and 2, pair 5 and 6.
  Whole stitch pair 3 and 2, pair 4 and 5.
  Pin in centre.
  Whole stitch pairs 1 and 2, pair 3 and 4, and pair 5 and 6.
  Whole stitch pairs 3 and 2, pair 5 and 4.
  Pull up all pairs (see fig. 38a).

39 A split six pair crossing.
Count each pair of threads as a single unit.

Cross pair 2 over 3, pair 4 over 5.
Twist pair 4 over 3.
Pin in centre (see fig. 39a).
Twist pair 2 over 1, pair 6 over 5.
Cross pairs 2 over 3, pair 4 over 5.
Pull up gently (see fig. 39b).

A split six pair crossing can also be worked in whole stitch.

Whole stitch pair 2 and 3, pair 4 and 5.
Whole stitch pair 4 and 3. Pin in centre.
Whole stitch pair 2 and 1, pair 6 and 5.

Whole stitch pair 2 and 3, lastly pair 4 and 5 (see fig. 39c).

40 An elaborate six pair crossing.
Treat each pair of threads as a single unit.

Fold back centre pairs 3 and 4 and recount, excluding these.
Twist pair 2 and 3.
Cross pair 1 and 2, pair 3 and 4.
Pin in centre, lay down the pairs left out, one on either side of the pin, and work over them.
Twist pair 2 and 3.
Pull up all pairs (see fig. 40a).

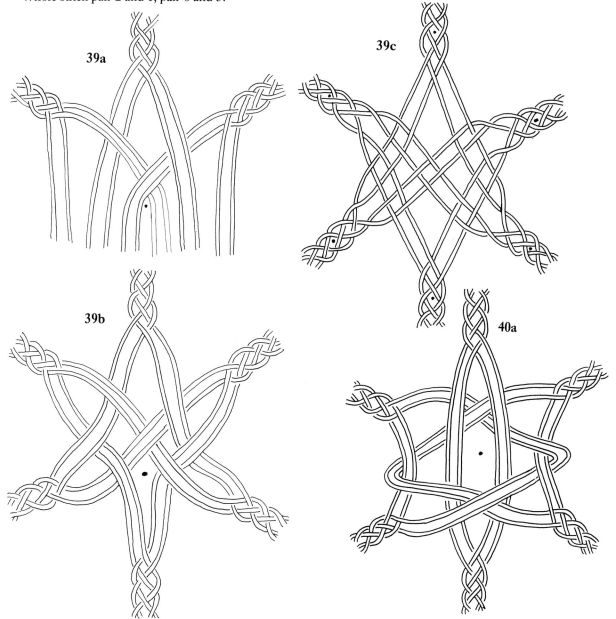

39a

39c

39b

40a

75

41a

42b

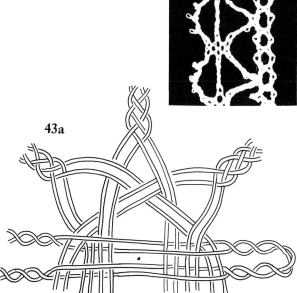

41b

43a

42a

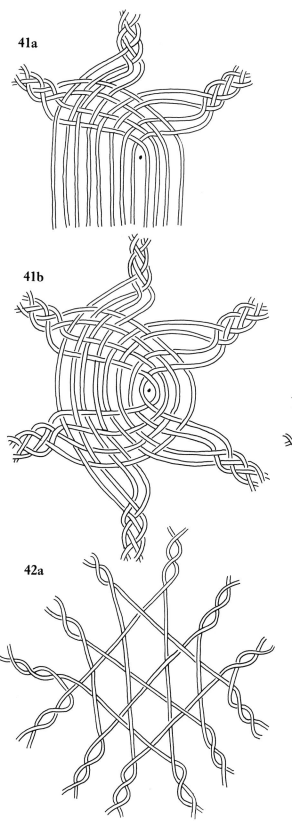

41 A six pair crossing where two pairs cross four pairs and return to the starting side.

Whole stitch pair 2 to the right, through pairs 3, 4, 5 and 6.

Whole stitch pair 1 to the right, through pairs 2, 3, 4 and 5.

Pin between pairs 4 and 5 (see fig. 41a).

Whole stitch pair 5 to the left, through pairs 4, 3, 2 and 1.

Whole stitch pair 6 to the left, through pairs 5, 4, 3 and 2.

Pull up all pairs gently (see fig. 41b).

42 A six pair starburst crossing.
Half stitch pairs 3 and 4.

Then half stitch pair 3 to the left, through pair 2 and 1.

Half stitch pair 5 to the left, through pairs 4, 3 and 2.

Half stitch pair 6 to the left, through pairs 5, 4 and 3.

This makes an attractive decorative crossing (see fig. 42a). See in use (fig. 42b).

43b

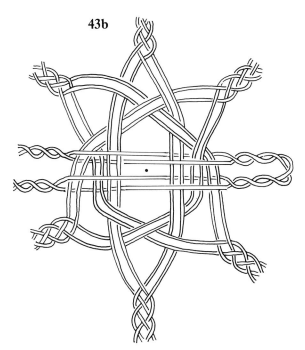

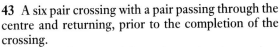

44a

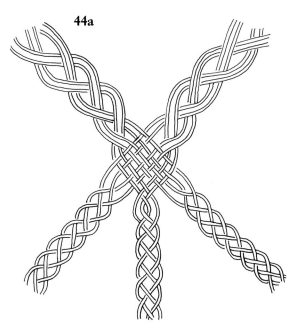

45a

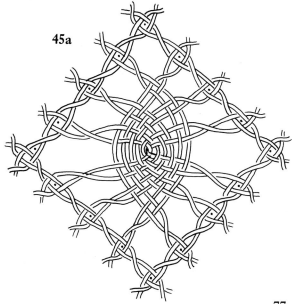

43 A six pair crossing with a pair passing through the centre and returning, prior to the completion of the crossing.

A pair can be crossed through any six pair crossing, always working to the centre stage, then crossing and if the pattern so dictates, returning, and then completing the crossing. In the example shown, a pair is working across Method 34 of the six pair crossing.

Treat each pair of threads in the crossing as one unit.

Cross pair 2 over 3, pair 4 over 5.

Twist pair 4 over 3.

Cross pair 4 over 5, pair 3 over 2.

Twist pair 2 over 1, pair 6 over 5.

Take the pair to be crossed and place one thread of this pair under pairs 1, 2 and 3. The other thread from that pair is placed over pairs 1, 2 and 3. Pin below both threads in the centre of the crossing.

Reverse the thread order of the single pair and pass the thread that was below over pairs 4, 5 and 6, whilst the other thread passes under pairs 4, 5 and 6. This pair then works the pattern; when this has been completed it returns through the crossing in the same manner. One thread passes under the first three pairs of the crossing, with the other thread over the first three pairs, then exchanging positions with the under-thread passing over the next three pairs and the other pair passing under the three pairs (see fig. 43a).

The crossing is then completed by crossing pair 2 over 3, pair 4 over 5.

Twist pair 4 over 3.

Lastly cross pair 2 over 3 and pair 4 over 5.

Pull up all pairs (see fig. 43b).

44 Crossing two sets of three plaits (six pairs) having three sets of two plaits on the completion of the crossing.

Whole stitch pair 3 to the right, through pairs 4, 5 and 6.

Whole stitch pair 2 to the right, through pairs 3, 4 and 5.

Lastly, whole stitch pair 1 to the right, through pairs 2, 3 and 4.

This crossing can be made with any six pairs. It leaves a small whole stitch block in the centre, which can prove to be a pleasing feature in the lace (see fig. 44a).

45 Elaborate six pair crossings can be used anywhere, but are frequently used in net grounds. (The simple spider.)

All pairs are usually twisted three times but can be twisted only once or twice. It does depend on the desired position of the spider. The more twists prior to the start, the more central and tighter the spider.

Whole stitch pair 3 to the right, through pairs 4, 5 and 6.

Whole stitch pair 2 to the right, through pairs 3, 4 and 5.

Whole stitch pair 1 to the right, through pairs 2, 3 and 4.

Pin in the centre. Pull up all pairs, being careful not to move the position of the bobbins in relation to each other.

Then commencing with the centre pairs again, whole stitch pair 3 to the right, through pairs 4, 5 and 6.

Whole stitch pair 2 to the right, through pairs 3, 4 and 5.

Whole stitch pair 1 to the right, through pairs 2, 3 and 4.

Pull all pairs up gently so that the spider is quite tight, and then twist all pairs to correspond with the start (see fig. 45a).

46 A six pair spider with an eye.
Twist all pairs.

Whole stitch pair 3 to the right, through pairs 4, 5 and 6.

Whole stitch pair 2 to the right, through pairs 3, 4 and 5.

Whole stitch pair 1 to the right, through pairs 2 and 3.

Pin between pairs 2 and 3 in the left-hand side of the spider and then whole stitch pair 3 to the left, through pairs 2 and 1.

Pin between 4 and 5 and work pair 4 to the right, through pairs 5 and 6.

Whole stitch pair 3 to the right, through pairs 4 and 5.

Whole stitch pair 2 to the right, through pairs 3 and 4.

Pull up all pairs gently and twist each pair to correspond with the start (see fig. 46a).

47 A six pair haloed spider.
Twist all pairs.

Halo; whole stitch and twist pairs 3 and 4, then whole stitch and twist pairs 4 and 5.

Whole stitch and twist pairs 5 and 6.

Whole stitch and twist pairs 2 and 3; whole stitch and twist pairs 2 and 1.

Spider; whole stitch centre pairs 3 and 4, 4 and 5.

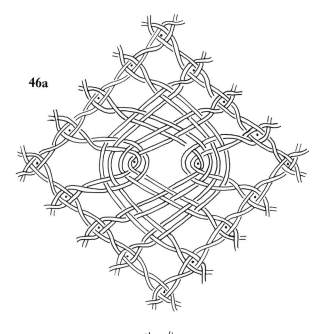

46a

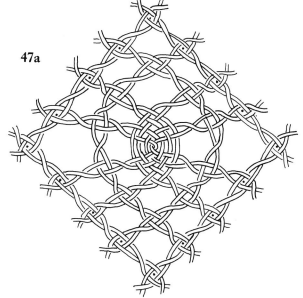

47a

Whole stitch pairs 2 and 3, 3 and 4.

Pin in centre; pull up all pairs.

Repeat the spider centre, whole stitch pairs 3 and 4, 4 and 5.

Whole stitch pairs 2 and 3, 3 and 4.

Twist pairs 2, 3, 4 and 5.

Halo; whole stitch and twist pairs 1 and 2, whole stitch and twist pairs 2 and 3.

Whole stitch and twist pairs 5 and 6 and whole stitch and twist pairs 4 and 5.

Lastly, whole stitch and twist pairs 3 and 4.

Twist all pairs to correspond with the start (see fig. 47a).

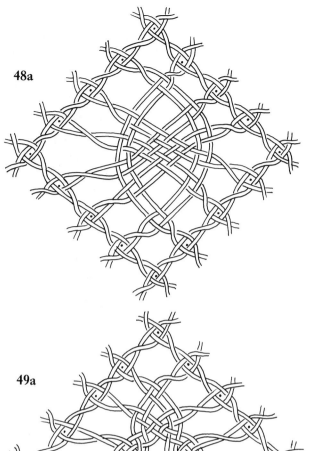

48a

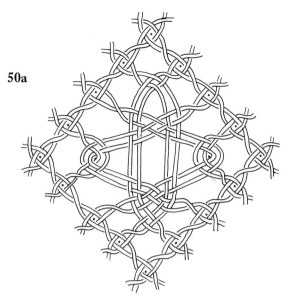

50a

49 A six pair narrow-eyed spider.
Twist all pairs to start.

Whole stitch pairs 3 and 4 and 4 and 5.

Whole stitch pairs 2 and 3.

Whole stitch pairs 3 and 4 and take 4 to the right, through pairs 5 and 6.

Whole stitch pairs 5 and 4.

Pin between pairs 5 and 6.

Whole stitch pair 6 to the left, through pairs 5 and 4, and work the left-hand side of the eye.

Whole stitch pair 3 to the left, through pairs 2 and 1, and pin between pairs 1 and 2.

Whole stitch pairs 2 and 3.

Whole stitch pair 1 to the right, through pairs 2, 3, 4 and 5.

Whole stitch pairs 2 and 3.

Lastly, whole stitch pairs 3 and 4 and twist all pairs and pull up (see fig. 49a).

50 A six pair wide-eyed spider.
Twist all pairs to start.

Whole stitch pair 3, through pairs 4, and 5.

Whole stitch pairs 3 and 2.

Whole stitch pair 3 to the right, through pairs 4, 5 and 6.

Pin between pairs 5 and 6.

Whole stitch pair 6 to the left, through pairs 5 and 4.

Work the left-hand side. Whole stitch pair 3 to the left, through pairs 2 and 1.

Pin between pairs 2 and 1.

Whole stitch pair 1 to the right, through pairs 2, 3, 4 and 5.

Whole stitch pairs 2 and 3.

Lastly, whole stitch pairs 3 and 4.

Twist all pairs to correspond to the start (see fig. 50a).

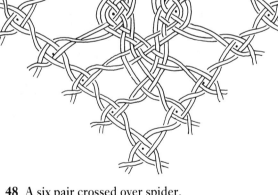

49a

48 A six pair crossed over spider.
Twist all pairs to start.

Whole stitch pair 3 to the right, through pairs 4, 5 and 6.

Whole stitch pair 3 to the left, through pairs 2 and 1.

Whole stitch pair 3 to the right, through pairs 4 and 5.

Whole stitch pair 2 to the right, through pairs 3 and 4.

Whole stitch pair 6, through pairs 5 and 4.

Whole stitch pair 1, through pairs 2, 3 and 4.

Pull up all pairs and twist each pair to correspond with the start (see fig. 48a).

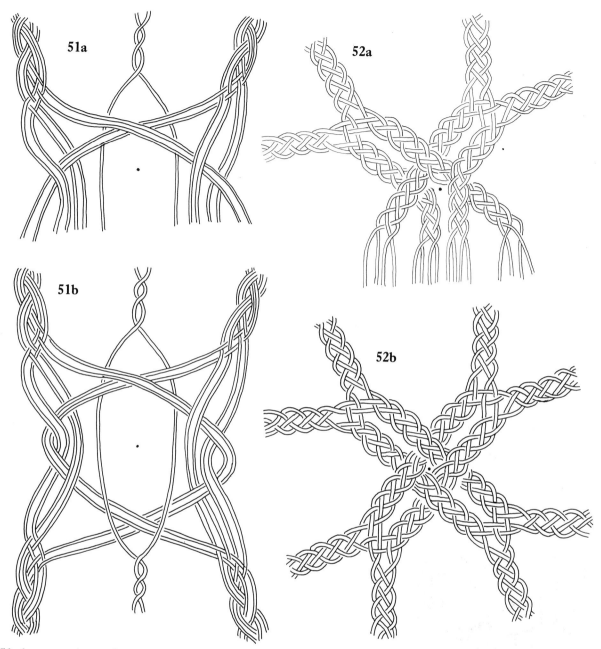

51a

52a

51b

52b

51 A seven pair crossing.

Count each pair of threads as a single unit.

Separate the centre pair and work over it but exclude it when counting the position of bobbin units.

Cross pair 3 over pair 4.

Twist pair 3 over 2 and cross pair 1 over 2.

Twist pair 5 over 4 and cross pair 5 over 6.

Pin in the centre of the split pair and all other pairs (see fig. 51a).

Lay the split pair back up the pillow.

Cross pair 1 over 2 and pair 5 over 6.

Lastly, cross pair 3 over pair 4.

Lay down the split pair.

Pull all pairs evenly. The pairs are now crossed (see fig. 51b).

52 An eight pair crossing (a large windmill).

Treat each group of two pairs as a single unit.

Cross group 2 over group 3.

Twist group 2 over 1 and group 4 over 3.

Pin in the centre (see fig. 52a).

Finally, cross group 2 over 3. This is actually a very large whole stitch with a pin in the centre (see fig. 52b).

53 A woven eight pair crossing.
Treat each pair of threads as a single unit.

Working to the right, cross pair 4 over pair 5, under pair 6, over pair 7 and under pair 8.

Weave pair 3 under pair 4 and over pair 5, under pair 6 and over pair 7.

Cross pair 2 over pair 3, under pair 4, over pair 5 and under pair 6.

Lastly, weave pair 1 under pair 2, over pair 3, under pair 4 and over pair 5.

Pull up all pairs (see fig. 53a).

54 An enclosed eight pair crossing.
Treat each pair of threads as a single unit.

Cross pair 4 over 5.
Twist pair 4 over 3, pair 6 over 5.
Cross pair 2 over 3, pair 6 over 7.
Twist pair 4 over 3, pair 6 over 5.
Cross centre pair 4 over 5.
Twist pairs 2 over 1, 4 over 3, 6 over 5, 8 over 7.
Cross pairs 2 over 3, pairs 6 over 7.
Pin in the centre (see fig. 54a).
Twist pairs 2 over 1, 3 over 4, 5 over 6, 8 over 7.
Cross pairs 4 over 5.
Twist pair 4 over 3, pair 6 over 5.
Cross pair 2 over 3, pair 6 over 7.
Twist pair 4 over 3, pair 6 over 5.
Finally, cross centre pair 4 over 5 (see fig. 54b).

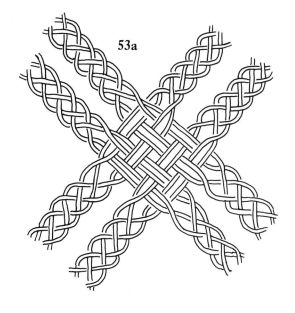

53a

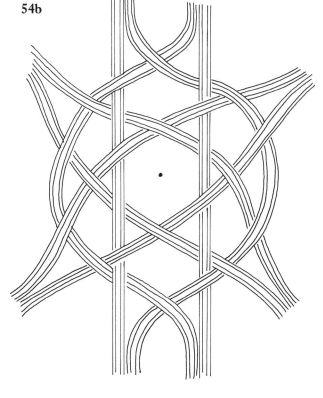

54b

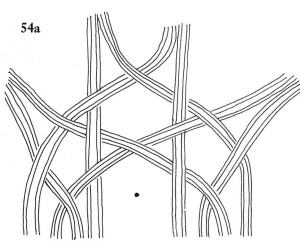

54a

55 An eight pair double enclosed crossing.
Treat each pair as a single unit.

Cross pair 4 over pair 5, under pair 6, over pair 7 and under pair 8.

Weave pair 3 under pair 4, over pair 5, under pair 6 and over pair 7.

Cross pair 2 over pair 3, under pair 4, over pair 5, under pair 6, over pair 7 and under pair 8. Pin in the centre.

Weave pair 1 under pair 2, over pair 3, under pair 4, over pair 5, under pair 6 and over pair 7.

55a

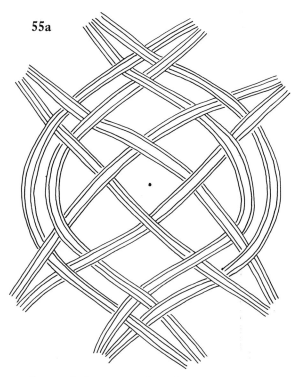

Cross pair 2 over pair 3, under pair 4, over pair 5, under pair 6.

Finally, weave pair 1 under pair 2, over pair 3, under pair 4 and over pair 5.

Pull all pairs up evenly (see fig. 55a).

56 An eight pair star crossing.

Eight pins are needed in the centre of this crossing in a diamond formation.

Whole stitch pairs 4 and 5, pin and whole stitch pairs 4 and 5 again.

Whole stitch pairs 2 and 3, pin and whole stitch pairs 2 and 3 again.

Whole stitch pairs 6 and 7, pin and whole stitch pairs 6 and 7 again.

Whole stitch pairs 3 and 4, and pairs 5 and 6.

Whole stitch centre pairs 4 and 5.

Whole stitch pair 4 to the left, through pairs 3, 2 and 1; pin and whole stitch to the right with pair 2. Whole stitch pairs 3 and 4.

Return to the other centre pair 5 and whole stitch to the right, through pairs 6, 7 and 8. Pin and whole stitch pairs 7 and 8 again.

Whole stitch pairs 5 and 6 and whole stitch pair 2 with pairs 3 and 4.

Whole stitch pair 7 through 6, 5, 4, 3 and 2. Pin between the last whole stitch made, and whole stitch again.

Work pair 5 to the right through pair 6, whole stitch with pair 7. Pin and whole stitch with pair 7 again.

Whole stitch the last pin hole at the centre bottom

with pairs 4 and 5, pin and whole stitch again with the same pairs.

This makes a very decorative crossing. The diamond formation of the pins can be placed very tightly together, or space out to suit the pattern (see fig. 56a).

57 An eight pair double edged eye.

Twist all pairs evenly; the number of twists will depend on the space to be filled and the tightness of the finished spider.

Whole stitch pair 4 to the right, through 4 pairs; pairs 5, 6, 7 and 8.

Whole stitch pair 3 to the right, through 4 pairs; pairs 4, 5, 6 and 7.

Whole stitch pair 2 through pairs 3 and 4.

Whole stitch pair 1 through pairs 2 and 3 and place a pin between the last whole stitch made and then whole stitch pair 3 to the left, through pairs 2 and 1.

Then whole stitch pair 4 to the left, through pairs 3 and 2.

On the right-hand side pin between the last whole stitch made and whole stitch pair 6 to the right, through pairs 7 and 8.

Whole stitch pair 5 to the right through pairs 6 and 7.

Whole stitch pairs 5 and 4 and then pairs 3 and 4 and then pairs 5 and 6.

Lastly, whole stitch the centre pairs 4 and 5. Twist the pairs to correspond with the start and pull up evenly (see fig. 57a).

56a

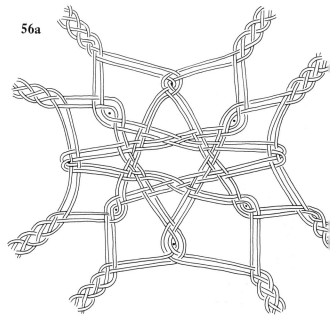

57a

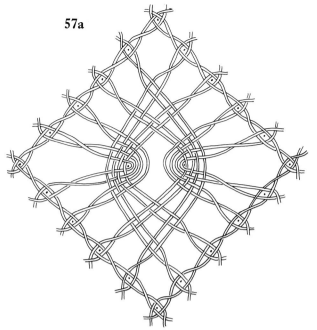

58a

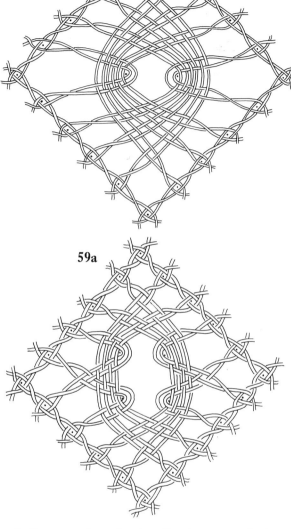

58 An eight pair triple edged eye.
Twist all pairs.

Whole stitch pair 4 through pairs 5, 6, 7 and 8.

Whole stitch pair 3 through pairs 4, 5, 6 and 7.

Whole stitch pair 2 through pairs 3, 4, 5 and 6.

Whole stitch pair 1 through pairs 2, 3 and 4.

Twist around the pin and whole stitch back through pairs 3, 2 and 1.

Take pair 5 around the pin and whole stitch back out through pairs 6, 7 and 8.

Whole stitch pair 4 through pairs 5, 6 and 7.

Whole stitch pair 3 through pairs 4, 5 and 6.

Whole stitch pair 2 through pairs 3, 4 and 5.

Twist all pairs as at the commencement of the eye (see fig. 58a).

59 An eight pair double eye.
Twist all the pairs to start.

Whole stitch pair 4 through pairs 5, 6 and 7.

Whole stitch pair 3 through pairs 4, 5 and 6.

Whole stitch pair 2 through 2 pairs 3 and 4, and pin.

Whole stitch back through pairs 3 and 2.

Whole stitch pair 1 with pair 2.

Whole stitch pair 2 through pairs 3 and 4 and then around the pin and back through 2 pairs; 3 and 2.

Work the right-hand side of the eye.

Take pair 5 around the pin and whole stitch it out to the right through pairs 6 and 7.

Whole stitch with pair 8.

Whole stitch pair 7 through pairs 6 and 5 and take that pair around the pin. Whole stitch back through pairs 6 and 7.

Whole stitch pair 4 through pairs 5 and 6.

Whole stitch pair 3 through pairs 4 and 5.

59a

Pull up evenly and twist all pairs to match the commencement (see fig. 59a).

60 An eight pair centre crossed spider.
Twist all pairs.

Whole stitch pair 4 to the right, through pairs 5, 6, 7 and 8.

Whole stitch pair 3 to the right, through pairs 4, 5, 6 and 7.

Whole stitch pair 2 to the right, through pairs 3, 4, 5 and 6.

Whole stitch pair 1 to the right, through all pairs 2, 3, 4, 5, 6, 7 and 8.

Whole stitch pair 4 to the left, through pairs 3, 2 and 1.

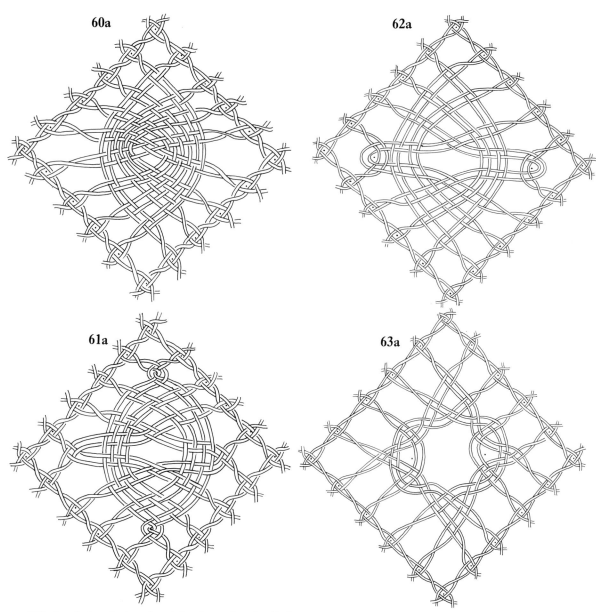

60a

62a

61a

63a

Whole stitch pair 4 to the right, through pairs 5, 6 and 7.

Whole stitch pair 3 to the right, through pairs 4, 5 and 6.

Whole stitch pair 2 to the right, through pairs 3, 4 and 5.

Pull up and twist all pairs to correspond to the commencement of the spider (see fig. 60a).

61 An eight pair double centre crossed spider.
Twist all pairs.

Whole stitch pairs 4 and 5, pin and whole stitch pairs 4 and 5 again.

Whole stitch pair 5 with pairs 6 and 7.

Whole stitch pair 3 with pairs 4, 5 and 6.

Whole stitch pair 2 with pairs 3, 4, 5, 6, 7 and 8.

Whole stitch pair 4 to the left with pairs 3, 2 and 1.

Whole stitch pair 2 to the right with pairs 3 and 4.

Whole stitch pair 7 to the left with pairs 6, 5, 4, 3 and 2.

Whole stitch pair 5 with pairs 6 and 7.

Whole stitch pair 4 with pairs 5 and 6.

Whole stitch pair 3 with pairs 4 and 5. Pin between pairs 4 and 5 and whole stitch these pairs again.

Twist all pairs (see fig. 61a).

62 An eight pair eye crossing.
Twist all pairs to start.

Whole stitch pair 4 with pairs 5, 6 and 7.

Whole stitch pair 3 with pairs 4, 5 and 6.

Whole stitch pair 2 with pairs 3, 4, 5, 6, 7 and 8.
Pin and whole stitch pair 8 with pairs 7, 6 and 5.
Whole stitch pair 4 with pairs 3, 2 and 1.
Pin and whole stitch pair 1 to the right side with pairs 2, 3, 4, 5, 6 and 7.
Whole stitch pair 3 with pairs 4, 5 and 6.
Whole stitch pair 2 with pairs 3, 4 and 5.
Twist all pairs (see fig. 62a).

63 An eight pair double eye crossing.
Twist all pairs.
Whole stitch pair 4 with pairs 5 and 6.
Whole stitch pair 3 with pairs 4 and 5.
Work the left-hand side and whole stitch pairs 3 and 4.
Whole stitch pair 2 with pairs 3 and 4, pin under the last whole stitch made.
Whole stitch pairs 2 and 3.
Whole stitch pairs 1 and 2.
Whole stitch pairs 2 and 3.
Whole stitch pair 4 with pairs 3 and 2.
Whole stitch pairs 3 and 4.
Work the right-hand side and whole stitch pairs 5 and 6.
Whole stitch pair 7 with pairs 6 and 5. Pin under the last whole stitch made.
Whole stitch pairs 6 and 7.
Whole stitch pair 8 with pairs 7, 6 and 5.
Whole stitch pairs 7 and 6.
Whole stitch pairs 5 and 6.
Whole stitch the centre pairs 4 and 5.
Whole stitch pairs 3 and 4 and 5 and 6.
Lastly, whole stitch pairs 4 and 5.
Twist all pairs (see fig. 63a).

64 An eight pair haloed spider.
Twist all pairs to be crossed.
Whole stitch and twist pair 4 with pairs 5, 6, 7 and 8.
Whole stitch and twist pair 4 with pairs 3, 2 and 1.
Whole stitch pair 4 with pairs 5, 6 and 7.
Whole stitch pair 3 with pairs 4, 5 and 6.
Whole stitch pair 2 with pairs 3, 4 and 5.
Pin in the centre and pull up all the pairs evenly.
Whole stitch pair 4 with pairs 5, 6 and 7.
Whole stitch pair 3 with pairs 4, 5 and 6.
Whole stitch pair 2 with pairs 3, 4 and 5.
Twist pairs 2, 3, 4, 5, 6 and 7.
Whole stitch and twist pair 1 with pairs 2, 3 and 4.
Whole stitch and twist pair 8 with pairs 7, 6, 5 and 4.
Pull all up evenly (see fig. 64a).

65 An eight pair open spider crossing.
This crossing comprises four open spiders.
Twist all pairs to start.

Top spider
Whole stitch pairs 3 and 4, 5 and 6.

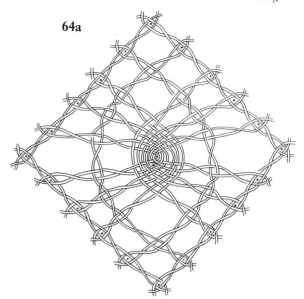

64a

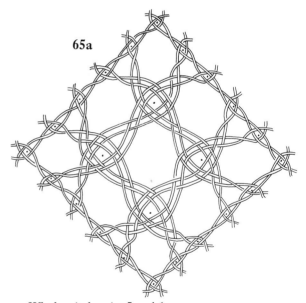

65a

Whole stitch pairs 5 and 6.
Whole stitch pairs 3 and 4, 5 and 6.
Whole stitch pairs 4 and 5.

Left-hand side spider
Whole stitch pairs 1 and 2, 3 and 4.
Whole stitch pairs 2 and 3.
Whole stitch pairs 1 and 2, 3 and 4.
Whole stitch pairs 2 and 3.
Whole stitch pairs 1 and 2.

Right-hand side spider
Whole stitch pairs 5 and 6, 7 and 8.
Whole stitch pairs 6 and 7.
Whole stitch pairs 5 and 6, 7 and 8.
Whole stitch pairs 6 and 7.
Whole stitch pairs 7 and 8.

66a

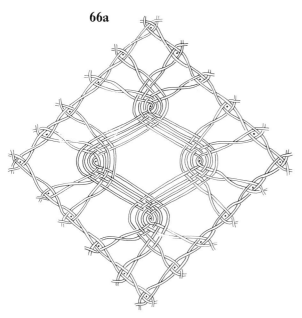

67a

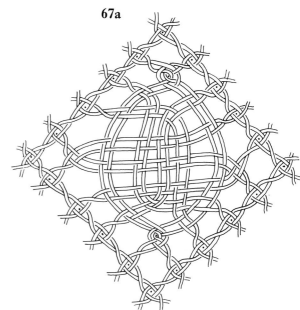

Bottom spider
> Whole stitch pairs 3 and 4, 5 and 6.
> Whole stitch pairs 4 and 5.
> Whole stitch pairs 3 and 4, 5 and 6.
> Whole stitch pairs 4 and 5.

> Lastly, whole stitch pairs 3 and 4, 5 and 6.
> Pull all the pairs evenly (see fig. 65a).

66 An eight pair spotted spider crossing.
This is four small spiders combined to create an all over crossing.
> Twist all pairs to start.
> Whole stitch pair 4 with pairs 5 and 6.
> Whole stitch pair 3 with pairs 4 and 5.
> Pin in the centre of the top spider.
> Whole stitch pair 4 with pairs 5 and 6.
> Whole stitch pair 3 with pairs 4 and 5.

Left-hand spider
> Whole stitch pair 2 with pairs 3 and 4.
> Whole stitch pair 1 with pairs 2 and 3.
> Pin in centre.
> Whole stitch pair 2 with pairs 3 and 4.
> Whole stitch pair 1 with pairs 2 and 3.

Right-hand spider
> Whole stitch pair 6 with pairs 7 and 8.
> Whole stitch pair 5 with pairs 6 and 7.
> Pin in the centre.
> Whole stitch pair 6 with pairs 7 and 8.
> Whole stitch pair 5 with pairs 6 and 7.

Bottom spider
> Whole stitch pair 4 with pairs 5 and 6.
> Whole stitch pair 3 with pairs 4 and 5.

Pin in the centre.
> Whole stitch pair 4 with pairs 5 and 6.
> Whole stitch pair 3 with pairs 4 and 5.
> Twist all pairs and pull out evenly (see fig. 66a).

67 An eight pair encircled whole stitch spider.
Twist all pairs.
> Whole stitch, pin, whole stitch pairs 4 and 5.
> Whole stitch pairs 3 and 4, 5 and 6.
> Whole stitch pair 2, through pairs 3, 4 and 5.
> Whole stitch pair 7, through pairs 6, 5, 4, 3, 2 and 1.
> Whole stitch pair 2, through pairs 3, 4, 5, 6, 7 and 8.
> Whole stitch pair 7, through pairs 6, 5, 4, 3 and 2.
> Whole stitch pair 3, through pairs 4, 5 and 6.
> Whole stitch pairs 3 and 4, 5 and 6.
> Whole stitch, pin and whole stitch pairs 4 and 5.
> Twist all pairs and pull up evenly (see fig. 67a).

68 An eight pair whole stitched block.
Twist all pairs to start.
> Whole stitch pairs 4 and 5; pin.
> Whole stitch pair 5 through pairs 4, 3 and 2; pin.
> Whole stitch pair 2 through pairs 3, 4, 5, 6 and 7; pin.
> Whole stitch pair 7 through pairs 6, 5, 4, 3, 2 and 1.
> Pin in the centre of the last wholestitch worked.
> Whole stitch pair 2 through pairs 2, 3, 4, 5, 6, 7 and 8.
> Pin in the centre of the last whole stitch.
> Whole stitch pair 7 through pairs 6, 5, 4, 3 and 2; pin.
> Whole stitch pair 2 through pairs 3, 4, 5, 6 and 7; pin.

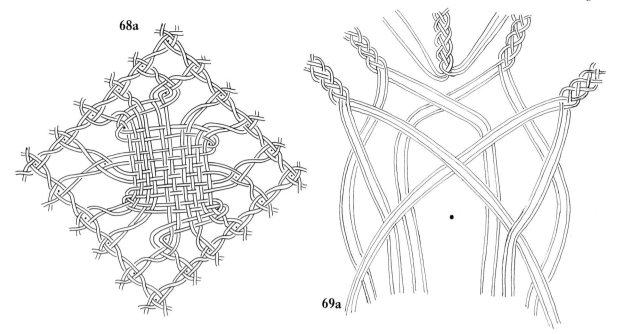

68a

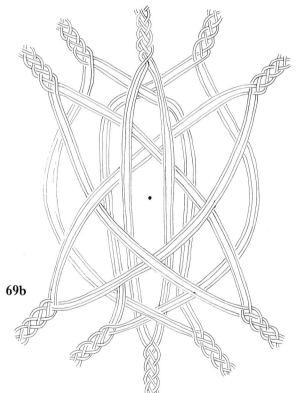

69a

69b

Whole stitch pair 7 through pairs 6, 5 and 4; pin.
Whole stitch pairs 4 and 5.
Twist all pairs (see fig. 68a).

69 A ten pair windmill crossing.
Lay back the centre pairs, 5 and 6.
These two pairs are excluded from the left to right count. Each pair is to count as a single unit.
Cross pair 4 over 5.
Cross pair 7 over pairs 6 and 5.
Twist pair 7 over pairs 6 and 5.
Cross pair 2 over pairs 3, 4 and 5.
Twist pair 4 over pairs 3, 2 and 1.
Cross pair 5 over 6.
Twist pair 7 over 6.
Cross pair 7 over 8 (see fig. 69a).

Lay down the central uncounted two pairs, pin in the centre of all the pairs and work the rest of the crossing over the two uncounted pairs, again not counting them in during any movement.

Twist pair 6 over 5.
Twist pair 7 over 6.
Cross pair 3 over pairs 4, 5, 6 and 7.
Twist pair 4 over pairs 3 and 2.
Twist pair 4 over 3.
Lastly, cross pair 4 over 5.
When all the pairs are crossed and pulled up, this makes a neat centre.

It will be found that each pair has passed through the crossing to lie in its opposite position (see fig. 69b).

70 A ten pair wrap around crossing.
This crossing can be used for any number of pairs. It is a simple process where the pairs are folded over and under each other before the pin and this action is repeated on the lower half.

87

70a

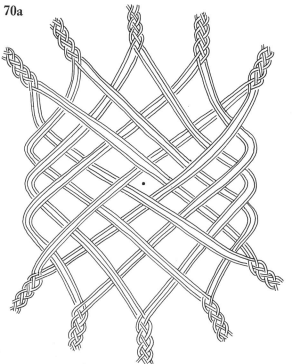

71a

72a

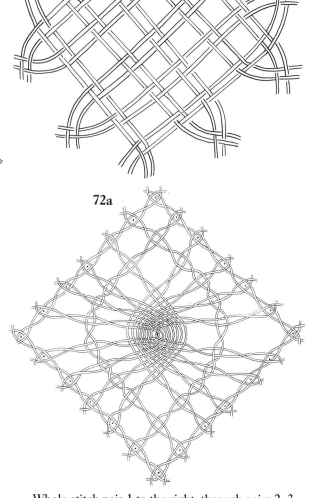

Cross pairs 2 over 3, 4 over 5, 6 over 7 and 8 over 9.

Cross pairs 3 over 4, 5 over 6 and 7 over 8.

Cross pairs 4 over 5 and 6 over 7.

Cross centre pairs 5 over 6.

Pin in the centre.

Left hand side

Twist pairs 2 over 1, 3 over 2 and 2 over 1.

Twist pairs 5 over 4, 4 over 3, 3 over 2 and 2 over 1.

Right hand side

Twist pairs 10 over 9, 9 over 8 and 8 over 7.

Twist pairs 10 over 9 and 9 over 8.

Twist pairs 10 over 9.

Cross pairs 5 over 6, 6 over 7, 7 over 8, 8 over 9 and 9 over 10.

Cross pairs 4 over 5, 5 over 6 and 6 over 7.

Cross pairs 3 over 4 and 4 over 5.

Lastly, cross pair 2 over 3.

Pull up evenly (see fig. 70a).

71 A ten pair whole stitch crossing.

Whole stitch pair 5 to the right, through pairs 6, 7, 8, 9 and 10.

Whole stitch pair 4 to the right, through pairs 5, 6, 7, 8 and 9.

Whole stitch pair 3 to the right, through pairs 4, 5, 6, 7 and 8.

Whole stitch pair 2 to the right, through pairs 3, 4, 5, 6 and 7.

Whole stitch pair 1 to the right, through pairs 2, 3, 4, 5 and 6.

Pull up all pairs evenly (see fig. 71a).

72 A ten pair haloed spider.

Twist all pairs.

Whole stitch and twist pairs 5 and 6, then pairs 6 and 7, 7 and 8, 8 and 9, 9 and 10.

Whole stitch and twist pairs 4 and 5 and then pairs 4 and 3, 3 and 2 and 2 and 1.

Whole stitch to the right pair 5, through pairs 6, 7, 8 and 9.

Whole stitch to the right pair 4, through pairs 5, 6, 7 and 8.

73a **74a**

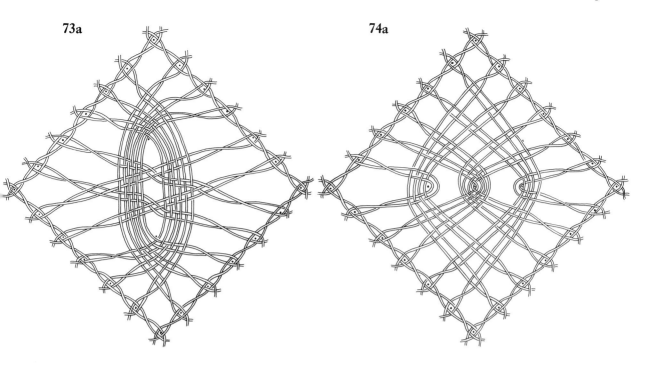

Whole stitch to the right pair 3, through pairs 4, 5, 6 and 7.

Whole stitch to the right pair 2, through pairs 3, 4, 5 and 6.

Pin in the centre and pull up evenly.

Whole stitch to the right pair 5, through pairs 6, 7, 8 and 9.

Whole stitch to the right pair 4, through pairs 5, 6, 7 and 8.

Whole stitch to the right pair 3, through pairs 4, 5, 6 and 7.

Whole stitch to the right pair 2, through pairs 3, 4, 5 and 6.

Twist pairs 2, 3, 4, 5, 6, 7, 8 and 9.

Whole stitch and twist pairs 1 and 2, 2 and 3, 3 and 4, 4 and 5, 10 and 9, 9 and 8, 8 and 7, and 7 and 6.

Lastly, whole stitch and twist pairs 5 and 6.

Pull up evenly (see fig. 72a).

73 A ten pair crossed over spider.
Twist all pairs to start.

Whole stitch to the right pair 5, with pairs 6, 7, 8 and 9.

Whole stitch to the right pair 4, with pairs 5, 6, 7 and 8.

Whole stitch to the right pair 3, with pairs 4, 5, 6 and 7.

Support whole stitch block with a pin.

Whole stitch pair 2 to the right, with pairs 3, 4, 5, 6,

7, 8, 9 and 10.

Whole stitch pair 5 to the left, with pairs 4, 3, 2 and 1.

Whole stitch pair 2 to the right, with pairs 3, 4 and 5.

Whole stitch pair 9 to the left, with pairs 8, 7, 6, 5, 4, 3 and 2.

Whole stich pair 6 to the right, with pairs 7, 8 and 9.

In order to separate the next small whole stitch block, place a pin in the centre of all the threads.

Whole stitch to the right pair 5, with pairs 6, 7 and 8.

Whole stitch to the right pair 4, with pairs 5, 6 and 7.

Whole stitch to the right pair 3, with pairs 4, 5 and 6.

Twist all pairs evenly (see fig. 73a).

74 A ten pair triple spider
Twist all pairs to start.

Whole stitch pair 5 to the right, through pairs 6, 7, 8, 9 and 10.

Whole stitch pair 4 to the right, through pairs 5, 6, 7, 8 and 9.

Pin between pairs 8 and 9.

Whole stitch pair 8 to the right, through pairs 9 and 10.

Whole stitch pair 3 to the right, through pairs 4, 5, 6 and 7.

75a　　　　　　　　　　　　　　　**76a**

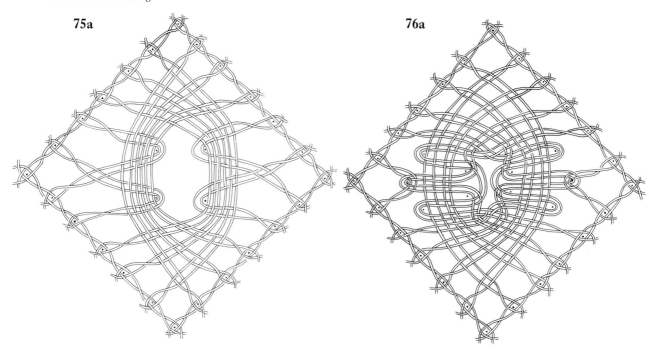

Whole stitch pair 2 to the right, through pairs 3, 4, 5 and 6.

Pin in the centre of all the pairs.

Whole stitch pair 5 to the right, through pairs 6, 7, 8 and 9.

Whole stitch pair 4 to the right, through pairs 5, 6, 7 and 8.

Whole stitch pair 1 through pairs 2 and 3, pin between pairs 2 and 3.

Whole stitch pair 3 through pairs 2 and 1.

Whole stitch pair 4 through pairs 3 and 2.

Whole stitch pair 5 through pairs 4 and 3.

Whole stitch pair 5 through pairs 6 and 7.

Whole stitch pair 4 through pairs 5 and 6.

Twist all pairs and pull up evenly (see fig. 74a).

75　A ten pair double eye crossing.

Twist all pairs to start.

Whole stitch pair 5 to the right, through pairs 6, 7, and 8.

Whole stitch pair 4 to the right, through pairs 5, 6 and 7.

Whole stitch pair 3 to the right, through pairs 4, 5 and 6.

Whole stitch pair 2 to the right, through pairs 3, 4 and 5.

Pin between pairs 4 and 5.

Whole stitch to the left pair 5, through pairs 4, 3, 2 and 1.

Whole stitch pair 2 to the right, through pairs 3, 4 and 5.

Pin between pairs 4 and 5.

Whole stitch to the left pair 5, through pairs 4, 3 and 2.

Pin between pairs 6 and 7.

Whole stitch pair 6 to the right, through pairs 7, 8, 9 and 10.

Whole stitch pair 9 to the left, through pairs 8, 7 and 6.

Pin between pairs 6 and 7.

Whole stitch pair 6 to the right, through pairs 7, 8 and 9.

Whole stitch pair 5 to the right, through pairs 6, 7 and 8.

Whole stitch pair 4 to the right, through pairs 5, 6 and 7.

Whole stitch pair 3 to the right, through pairs 4, 5 and 6.

Pull up evenly (see fig. 75a).

76　A ten pair cluny spider.

Twist all pairs to start.

Whole stitch pair 5 to the right, through pairs 6, 7, 8 and 9.

Whole stitch pair 4 to the right, through pairs 5, 6, 7 and 8.

Whole stitch pair 3 to the right, through pairs 4, 5, 6 and 7.

Whole stitch pair 2 right across the spider, through pairs 3, 4, 5, 6, 7, 8 and 9, and pin between pairs 8 and 9.

Whole stitch pair 9 to the left, through pairs 8, 7 and 6.

Pin on the inside of pairs 6 and 7.

Whole stitch pair 7 to the right, through pairs 8, 9 and 10.

Pin between pairs 9 and 10.

Whole stitch pair 10 to the left, through pairs 9, 8, 7 and 6.

Pin on the inside of pairs 6 and 7.

Whole stitch pair 7 to the right, through pairs 8 and 9.

Pin and whole stitch to the left pair 9, through pairs 8, 7 and 6.

Work the left-hand side.

Whole stitch pair 5 to the left, through pairs 4, 3 and 2.

Pin between pairs 2 and 3.

Whole stitch pair 2 to the right, through pairs 3, 4 and 5.

Pin on the inside of both pairs 4 and 5.

Whole stitch pair 4 to the left, through pairs 3, 2 and 1.

Pin between pairs 1 and 2.

Whole stitch pair 1 to the right, through pairs 2, 3, 4 and 5. Pin on inside of pairs 4 and 5.

Whole stitch pair 4 to the left through pairs 3 and 2.

Pin between pairs 2 and 3.

Whole stitch pair 2 across the spider to the right side through pairs 3, 4, 5, 6, 7, 8 and 9.

Whole stitch to the right pair 4 through pairs 5, 6, 7 and 8.

Whole stitch to the right pair 3 through pairs 4, 5, 6 and 7.

Whole stitch to the right pair 2 through pairs 3, 4, 5 and 6.

Twist all pairs evenly (see fig. 76a).

77 Windmill crossing.

Each group of four threads is counted as one unit. The groups may be plaited or left loose. In the diagram it will be noted that eight are plaited and four pairs are worked open in order to show the difference.

Lay back centre two groups and do not include these in the numbering.

Cross group 2 over group 3.

Twist group 4 over group 3 and group 2 over group 1.

Lay down left-out groups

Pin in centre of all threads.

Lastly, working over the laid-down two groups, cross group 2 over group 3.

Pull up evenly (see fig. 77a).

78 A twelve pair gimp-style spider.

Twist all pairs to start.

Two pairs of the spider are passed between pairs to form the gimp effect.

Whole stitch pairs 6 and 7 and then pairs 7 and 8.

Whole stitch pairs 5 and 6 and then pairs 6 and 7.

These two pairs on either side now act as gimps until they meet at the bottom of the spider.

Pair 4 is opened up and the two left-hand pairs are laid between them before pair 4 is twisted.

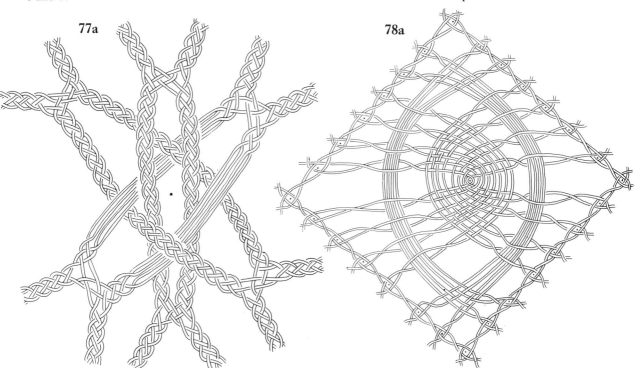

77a   78a

Repeat this in turn with pairs 3, 2 and 1.

On the right-hand side again, repeat in turn with pairs 9, 10, 11 and 12.

The twisted pairs in the centre now work a simple spider.

Whole stitch pair 6 to the right, through pairs 7, 8, 9 and 10.

79a

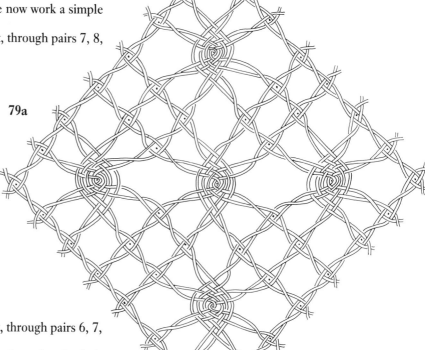

Whole stitch pair 5 to the right, through pairs 6, 7, 8 and 9.

Whole stitch pair 4 to the right, through pairs 5, 6, 7 and 8.

Whole stitch pair 3 to the right through pairs 4, 5, 6 and 7.

Pin in the centre.

Whole stitch pair 6 to the right, through pairs 7, 8, 9 and 10.

Whole stitch pair 5 to the right, through pairs 6, 7, 8 and 9.

Whole stitch pair 5 to the right, through pairs 6, 7, 8 and 9.

Whole stitch pair 4 to the right, through pairs 5, 6, 7 and 8.

Whole stitch pair 3 to the right through pairs 4, 5, 6 and 7.

Twist pair 3, open the pair up and place the two last pairs (false gimps) between pair 3 and twist pair 3 prior to leaving it.

Repeat this process, twisting and opening up a pair and placing the two pairs between that pair and then twisting that pair.

Do this in turn with pairs 4, 5 and 6 and then, on the right-hand side, with pairs 8, 7, 6 and 5.

Whole stitch pairs 6 and 7 and then pairs 7 and 8.

Whole stitch pairs 5 and 6 and then pairs 6 and 7.

Twist pairs 5, 6, 7 and 8 and pull up evenly.

This spider can be made with more threads in either the gimp-like edge or in the spider itself (see fig. 78a).

92

79 A twelve pair baby grid and spider crossing. This crossing can be made with all baby spiders or, alternatively, with a small grid to divide them.

Twist all pairs to start.

Top Spider

Whole stitch pair 6 through pairs 7 and 8.

Whole stitch pair 5 through pairs 6 and 7.

Pin in the centre.

Whole stitch pair 6 through pairs 7 and 8.

Whole stitch pair 5 through pairs 6 and 7.

Twist all pairs.

Half stitch, pin, half stitch pairs 4 and 5.

Half stitch, pin, half stitch pairs 3 and 4, 5 and 6.

Half stitch, pin, half stitch pairs 4 and 5.

The grid has been constructed.

Repeat the spider method for each of the small spiders, and in between repeat the method for the small grid.

Twist all the pairs and pull up evenly on the completion of the entire crossing (see fig. 79a).

81a

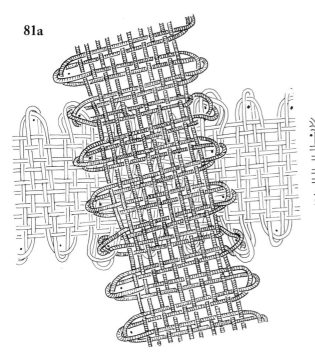

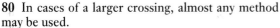

82a

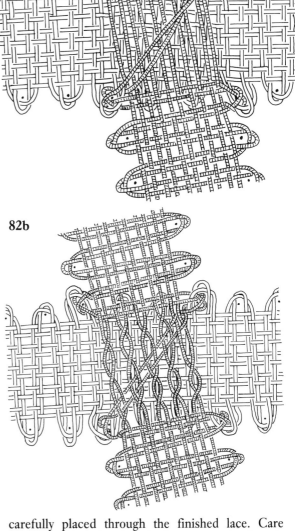

80 In cases of a larger crossing, almost any method may be used.

The simple spider works to at least 60 pairs. See Section IV Method 45. Care has to be taken to pull evenly throughout, in order to retain the flatness, but with care this is not too difficult.

Alternatively, Section IV Method 70, which is the wrap-around crossing, will work easily and remain flat.

BRAID CROSSINGS

81 Crossing a braid over a completed piece of lace. Remove the pins of the underbraid where the next braid will tend to cover them. The lace will not therefore be damaged by having to dig in for the pins, which have been trapped between the two layers of lace.

The most straightforward method of crossing the braid is to work the second braid up to the point where a pin hole of the second braid falls directly over the pin of the edge of the underbraid. Into this pin hole, make a sewing with the workers of the second braid and work back across the second braid to the edge pin hole of the underbraid, on its other side. If the braid is very narrow, only two sewings will be necessary to marry the two braids together. If a broad braid is to be crossed, then all four edge pin holes need to have a sewing in order to hold the top braid firmly to the lower one. In fig. 81a a sewing is made at all four corner pin holes.

In the overlap part of the two braids, work the worker across the lace and around the pin, which is

82b

carefully placed through the finished lace. Care should be taken that this pin does not cut the threads of the lace below.

Work back and forth, always taking care with the placing of the pins in the underlying lace, until the edge pin hole of this is reached. At this point a sewing is made with the worker from the top piece of lace. Work across to the last edge pin hole and make a sewing in that edge pin hole.

This crossing is very neat and is ideal where the work has to be viewed from either side (see fig. 81a).

82c

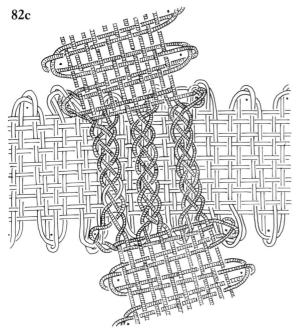

82 Crossing a braid over a finished piece of lace, where the crossing will be the underside when the lace is completed.

A sewing is made in all four corners of the underbraid with the worker from the top braid. The passives and the worker are carried straight across to the other side of the underlying lace. This can only be used if the underlying lace is not too wide, as it leaves long loops which can become unsightly (see fig. 82a).

Alternatively, the braids can be crossed (as in fig. 82a) except that the passives are twisted and the worker from the top lace is whole stitched through

them. This twisting reduces the loose loop effect on the finished lace (see fig. 82b).

Another variation to 82 is to plait all the passives and the worker after the first two sewings have been made in groups across the underlying piece of lace, before they are separated out again and the lower two sewings worked (see fig. 82c).

83 Braid Sewing. At the point of making the sewing, when crossing the braid over a completed piece of lace, both of which have footside edges.

The whole stitch of the edge-pairs must be made before the pair which was on the outside edge makes the sewing. After the sewing, the sewing pair is worked across the braid. On the opposite side of the lace the whole stitch edge is made up, and the pair which has been on the outer edge then makes a sewing and is worked across the lace. This keeps good straight edges to both pieces of lace (see fig. 83a).

84 Crossing two pieces of braid whilst working both at the same time.

Work the braids to where they meet. The worker from braid 1 is worked across the braid to the far side and is then taken around the corner pin to become the worker of braid 2.

Similarly, the worker from braid 2 works across the braid and around the corner pin to become the worker

83a

84a

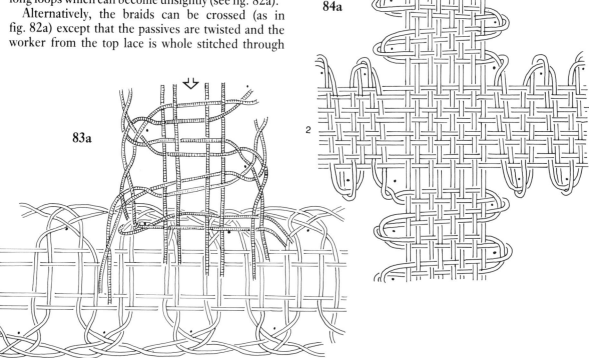

of braid 1. However, before doing so, the passives from both braids whole stitch through each other (see fig. 84a).

An alternative method to make a firmer join between the two braids

The workers from both braids are whole stitched, pinned, whole stitched in the first corner and each worker then works across its own braid. The passives

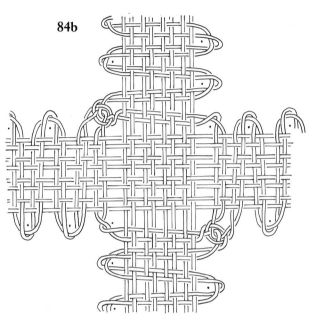

84b

are then whole stitched through each other, and each of the workers turn around a pin at the corners and become the workers for the opposite braids. Work each across the braids and at the last corner, where the two workers meet, whole stitch, pin, whole stitch them together before each continues to work its own braid (see fig. 84b).

85 Crossing two braids, but keeping the appearance of a twisted footside to both braids. The finished appearance is as if one was stopped and another started on the other side of the crossing.

Work braid 1 and leave the worker on the left; twist and support by a pin. Wholestitch the first two passives together, pin to support; twist the third passive and whole stitch and twist with the twisted edge-pair. Support this on a corner pin.

Work braid 2 to the last pin hole on the right, work through the passives but not through the twisted edge-pair. Leave the worker of braid 2, in order to become passive, lying between the last passive worked and the twisted edge-pair.

Work the waiting pair left, at the pin between the two braids, and whole stitch and twist this with the edge-pair; whole stitch across the four passives. Twist the worker, whole stitch and twist with edge-pair. Pin in the corner and leave.

Working from the left, take the pair that was the twisted footside pair and work across braid 2. Whole stitch, twist the right-hand pair; repeat with each passive from braid 2 in sequence across the braid.

Whole stitch the right-hand central passive of braid one through six pairs to the right, and then the second pair through six pairs to the right. On the completion of that movement, pin between the two pairs and whole stitch them together.

Work the left-hand twisted footside pair of braid one across braid 2; whole stitch and twist each passive pair in sequence. The pair that was supported on the pin, working from the left, is whole stitched and twisted with the first pair. Then it is whole stitched through the next four pairs, twisted and whole stitched and twisted with the edge-pair.

Supported on a pin, it is then whole stitched and twisted with the edge-pair of braid 1, where it is left as a passive. The worker for braid 1 has already been whole stitched and twisted with the edge-pair on the opposite side. It is then whole stitched through 3 pairs to the left, twisted and whole stitched and twisted and then taken around the edge pin.

The worker for braid 2 is the second passive on the right. This is twisted, whole stitched and twisted with the edge-pair, pinned, and is then ready to continue the work down braid 2 (see fig. 85a).

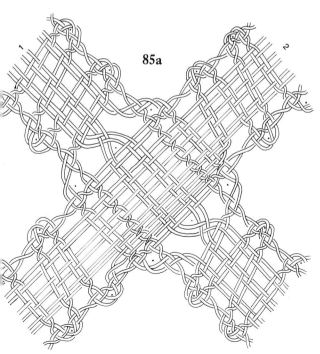

85a

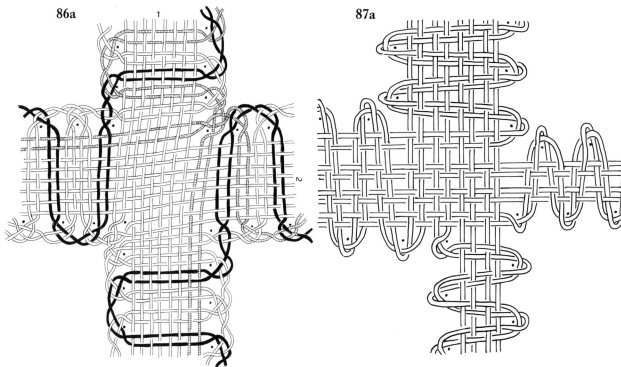

86a

87a

86 Crossing two braids both with footside edges.

In this method there is a slight distortion of the position of the passives, but it is so slight that in the overall appearance it will not be visible.

Work braid 1 to the left-hand side and make up the edge; pin and leave both pairs.

Work braid 2 to the right-hand side and make up the edge, pin and leave.

In the corner between the two braids, whole stitch and twist the two edge-pairs together, one from each braid, and support that whole stitch on a pin.

Whole stitch the pair that was the edge-pair of braid 2 across all the passives of braid 1, and including the pair supported on a pin that was the edge-pair of braid 1.

Return to the pair left at the union of the two braids and whole stitch through all the passives together with the edge-pair of braid 2.

Whole stitch all the passives from both braids through each other in their correct sequence.

To work the last corner, twist the last two pairs from both braids, pin between the inner two pairs and whole stitch them together. Twist them both.

Twist the next pair to the left and whole stitch and twist the left-hand pair from the corner with it; pin on the inside of both pairs. Then take the inner pair across the work.

Repeat this with the other edge-pairs to achieve a worker and an edge-pair for both braids.

Pull all the pairs evenly. Each braid will now have a worker and two edge-pairs (see fig. 86a).

87 To cross two braids of uneven width at the end of a crossing, having changed the position of the width of the braids.

Whole stitch the worker from the widest braid across the braid to the left-hand side. Leave this worker to hang as a passive.

Whole stitch the worker from the narrow braid across that braid to the right, twist and support it on a pin. Allow it to hang as a passive.

Whole stitch the central pairs in sequence through each other. The first passive on the left of the two braids is twisted around the pin and then whole stitches the widest braid.

To obtain a worker for the narrow braid, take the second passive on the left and twist and support on the pin. This passive then works in whole stitch across the narrow braid (see fig. 87a).

88 Decorative union of two braids.

When the two braids to be joined have twisted footsides, a decorative join can be made to give the appearance of each braid meeting and turning – but not crossing.

Work the worker from braid 1 across the lace to the left-hand side and make up the edge.

Whole stitch and twist the left-hand twisted foot-side pair of braid 2 through the next three pairs on the left-hand side.

Whole stitch and twist the two centre passives of braid 1, whole stitch and twist the twisted footside pair of braid 1 through two passives of braid 2.

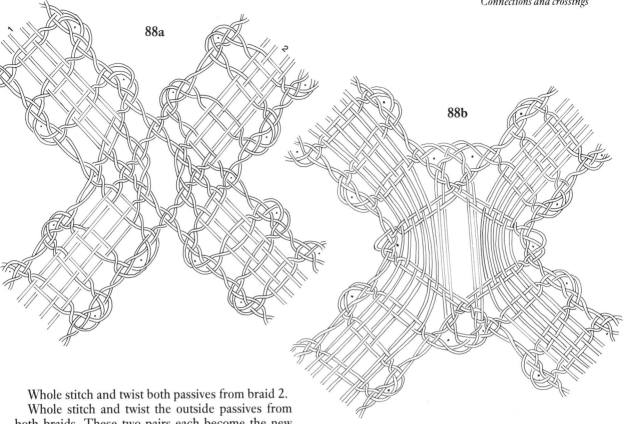

88a

88b

Whole stitch and twist both passives from braid 2.

Whole stitch and twist the outside passives from both braids. These two pairs each become the new twisted footside pairs – one for each braid.

The outside twisted foot side-pair on both braids now works across its own braid as their workers (see fig. 88a).

Alternative crossing and turn

Whole stitch the two outside workers from both braids to the centre and whole stitch them together.

Whole stitch each with the central twisted edge-pairs.

Twist the central pair and whole stitch. Then whole stitch one pair to the left and one to the right, across each braid.

Make up the edge and whole stitch both pairs back to the centre. Whole stitch them together. Twist both.

Whole stitch left-hand central pair with the pair to the left of it and twist both.

Whole stitch the right-hand central pair with the pair to the right of it and twist both.

Whole stitch the central pair and twist both. Pin to support each pair, then work one pair across each braid (see fig. 88b).

89 Connecting two braids and subsequently separating them.

Work the worker from the footside edge to the pin where the two braids meet.

Twist the worker around the pin and allow it to hang as a passive.

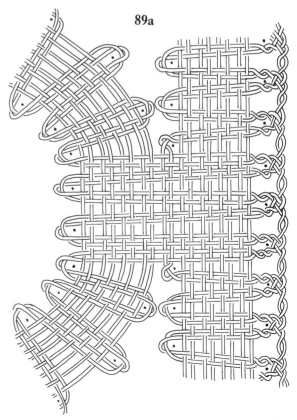

89a

Work the worker of the second braid across both braids, make up the edge on both sides for as long as the two braids are together.

At the point where the braids separate again, work across to the second braid. The worker continues with that braid.

The outside passive of the first braid is then twisted around the edge-pin and taken as a worker across the braid to the footside edge, where the usual exchange will take place.

This method leaves a neat appearance without any obvious holes (see fig. 89a).

90 Dividing a braid with an added cordonnet or coarse thread.

This method, if to be divided evenly, requires to be made with an odd number of pairs in the braid.

Weave a cordonnet pair across the central four threads. (It will be noted that the four threads were not pairs.)

Whole stitch the four central threads together and twist both. This secures the cordonnet.

Whole stitch the worker from the left through three pairs and the fourth pair, which is a single thread and a cordonnet thread. These two threads are now used as a pair. Twist the worker and add a new pair on to this worker. Make up the edge with the nearest edge pair.

Pin on the inside of both pairs and work back through the braid to the left, excluding the new pair which has just been added.

The new pair is then twisted and whole stitched and twisted with the right-hand central pair, and a pin placed on the inside of both pairs. The inner pair is worked to the right through pairs including the cordonnet thread pair and all the other pairs. The two braids are now worked individually from each other (see fig. 90a).

91 Joining two braids and keeping the illusion of a footside on both until they are completely joined.

Work both braids to the point where they join. Take each worker to the outside edge and make up both edges.

Whole stitch the central edge-pairs together and pin between them to support these two pairs now hanging down, which become the inner edge-pairs of both braids.

Whole stitch the left-hand inner edge-pair across the first braid and its edge-pair. Twist the worker once and whole stitch across the second braid to the right to the last pair, and leave. This pair will be cut off later. Whole stitch the right-hand inner pair across the two braids, but twisting once between them between the inner edge-pair.

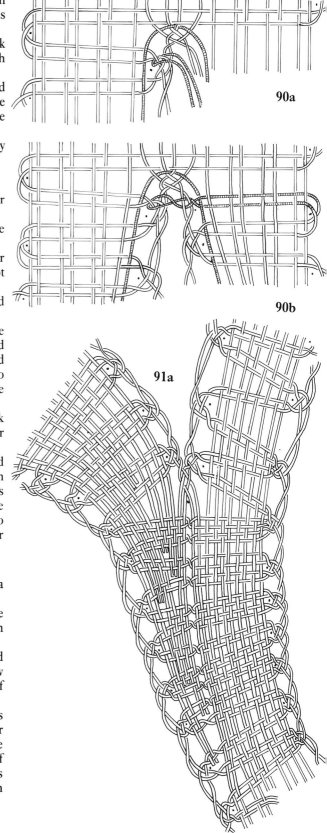

90a

90b

91a

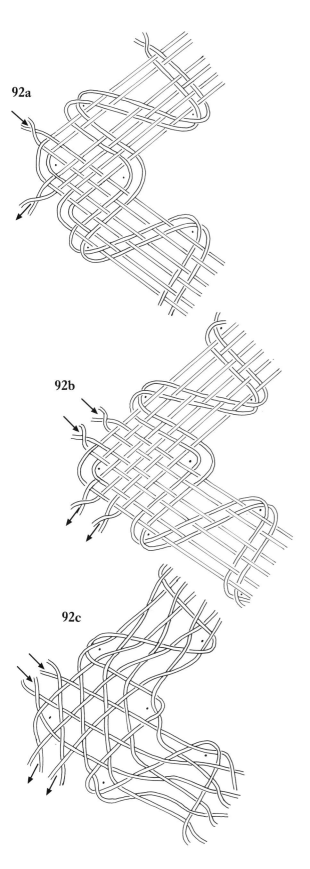

92a

92b

92c

Work back and forth, removing the pairs from the left-hand braid and always twisting between the braids until all the pairs except the edge-pair have been removed.

This gives a very neat union and the removal of one braid (see fig. 91a).

92 Taking in one pair and leaving another at the widest edge of a pattern of a trail.

Right-hand bend
Take the worker to the right pin and leave.

Enter the new pair from the left and work across all the passives.

Turn the left-hand passive around the corner pin and work through two passives to the right.

Leave out one pair, then take the worker pair from the right-hand side to the left, through all the passives. The corner is now completed, with a pair having entered and another pair having left on the widest point of the bend (see fig. 92a).

An alternative turned corner of a trail with two pairs entering and two pairs leaving again, on the widest curve.
Work the worker to the right-hand side, pin on the inside of that pair and leave.

Enter a new pair from the left-hand side, work this across to the right-hand side.

Enter a second new pair from the left-hand side and work back across to the right-hand side through three pairs.

Turn the outside left-hand passive pair around the pin and work to the right-hand side through two pairs.

The two pairs on the left-hand side are now left out to work the ground.

Work the worker from the inside across all the pairs to the left (see fig. 92b).

Many patterns using this method are worked in half stitch. It will be realized that this is not so easy to follow diagramatically; the diagram at fig. 92b showed how it worked in whole stitch. Fig. 92c does, however, show the piece worked in half stitch.

PICOTS, TALLIES, VENETIAN CORDS, PLAITS AND BRAIDS

1 Simple picot.

Right-hand side picot
Place the pin under the outside thread, twist the thread with the pin in an anti-clockwise direction. Place the pin in the required position beside the work. The thread can then be taken back into the work (see fig. 1a).

Left-hand side picot
Place the pin over the outside thread, twist the thread with a pin in a clockwise direction. Place the pin in the required position beside the work. The thread can then be taken back into the work (see fig. 1b).

To make a simple picot on either side of the plait, use the outside thread on either side to make the picot (see top of fig. 1c).

This sometimes leaves a loose plait.

If a firmer plait with picots is required, make the picot on the right-hand side with the outside right-hand thread. Whole stitch in the plait before making the picot with the outside thread on the left. This tightens up the plait (see the lower half of fig. 1c).

2 A knotted picot.   This is made with a pair.

Picot on the right-hand side
Place a pin under the first thread and over the second, which is then drawn to the right-side edge. This forms a loop on the pin. The pin is then placed between the two threads. The loop is drawn up between these threads.

Place the pin and picot in the required position beside the work. The pair can then be worked with the lace (see fig. 2a).

Picot on the left-hand side
This is worked in the same way as the right-hand picot, except that each movement is drawn to the left (see fig. 2b).

Making a picot on either side of the plait.

Make the picot with the outside pair of the plait nearest the required position of the picot (see the top picots in fig. 2c).

It will be seen that this sometimes produces a loose hole in the plait after the completion of the picots.

To avoid this occurence, make the right-hand side picot first, and whole stitch the pairs before making the left-hand side picot. This has the effect of drawing up the two sides and thus producing a smoother plait (see lower picots of fig. 2c).

3 Twisted picot.

A right-hand twisted picot
Cross the outside pair three, five or seven times. An odd number is needed.

Place the pin under the outside thread, twist the thread with the pin in an anti-clockwise direction. Place the pin and loop in the required position beside the work, keeping the loop loose.

The second thread from the twisted pair is then wrapped around the first loop in the same anti-clockwise direction and allowed to slip under the first loop.

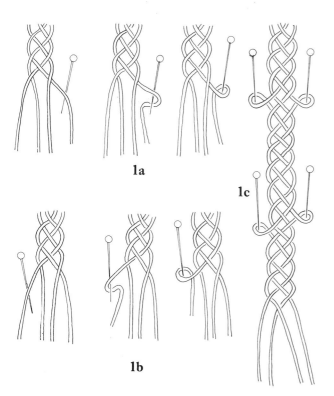

1a

1c

1b

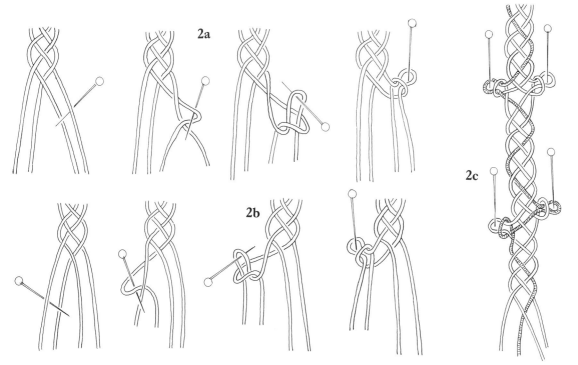

2a

2b

2c

When both threads are gently pulled tight the two threads will bind together to form a tight picot (see fig. 3a).

A left-hand twisted picot
Twist the outside pair three, five or seven times, depending on the size of the desired picot. An odd number is required. Place the pin under the outside thread and twist the thread and the loop in a clockwise direction. Place the pin and loop in the required position beside the work, keeping the loop loose.

Wrap the second thread from the twisted pair in the same clockwise direction, allowing the second loop to slip under the first loop on the pin. Pull both threads up evenly. The two loops will then interlock one with the other (see fig. 3b).

When making two picots on a plait, if one is made directly opposite to the other and both outside pairs are used, it will be found that a hole is left in between the picots (see top picots of fig. 3c).

It is preferable to make the right-hand picot, and then whole stitch the pairs before making the left-hand picot. In this way the hole is eliminated (see the lower picots of fig. 3c).

4 Triple picot where a single pair passes through a plait; three picots are constructed before it returns.

Whole stitch the single pair through the plait and make a picot with this pair.

Whole stitch the same pair together with the nearest pair to it from the plait. Picot with the outside pair and whole stitch the picot pair together with the nearest pair.

Picot with the outside pair and whole stitch that pair through two plait pairs (see fig. 4a).

5 Picot (apple blossom): the join of two plaits.
Make a picot in the central union of the two plait join with the right-hand pair of the left-hand plait.

Whole stitch the picot pair to the right through two plaits and picot on the right-hand side.

Whole stitch the two left-hand pairs and picot with the left-hand outside pair on the left-hand side.

Whole stitch both pairs together.

Whole stitch the pair that made the right-hand picot to the left through two pairs and make a picot with that pair at the same central bottom point.

Whole stitch the two left-hand pairs together and plait.

Whole stitch the two right-hand pairs together and plait (see fig. 5a).

Alternate join with crossover centre.
Make a picot in the central union to the two plait join, with right-hand pair of the left-hand plait.

Whole stitch the left-hand pair of the right-hand plait through the two pairs to the left, and make a picot on the left.

Picot on the right-hand side with the right-hand pair of the right-hand plait, and whole stitch the picot pair two whole stitches to the left.

Whole stitch the two left-hand pairs and plait, picot the next pair at the bottom union point.

Whole stitch with the right-hand pair and then plait both pairs (see fig. 5b).

101

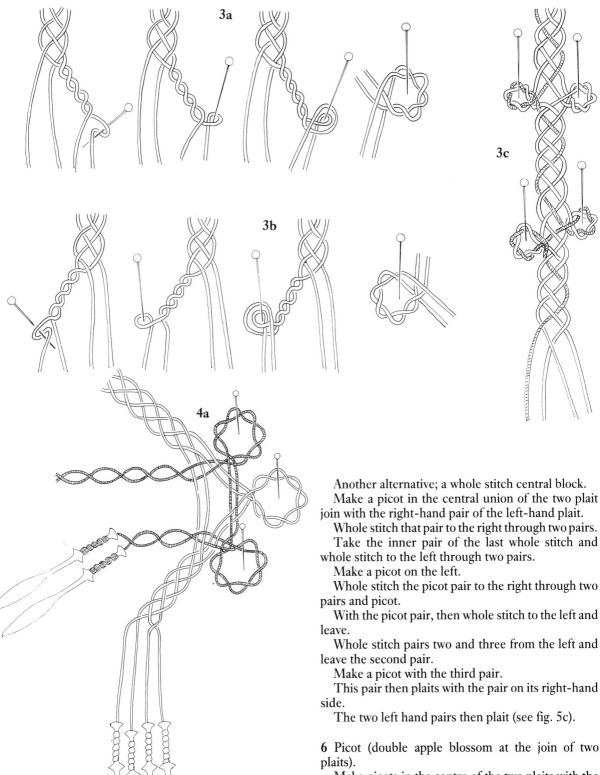

3a

3b

3c

4a

Another alternative; a whole stitch central block.

Make a picot in the central union of the two plait join with the right-hand pair of the left-hand plait.

Whole stitch that pair to the right through two pairs.

Take the inner pair of the last whole stitch and whole stitch to the left through two pairs.

Make a picot on the left.

Whole stitch the picot pair to the right through two pairs and picot.

With the picot pair, then whole stitch to the left and leave.

Whole stitch pairs two and three from the left and leave the second pair.

Make a picot with the third pair.

This pair then plaits with the pair on its right-hand side.

The two left hand pairs then plait (see fig. 5c).

6 Picot (double apple blossom at the join of two plaits).

Make picots in the centre of the two plaits with the inside pairs from each plait.

Whole stitch the picot pairs together.

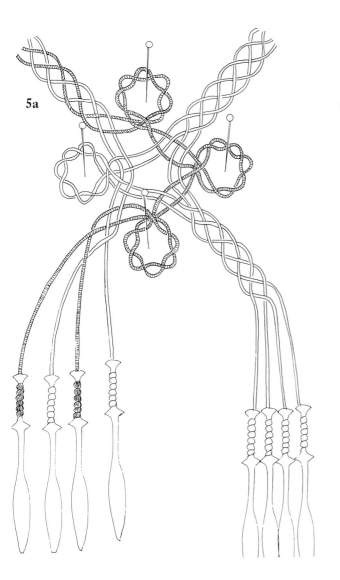

5a

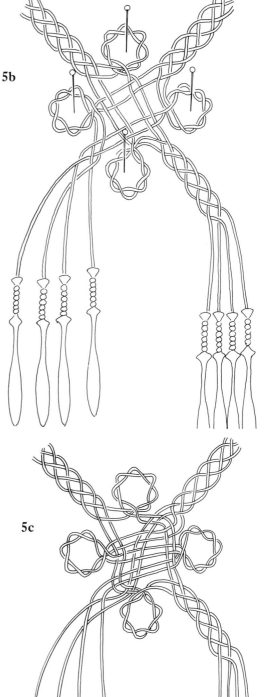

5b

5c

Take the left-hand pair to the left and whole stitch through the left-hand pair and picot.

Whole stitch the left-hand pairs together with the outside pair picot and whole stitch the left-hand pairs together again.

Whole stitch the central pair to the right through one pair and picot.

Whole stitch these pairs together and picot with the outside pair.

Whole stitch the same two pairs together.

Whole stitch the central pairs together. Each pair then picots at the bottom of the join. The right-hand pairs plait together and the left-hand pairs also plait together (see fig. 6a).

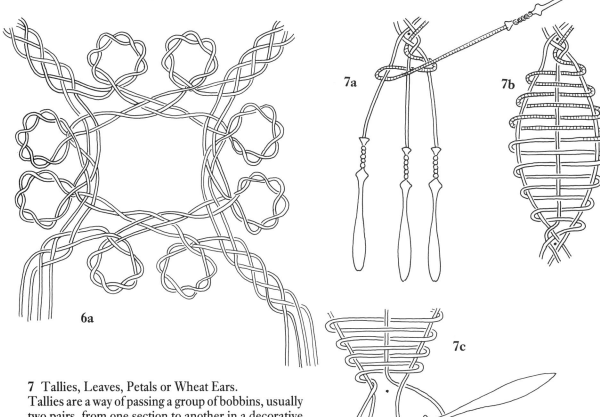

6a

7a

7b

7c

8a

7 Tallies, Leaves, Petals or Wheat Ears.
Tallies are a way of passing a group of bobbins, usually two pairs, from one section to another in a decorative woven form.

A leaf shape tally can be woven with any of the four threads but, in this diagram, the second thread becomes the weaver.

Whole stitch the pairs to start and secure by placing a pin in the centre of the whole stitch.

Take the second thread from the left and lengthen it so that the thread will always be loose.

Cross thread 2 over and under the two threads to the right.

Working the same thread to the left, take it over, under and over the three threads to the left.

When the weaver bobbin is back in its original position, pull this thread tightly up towards the pin, whilst holding the outside threads into the shape of the required tally (see fig. 7a).

The process is then repeated, until a full woven leaf shape is made. The overall shape of the leaf is controlled by the shape of the outside threads, whilst the weaver is tightened.

The weaver must not be pulled at any other time in the weaving as it is essential that the edge-pairs are held taut. Failing this the entire shape will distort.

End the tally with a whole stitch and with a central pin (see fig. 7b). If the pairs from the tally are not to be included into the ground work immediately, then a single knot with the outside passives will hold the tally together (see fig. 7c).

8 Tallies can be made in many shapes.
Tallies can be made in many shapes, but in the same way as a normal tally. It is merely the regulation of the outside threads that controls the shape obtained.

The lacemaker may find the single knot at the end of a shaped tally of even greater assistance in the overall shape retention. Another way of keeping the overall shape is to work the passive pair into the ground before the pair that contained the weaver. This is because there is still a tendency to pull the weaver and, if the outside pair is not held, it may still

104

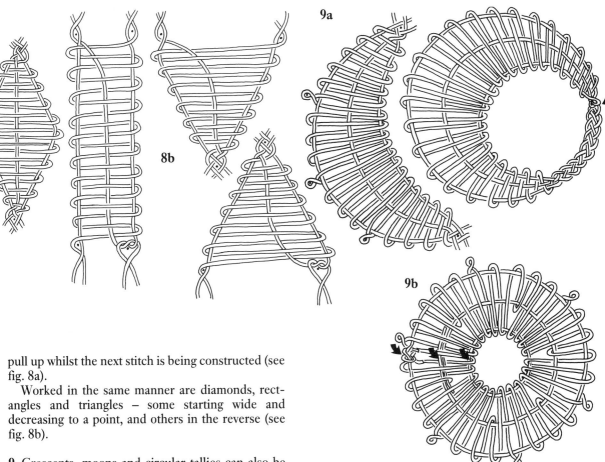

9a

8b

9b

pull up whilst the next stitch is being constructed (see fig. 8a).

Worked in the same manner are diamonds, rectangles and triangles – some starting wide and decreasing to a point, and others in the reverse (see fig. 8b).

9 Crescents, moons and circular tallies can also be made.

Crescents and moon-shaped tallies can also contain picots or can, at certain points, be joined to the lace with sewings.

Start as for a leaf shape with a whole stitch, and a pin in its centre for support.

Work as for a leaf, but allow the threads on the left-hand side to lie more loosely, whilst making sure that the threads on the right-hand side lie really close to each other.

When a picot is needed, make only a single picot. Any picots which use two threads to construct the picot distort the shape too greatly.

Pin the picot in place and continue working the shape.

The picots can help support the entire shape, so some lacemakers may have a preference for adding them.

Complete the crescent with a supportive whole stitch (see fig. 9a). A complete circle can also be made.

Commence the single threads on a supporting pin and work two or three complete movements.

On the third movement only pass over the centre thread and then back to the outside thread, before working the complete pattern of movements for another two or three repeats. Work another half row before repeating the full movements. In this way there will be less overcrowding in the centre, and an even overall woven appearance for the circle.

On completion of the circle, knot the start to the end and weave the loose ends into the tally where they will not show (see fig. 9b).

10 Four pair tallies (for example where two plaits meet).

There are four principal methods.

Method A

Place a pin between the outside two threads of the right-hand plait. The outside thread becomes the weaver.

The next thread to it and the left-hand outside thread are the two controlling passive threads.

All the other five threads are treated as one unit and lie in the centre. Take the weaver to the left over the first thread, under the group of five threads and over and under the edge thread.

105

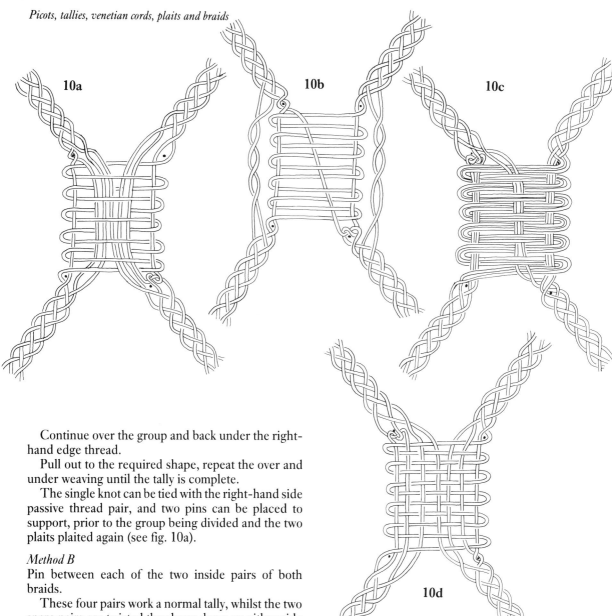

10a

10b

10c

10d

Continue over the group and back under the right-hand edge thread.

Pull out to the required shape, repeat the over and under weaving until the tally is complete.

The single knot can be tied with the right-hand side passive thread pair, and two pins can be placed to support, prior to the group being divided and the two plaits plaited again (see fig. 10a).

Method B
Pin between each of the two inside pairs of both braids.

These four pairs work a normal tally, whilst the two spare pairs are twisted they hang down on either side of the tally.

On the completion of the tally the two pairs that worked the tally are pinned (prior to their being united with the twisted pair) and are plaited into the two plaits (see fig. 10b).

Method C
This tightly woven block is very useful if the finished lace is to receive hard wear, as it retains its shape well.

Pin between the two outside pairs, one from each plait, and weave the right-hand thread over and under each single thread to the left.

This is repeated back and forth until the required length is achieved. Pull all the threads up evenly before pinning between the outside pairs. Then plait with their partners (see fig. 10c).

Method D
A double woven thread tally is very quick to make but does require a little practice in order to keep the tension of both threads evenly controlled.

Pin between both pairs of either plait and treat each pair as single unit.

Work the tally over, under, over and under until the required length is achieved.

Pin between the two pairs on either side and plait the two separate plaits (see fig. 10d).

11 Six pair tulip tallies.
Tallies may be added to or subtracted from whilst the

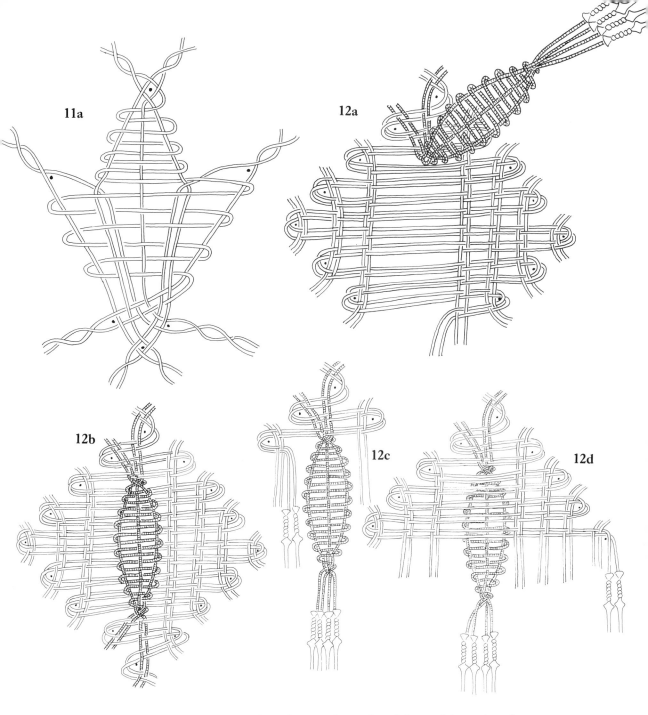

11a

12a

12b

12c

12d

construction is moving forward. For example, a four threaded tally may be started, then a pair added from either side and a wide tally may be then worked with the thread groups in any arrangement that the lacemaker finds most suitable (see fig. 11a).

12 Surface Tallies
Tallies may also be worked over the top of the work or below; the method is virtually the same. These are called surface tallies. Two adjacent pairs are left out of

the work and the work is continued.

The tally is then made (see fig. 12a).

The pairs from the tally can then be re-introduced into the work, thus making a tally over the work but fixed to it (see fig. 12b)

If the work is to be turned over, the tally will need to be made first and laid on the pillow (see fig. 12c).

Work is constructed over this until the end of the tally is reached, then the tally pairs will be re-introduced to the work (see fig. 12d).

107

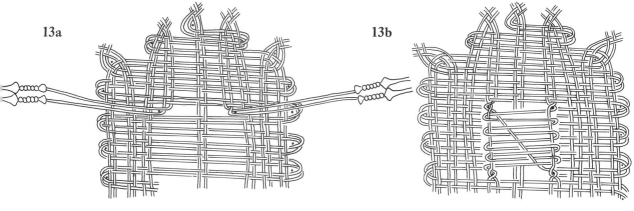

13a   **13b**

13 A wide square tally.

This can be worked over the top of the work, or below it. Two pairs can be used adjacent to each other and worked into a tally, as in Method 12, excluding the whole stitch to start.

Adjacent pairs, although producing a square tally if one is somewhat slim in order to keep the sides straight, can only be worked down the same width as the pairs which came out narrowly from the work.

If a solid square tally is required then leave out a pair on either side of the centre pair in order to make the tally and work the ground.

This method does not leave a large hole in the centre of the ground (see fig. 13a).

Work the tally over the ground to the required length and incorporate the tally pairs in the same position into the ground (see fig. 13b).

This wide tally can also be laid under the work if the final piece is to be turned over.

14 A raised rolled tally.

The rolled tally sits above or below the work like a small bump on the surface of the lace. This can be made with four adjacent threads out of the ground. If a slightly wider tally is required, then use three pairs of bobbins to construct the tally. Counting to the right-hand side, use threads 1 and 2 leave out the thread 3, use thread 4 in the tally and leave thread 5 out but use the thread 6.

If the tally is to be on top then work over the two spare threads. Weave a good long tally so that when it is rolled it will keep its firm raised shape.

Place a long pin over the two working pairs of the tally and take each pair in turn over the pin to hang down (see fig. 14a).

Push the pin up level to where the ground was stopped. Continue the ground, incorporating the loose threads and the tally pairs.

Where the tally is to be under the work lay back the two loose threads and work the tally. On its

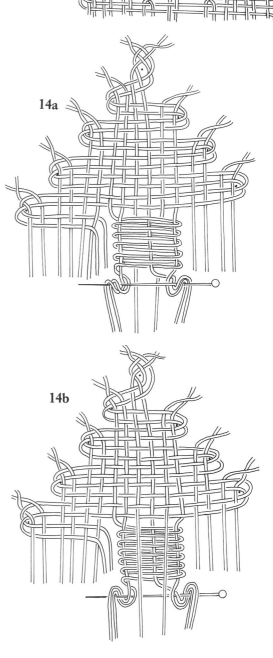

14a

14b

14c

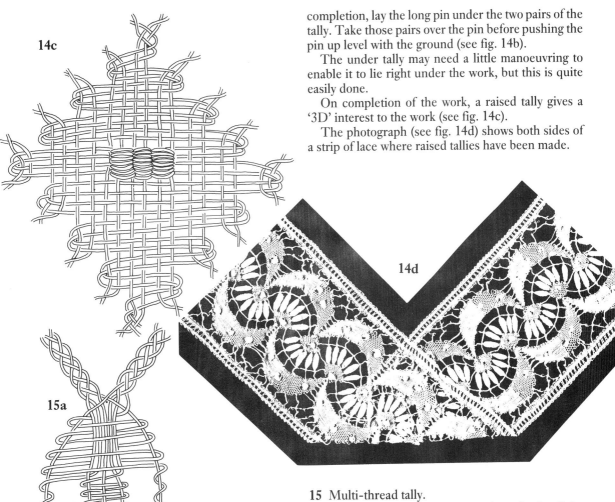

14d

completion, lay the long pin under the two pairs of the tally. Take those pairs over the pin before pushing the pin up level with the ground (see fig. 14b).

The under tally may need a little manoeuvring to enable it to lie right under the work, but this is quite easily done.

On completion of the work, a raised tally gives a '3D' interest to the work (see fig. 14c).

The photograph (see fig. 14d) shows both sides of a strip of lace where raised tallies have been made.

15a

15 Multi-thread tally.
Tallies can be made with any number of pairs. Pairs can also be altered within the tally in order to give different appearances (see fig. 15a and b).

16 To thicken a tally in very loose ground a spare thread is used in order to make the tally.

Weave the spare thread into the stitch of the net at the place where the tally is to be started. Spread out the four threads of the net and weave a tally with the spare thread, passing under, over, under and over, etc., until the tally is complete. To remove the spare thread, weave it into the union of the pair from the tally and the pair from the net (see fig. 16a).

17 False tally in net grounds.
A false tally can be made in the net, giving a decorative effect to the net but not changing the overall flow of the net.

Work the net to a diagonal line having three or four pairs hanging out of it. The tally is worked through these pairs before they make up the next diagonal line of the net.

15b

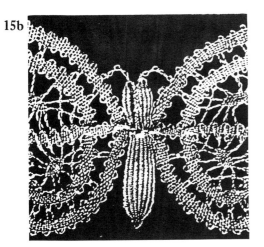

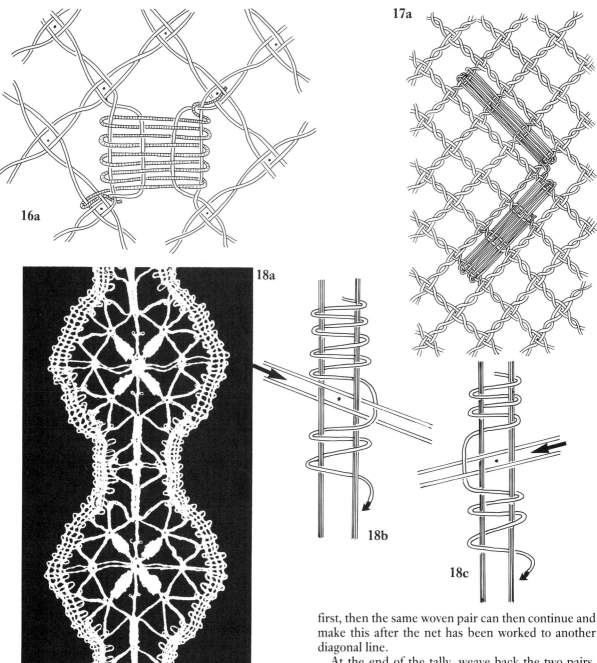

16a

17a

18a

18b

18c

first, then the same woven pair can then continue and make this after the net has been worked to another diagonal line.

At the end of the tally, weave back the two pairs. Cut off after some more net has been completed (see fig. 17a).

18 Venetian cord.

To make the cord, weave a single thread over and under and over and under, around two gimp threads or a group of threads. Push all the weaving up tight. The cord has a pleasant tallie appearance and is often used as an attractive embellishment to the lace (see fig. 18a).

Hang a new pair on a pin close to where the top of these pairs left the net. Weave or whole stitch this pair diagonally down through the four net pairs, whole stitch or weave back up the four pairs and down again. If this effect is now thick enough for the tally, then weave back through two pairs and cut off the weaving pair. Continue with the net.

If a second tally is required at right angles to the

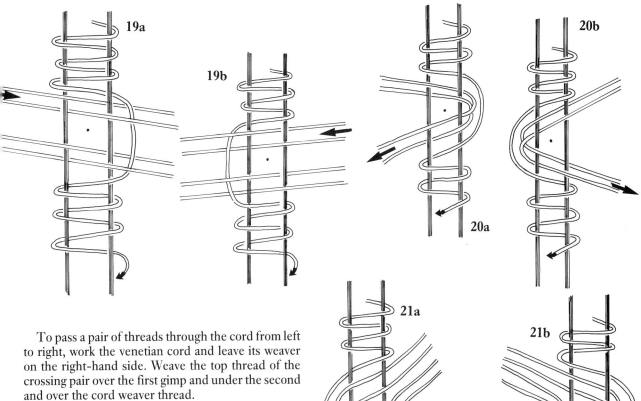

To pass a pair of threads through the cord from left to right, work the venetian cord and leave its weaver on the right-hand side. Weave the top thread of the crossing pair over the first gimp and under the second and over the cord weaver thread.

Take the lower thread of the crossing pair and pass this under the first gimp, over the second gimp and under the weaving thread.

The cord weaver then continues to weave over and under the gimps (see fig. 18b).

To pass the pair through the cord, from right to left, it is necessary to reverse the proceedings (see fig. 18c).

19 Passing two pairs through the venetian cord.
Passing from left to right, work the venetian cord to the passing through point and leave the weaver thread on the right-hand side.

Work as for Method 18 to cross pair 1.

Repeat this in the same sequence to cross pair 2.

The cord weaver can then continue to weave over and under the gimps (see fig. 19a).

To pass two pairs from left to right, reverse the process (see fig. 19b).

20 Attaching the cord to the ground by passing the worker through the cord and back into the ground.

Working from the left-hand side and back to the left-hand side, leave the cord weaver on the right-hand side of the cord.

Weave the top thread of the attaching pair over and under the two gimps working to the right.

Weave the lower thread of the attaching pair under and over the two gimps working to the right. Pin in the centre of the cord.

Twist the pair and work to the left. The first top thread passes under and over the two gimps, then the lower thread passes over and under the two gimps. The cord weaver can then continue to weave (see fig. 20a).

Working from right to left, merely reverse the entire process (see fig. 20b).

21 Attaching the cord to the ground where two pairs touch the cord. One passes through the cord before returning whilst the other merely meets the cord and then turns with the pair passed through.

Weave the top pair through the venetian cord, as in Method 20b.

On leaving the cord, the pair which passed through the cord now works under the pair that was simply turned (see fig. 21a and fig. 21b).

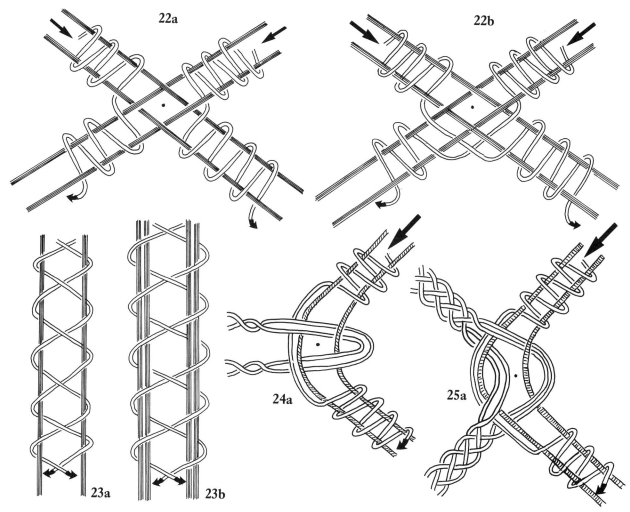

22 Crossing two venetian cords.

Weave the weaver from both cords to the outside edges and leave.

Cross the two cords by working the four gimp threads in whole stitch with a pin in the centre. The weavers can then continue to weave across their own cords (see fig. 22a).

An alternative method is to weave the weavers for both cords to the outer edges and leave.

Cross the two cords by working the four gimp threads in a whole stitch with a pin in its centre. Weave each weaver across its own cord and then cross the weavers before each works the alternate cord. In this way the two cords are held slightly more tightly together (see fig. 22b).

23 A grand venetian cord can be made by working a pair of threads in a woven formation.

Place the weaver threads in the centre of the two gimps and then take the right-hand thread under and over the right-hand gimp, and the left-hand thread over and under the left-hand gimp. Cross the two threads in the centre and continually repeat the movements (see fig. 23a).

Push all the threads close up to each other, so that the overall appearance is that of a tight tally.

A royal grand venetian cord can be made by using two pairs of gimps. These are worked over by two threads. The gimps are carefully handled so that they do not twist, but lie flat side by side (see fig. 23b).

Pairs can be crossed through the grand royal cords in the same way as for venetian cords, except a weaver thread from the cord is left out at either side of the cord. The pair to be crossed passes through a weaver thread before it crosses the gimps – as well as the weaver thread after it has passed through the cord.

24 Bending and joining a venetian cord.

A venetian cord will often need to be bent so that the cord itself can join with the edge and then return into the lace.

To work the union where the cord travels from the

112

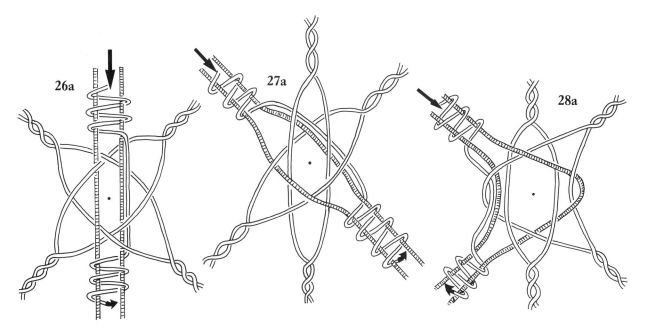

right-hand side to join the left-hand edge, weave the weaver to the left. Pass the pair as a unit, with both threads together, over the weaver and the first gimp and then under the second gimp. Pin below the worker pair between the two gimps.

Pass the worker pair over the first gimp and under the second. In this way the worker holds the cord close to the edge without distorting its shape. The weaver can then continue to weave (see fig. 24a).

To join a cord in the opposite direction it is necessary merely to work in reverse.

25 A plait and a cord meeting together and then working away in the original direction.

For a right-hand side cord, work the weaver to the left-hand side.

Pass a pair from the plait as one unit over the weaver and gimp, and under the second gimp. Pass the second pair from the plait under the weaver thread and the first gimp and back over the same gimp and the weaver. Pin in the centre of all threads.

Take the right-hand pair over the first gimp and under the second gimp and the weaver thread.

Both the venetian cord and plait are ready then to be continued (see fig. 25a).

26 Passing a cord through two diagonal pairs where the cord is in the central position.

Number the threads from left to right.

Counting a gimp with the weaver as one unit.

Twist 3 (gimp) over 2.

Cross 4 over 5.

Cross the centre threads 3 over 4.

Twist 3 over 2 and 4 over 5.

Twist 1 over 2 and 5 over 6.

Twist 3 over 2 and 5 over 4.

Cross centre threads 3 over 4.

Cross 2 over 3 and 4 over 5.

The cord has now passed through two pairs and the pairs are crossed (see fig. 26a).

27 Crossing a cord through two adjacent pairs.

Number threads from left to right, counting the gimp and weaver as one unit.

Twist 3 over 2 and cross 4 over 5.

Cross 3 over 4.

Twist 3 over 2 and 5 over 4.

Pin in the centre of all threads.

Twist 2 over 1 and 6 over 5.

Cross 2 over 3 and twist 5 over 4.

Cross 3 over 4.

Lastly twist 3 over 2 and cross 4 over 5.

The cord can then be continued (see fig. 27a).

28 Bending a cord with two adjacent pairs at a union.

Number the threads from left to right, counting a gimp with the weaver as one unit.

Twist 5 over 4.

Cross gimp thread 2 over 3, 4 and 5.

Twist 6 over 5 and 3 over 2 and 1.

Pin in the centre of all threads.

Twist the gimp and thread unit 2 over 1 and twist 6 over 5.

Twist 2 over 3 and cross 4 over 5.

Cross 3 over 4.

Cross 3 over 2 and twist 5 over 4.

This makes a tight join (see fig. 28a).

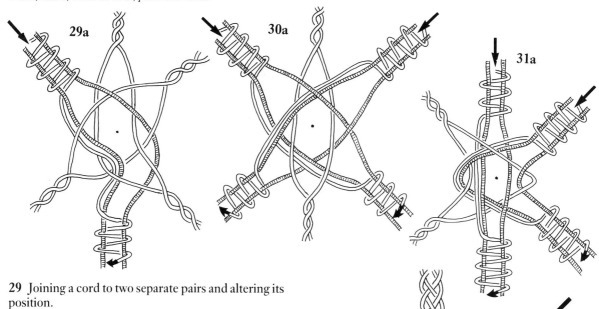

29 Joining a cord to two separate pairs and altering its position.

Number the threads from left to right, counting the gimp and weaver as one unit.

Cross 2 over 3 and twist 5 over 4.

Cross 3 over 4.

Twist 3 over 2 and then cross 4 over 5.

Twist 2 over 1 and then 6 over 5.

Pin in the middle of all the threads.

Cross 2 over 3 and 4 over 5.

Cross 3 over 4.

Cross 5 over 6 and then cross 2 over 3, 4 and 5.

The cord which was on the left-hand side is now to be worked straight down the lace and the single pairs are used one on each side (see fig. 29a).

If the cord entered on the right, then merely reverse the entire process.

30 Crossing two cords and a single pair.

Number the threads from left to right, counting the gimp and weaver as one unit.

Cross 2 over 3 and twist 4 over 3.

Cross 3 over 4.

Twist 3 over 2 and cross 4 over 5.

Twist 2 over 3 and twist 6 over 5.

Pin in the centre of all threads.

Twist 3 over 2 and cross 4 over 5.

Cross 3 over 4.

Cross 2 over 3 and twist 5 over 4.

Each cord can then be completed and the pair used in the lace (see fig. 30a).

31 Joining a single pair with two cords bending the right-hand cord.

Number the threads from left to right, counting the gimp and weaver as one unit.

Twist 5 over 4.

Cross 2 over 3, 4 and 5.

Twist 6 over 5.

Twist 3 over 2 and 1.

Pin in the centre.

Twist 2 over 1 and then 3 over 2.

Twist 6 over 5 and then cross 4 over 5.

Cross 3 over 4.

Cross 2 over 3 and twist 5 over 4.

The single pair has joined the two braids together and the right-hand braid bends towards the right again, whilst the straight cord continues straight down (see fig. 31).

If the cords lie the opposite way, then reverse the process.

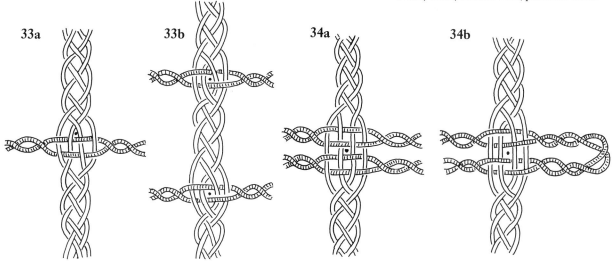

33a **33b** **34a** **34b**

32 Joining two plaits and a cord, with each returning to its original direction following the union.

Counting from the left-hand side, number each pair as a unit and each of the gimps as a single unit. The weaver from the cord remains on the outside edge of the join.

Cross 4 over 5.

Twist 6 over 5.

Cross 2 over 3, twist 4 over 3.

Cross 4 over 5 and pin in the centre.

Cross 4 over 5, twist 4 over 3 and cross 2 over 3.

Twist 6 over 5 and cross 4 over 3.

Plait the two plaits. The weaver can then continue weaving the cord (see fig. 32a).

If the cord is on the left-hand side at the start then reverse the entire method.

33 Passing pairs through plaits.

Place a pin in the centre of the plait at the position of the crossing.

Whole stitch the pair to be crossed through the two pairs of the plait. The plait can then be continued (see fig. 33a).

Alternative method

Work the plait to the position of the crossing and then take the top thread of the pair, to be crossed over the first pair of the plait and under the second.

Pin in the centre of the two plait pairs, supporting the single crossed thread. Take the lower thread of the crossing pair under the first pair and over the second pair of the plait. The plait can now be continued (see fig. 33b).

34 Crossing two single pairs through a plait.

Plait to the point of crossing. Whole stitch the first pair to be crossed through the two plait pairs. Pin in the centre of the plait under that pair. Whole stitch the second pair through. Continue the plait. These

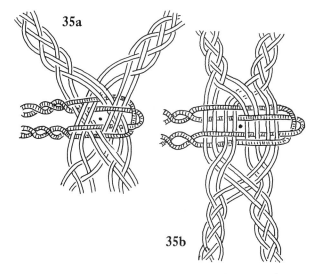

35a

35b

crossing pairs may travel in either direction (see fig. 34a)

Alternatively, plait to the point of crossing and take the top thread of the pair to be crossed over the first pair and under the second pair of the plait. Then take the lower thread under the first pair and over the second pair. Support in the centre of the plait with the pin. Another pair may be crossed in either direction in the same manner (see fig. 34b).

35 Crossing a pair back and forth through two plaits.

Work both plaits to the position of the crossing and then cross the centre two pairs of the plaits over each other.

Take the upper thread of the pair to be crossed over the first and second pairs and under the other two pairs of the plaits.

Take the lower thread under the first two pairs and over the second two pairs.

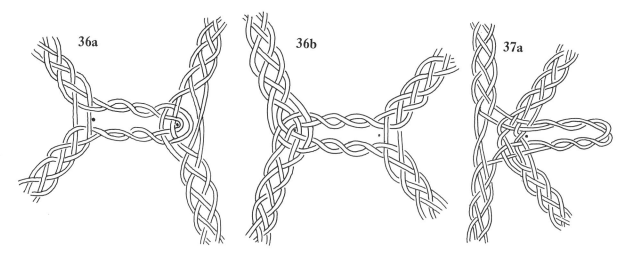

Twist the left-hand plait pairs together and then twist the right-hand pairs together. Pin in the centre.

If taking the same pair immediately back, twist that pair before taking the upper thread under the first two pairs and over the second two pairs. The lower thread passes over the first two pairs and under the next two pairs. Cross the centre two pairs, one from each plait, before continuing to work the plaits. This makes a very tight centre (see fig. 35a).

For a looser and more decorative crossing, cross the two centre pairs, one from each plait. Take the upper thread of the crossing pair over the first two pairs and under the second two pairs. Take the lower thread under the first two pairs and over the second two pairs and pin in the centre. Twist the pair before returning. Take the upper thread under two pairs and over the next two pairs, and then the lower thread over two pairs and under the next two pairs. Cross the centre two pairs, one from each plait, before continuing (see fig. 35b).

36 Linking plaits with the various spacings.
Work the plaits to the joining point. Separate the pairs of the left-hand plait with a pin. Take the right-hand pair of the left-hand plait and twist this pair if a space is required between the join. Whole stitch this pair with the left-hand pair of the right-hand plait, pin to support. Work another whole stitch with these pairs. Twist or not to correspond with the outward passage of these threads. Plait together with the hanging pair from the left-hand plait.

Twist the right-hand pair of the right-hand plait before continuing to plait with its partner (see fig. 36a).

Alternate linking
Work the plaits to the point of linking. Place a pin between the left-hand plait pairs, twist the right-hand pair of the left-hand plait only if a separation is required. Then whole stitch that pair through the two right-hand plait pairs. Pin on the inside of the last whole stitch made. Whole stitch the inner pair from the last whole stitch made to the left, through the pair. Repeat the twist or not (as on the outward journey). Continue plaiting both plaits (see fig. 36b).

37 Taking one pair from the plait through another plait and using it as required, and then returning the pair to its original position.

Whole stitch the right-hand pair from the left-hand plait through both pairs of the right-hand plait. Pin to the right of the right-hand plait. The pair that worked through the plait can now be used in the lace, or may be simply turned around the pin before the pair whole stitches to its original position (see fig. 37a).

If a separation is required between the pairs then the worker pair can be twisted before, and after, passing through the right-hand plait.

Alternative method
Take the right-hand pair of the left-hand plait. Twist as required, take the top thread of this pair over the first pair and under the second pair of the right-hand plait. Take the lower thread under the first pair and over the second pair. Pin under these threads in the centre of the two plait pairs. Use or not in the ground as required and return by taking the top thread under the first pair and over the second pair and the lower thread over the first pair and under the second pair. Twist to correspond with the outward journey and continue plaiting both pairs (see fig. 37b).

Windmill alternative
Number the pairs from left to right, counting each pair as a unit. Cross pair 2 over pair 3, twist pairs 2 over 1 and 4 over 3. Pair 4 can now be used in the lace. Pin in the centre of all pairs. Whole stitch pairs 3 and 4 and finally cross pairs 2 and 3. Continue each plait.

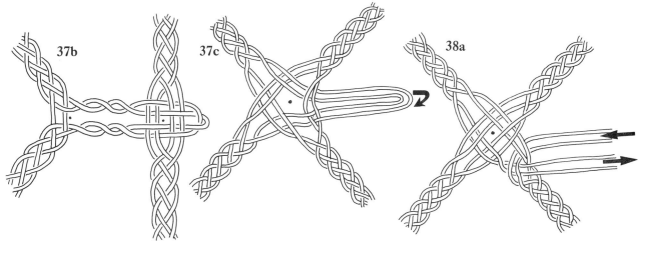

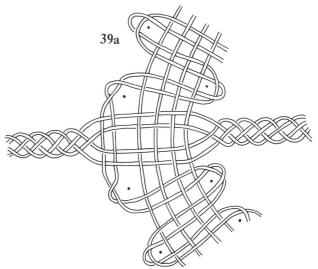

It will be noted that two pairs have changed position, and this forms a tighter join (see fig. 37c).

38 Crossing two plaits and exchanging a pair from the ground.

Number the pairs from left to right, counting each pair as a unit. Pair 5 is the pair from the ground. Cross pair 2 over pair 3. Twist pairs 2 over 1 and 4 over 3. Pin in the centre of all pairs. Cross pair 2 over 3. Pairs 1 and 2 can now be plaited. Cross pair 4 over 5 and twist pair 4 over 3. Cross pair 4 over 5 and continue plaiting pairs 3 and 4. Pair 5 can now work the lace (see fig. 38a).

39 Taking a plait or two pairs through a braid on a curve.

Work the braid, leaving the worker on the side where the two pairs will enter. Pin the worker and turn this to lie with the passives, and work the two pairs to be crossed through all the passive pairs of the braid. Place a pin on the inside of the first passive (previously the worker). Turn this pair around to work across the braid as the worker. It will be noted that the two pairs have passed through the braid and the pin arrangement of the braid has been kept even (see fig. 39a).

40 Taking pairs in and out of a braid without disturbing the edge pin holes.

At Z, the first interchange, the worker is left out to work into the lace on the right-hand side. A pin is placed in the normal edge pin hole and another pair from the lace can then enter from that side and become the worker. In this exchange it will be noted that

the pin is not enclosed. At the second interchange, Y, the worker, leaves the braid on the left and whole stitches with the pair entering. The pin is therefore enclosed. At the third interchange, X, a pair may leave the braid on one side, whilst another pair continues the braid entering from the opposite side. Work the first exit pair to the right. Support with the edge pin and leave.

Take in the new pair on the opposite side. Support this pair before working with the edge pin (see X in fig. 40a). At the fourth interchange, W, the worker leaves the braid on the left and the pin is placed under this in the edge pin hole for support. A pair may enter from this side. Work straight across and exit on the other side, a pin being placed for support in the edge

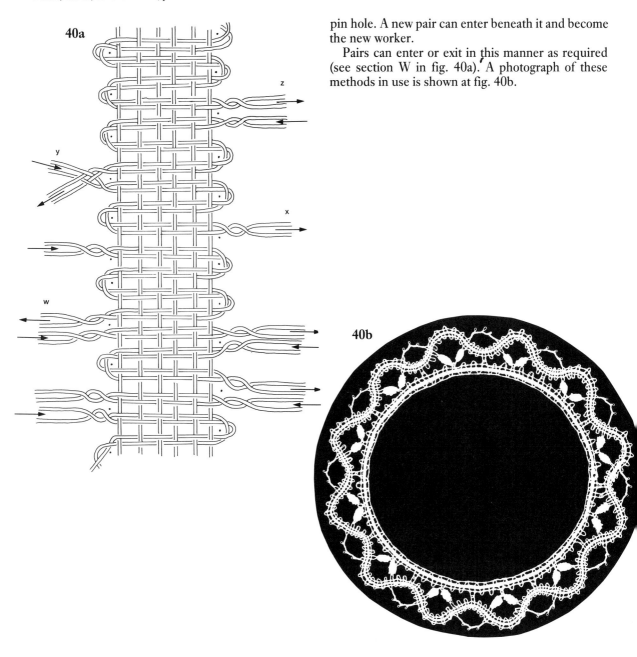

40a

40b

pin hole. A new pair can enter beneath it and become the new worker.

Pairs can enter or exit in this manner as required (see section W in fig. 40a). A photograph of these methods in use is shown at fig. 40b.

CARRYING PAIRS, RAISED WORK, FILLINGS

This section covers the carrying of pairs from one area of lace to another. It also includes raised work and using pairs from the work for fillings and returning them to their original positions.

1 To carry a single pair between two sections of the work it is necessary for these to be twisted for strength, appearance and tension (see fig. 1a).

2 To carry two pairs from one area of lace to another the pairs can be plaited. There are two methods of plaiting. In the first the pairs must be twisted in order to start, then worked continuously in half stitch to the required length.

Note that this will leave the pairs twisted at the end. The second method is to whole stitch and twist repeatedly for the required length, thus leaving the pairs untwisted (see fig. 2a). An alternative method of carrying two pairs is simply to twist the pairs around each other (see fig. 2b).

3 To carry three pairs.
Treating each pair as a unit, cross the centre pair over the left-hand pair, then cross the pair that is now in the centre over the right-hand pair. Repeat these two movements until the required length is worked (see fig. 3a).

Flat plait. Whole stitch the right-hand pair through the two pairs to the left.

Twist the outside pairs, whole stitch the right-hand pair through the left, twist the outside pairs and repeat to the required length (see fig. 3b).

For the third method, take the outer pairs as single units. The two threads from the centre pair are worked singly. Work these four units as a half stitch continuous plait (see fig. 3c).

Lastly, for the fourth alternative half stitch the right-hand and centre pair, then half stitch the left-hand and centre pair. Worked continuously this will give a decorative plait (see fig. 3d).

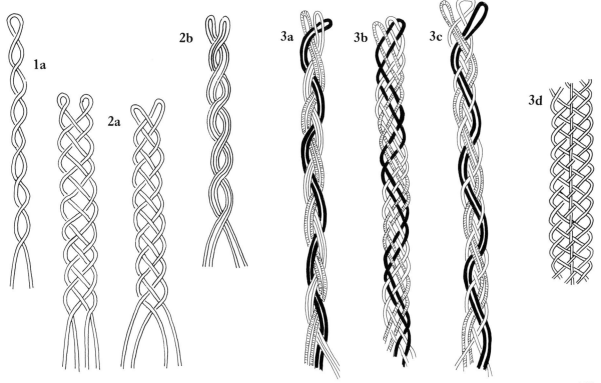

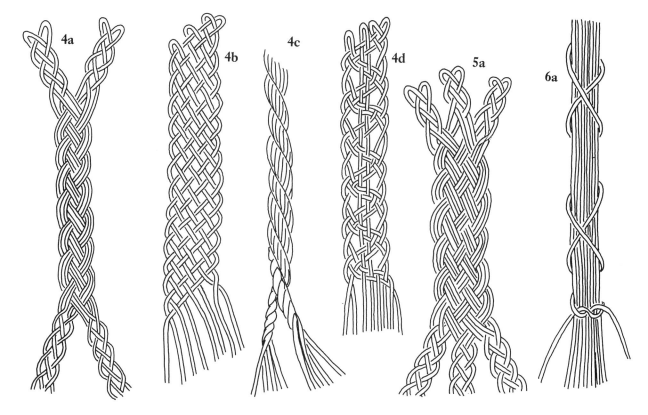

4 To carry four pairs.

Four pairs can be carried in a windmill plait. Using each pair as a single unit, whole stitch and twist continuously to the desired length (see fig. 4a).

To make a flat plait, whole stitch from the right to the left across three pairs. Twist the outside pairs and repeat to the desired length (see fig. 4b).

Four pair cord. Divide the four pairs into two groups of two pairs. Twist both groups tightly and then twist the two groups together. This will form a tightly wound cord. The pairs can then be separated and used as required (see fig. 4c).

An alternative method is to whole stitch the right-hand pair through to the left, through three pairs. Twist the outside pairs, then *whole stitch the second pair from the left to the right, through two whole stitches; then twist this pair. Take the second pair from the right through two pairs and twist*. Repeat steps * to * until the desired length is reached (see fig. 4d).

5 This method may be used to carry any number of pairs.

Group the pairs together and take an outside thread from either side of the group. Cross this pair over the top and then under the group, crossing again and thus binding the group together. This wrapping is repeated several times; the more repeats the tighter the

binding. At the required length the two wrapping threads must be knotted before they and the other threads are separated into pairs for further use (see fig. 5a).

6 Six pair crossings.

Number the pairs from the left to the right, counting each pair as a unit. Cross pairs 2 over 3 and 4 over 5. Twist pair 6 over 5, 4 over 3 and 2 over 1. Repeat these two movements to the desired length. Finish with the movement 2 over 3 and 4 over 5 (see fig. 6a). This method is used in photograph 6b.

7 Crossing many pairs.

Divide the pairs into three groups. One group will always have an odd pair. Braid these groups as for method 3 (see fig. 7a).

8 Carrying pairs in a roll.

To make a roll, at least six or seven pairs are needed. Whole stitch from the left through all pairs (see fig. 8a). When the right-hand side is reached, the worker is laid over the pairs, and on this left-hand side a temporary support pin is placed under them.

It is essential that the pairs are retained in their correct order. The worker is then worked through to the right (see fig. 8b). The worker is then taken back over the roll and the temporary support pin is moved

6b

7a

8a

down one stage. After each crossing the pairs must be gently tightened in order to keep an even roll (see fig. 8c).

9 A roll can be worked around a centre cord.
Bunch the core pairs and tie a temporary thread around them in order to secure as a bunch.

This temporary thread can slide down the core below the work, as the work progresses. A minimum of five pairs will be required for the outer casing. Whole stitch from the left through the casing pairs and lay the core on these. Take the worker over the core and support on a pin on the left-hand side. Whole stitch the pairs to the right under the core and replace the core centrally on the work.

Take the worker over to the left-hand side and remove the temporary pin from the previous row and replace it to support the worker. It will be found that the whole stitched pairs will form a woven outer wrap to the core.

At the end of the work, secure the core and wrapping by tying the worker threads once around the bunch and secure with a reef knot. Remove the temporary pin and the temporary tie thread from the core pairs. The threads can now be separated into pairs and used as required (see fig. 9a).

8b **8c** **9a**

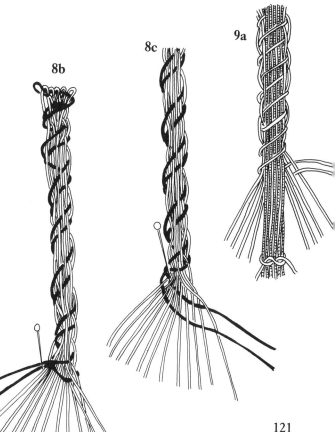

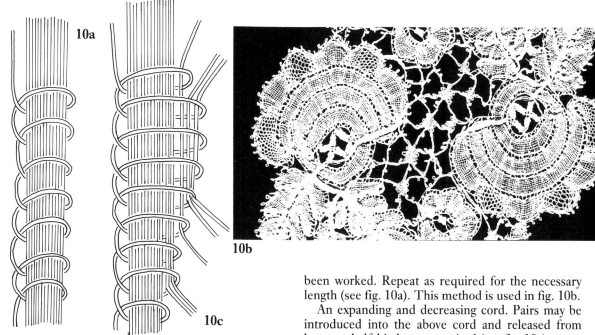

10a

10b

10c

been worked. Repeat as required for the necessary length (see fig. 10a). This method is used in fig. 10b.

An expanding and decreasing cord. Pairs may be introduced into the above cord and released from between half-hitches as required (see fig. 10c).

10 Carrying pairs in a half hitched cord.
Group the pairs to be carried together and, taking the outside thread from the left, pass this thread under and then over the group. Pass the bobbin down the loop that this thread has made. A half hitch will have

11 Where a rib and roll are working side by side, the roll may be taken out and worked into either a tendril or a flower, before being returned to accompany the rib.

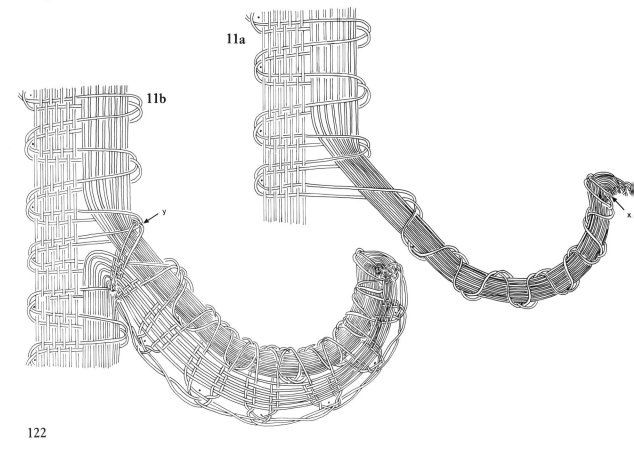

11a

11b

y

x

The rib and roll are worked by whole stitching the rib, separating the worker pairs and passing the top thread over and the bottom one under the roll, followed by a twisting of the workers and repeating by taking the top thread over and the bottom one under the roll, before whole stitching across the rib. A footside may be added on the rib side if desired or not.

When the roll is to be separated, work the worker across the rib, over and under the roll. Twist once; this worker continues to wrap over and under the roll, twisting on either side. Support pins are placed on the outer edge of the curve in order to assist in the shaping of that curve.

At the turning point – mark x on the diagram – wrap the workers for the last time to this point. Place a pin under the workers and, neatly turning all the pairs, whole stitch this worker through them. Put one twist on each of the outside two pairs and pin on the inside of these pairs (see fig. 11a). Whole stitch the inner pair back through the pairs. Then make a sewing around the roll with the worker pair. Whole stitch back through the rib pairs to the edge-pair. Twist the worker, whole stitch with the edge-pair, pin on the inside of both pairs and twist both pairs. Whole stitch the inner pair back through the rib and make a sewing with this pair around the roll.

Proceed in this manner until the rib reaches the place where the roll separated from the original rib. The temporary pins, used to support the curved roll, must be removed as the rib progresses. Care must be taken with the tension, as there is a tendency to over tighten the worked sewings and thus distort the curved shape.

Having worked the rib edge-pin hole at the position where it is to be reconnected to the original roll. Whole stitch through the rib and make a sewing around the roll and through the loop of the pair wrapping the original roll, before the divide marked y on fig. 11b. Whole stitch back through the rib pairs and whole stitch with the rib edge-pair. Pin on the inside of the outside pair only.

Turn all the rib pairs in sequence; the inner edge-pair now becomes one of the roll alongside the main rib. The pair supported by the pin is twisted once and separated in order to pass one thread over and one under the roll, and is then whole stitched across the rib – becoming the worker for the rib and the roll together (see fig. 11b). Its use is shown in lace construction in fig. 11c.

12 Carrying spare pairs around with a gimp.
Pairs are often used within an enclosed part of the design, which are not then required for the following section; a whole stitched block followed by a honeycomb ring – the whole stitch block to be filled requiring more pairs than the honeycomb. These

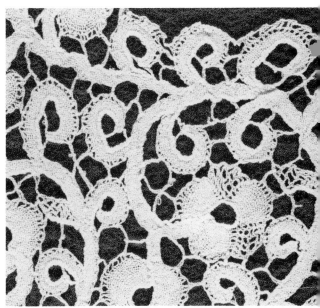

11c

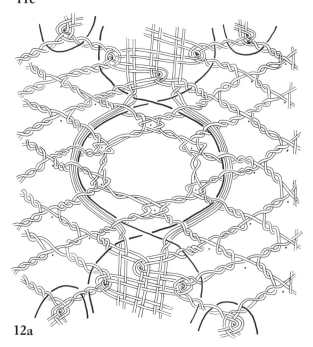

12a

spare pairs can be carried with the gimp alongside it as one unit. They can then be separated and used as required (see fig. 12a).

13 Carrying spare pairs across the net from one section of work to another.

To fill the whole stitch blocks more pairs are required than for some net grounds. To carry these spare pairs across the net the spare pair is worked with one of the net pairs as a single unit. At the crossing of

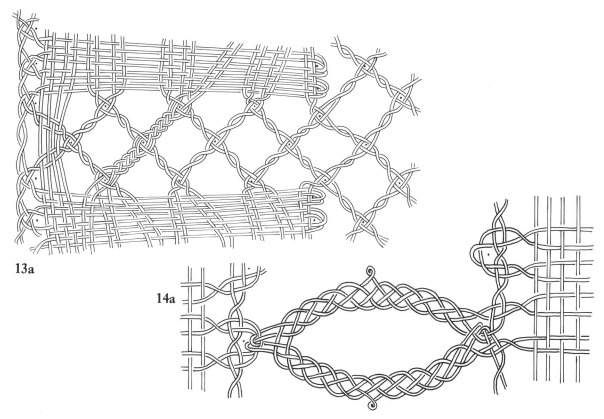

13a

14a

the net, the two pairs work as one pair and work the net stitch. Insert a pin, then the two united pairs are plaited to the next crossing point. They may be carried in this manner across any net and then used as required (see fig. 13a).

14 Making the filling while the work is in progress. Several fillings can be made within the two sections of work by using the edge-pair with the worker pair. Work the edge-pairs together and place a pin between these two pairs. Plait out with these pairs to the picot, construct this and plait on to the edge of the next section of lace with the nearest pair of the plait to the edge. Make a sewing into that edge. Continue plaiting to the other picot, construct this and plait back to the start. In the hole – left by the pin that was placed between the pairs at the commencement of the plait – make a sewing. Whole stitch the sewn pair with the other plait pair. Work the plait pair across the work as the worker. The sewn plait pair is left at the edge as the edge-pair (see fig. 14a). There are two methods of working this type of filling, as illustrated in figs 14b and 14c. If more filling is required the method of work is as fig. 14a. The pairs work in and out, with a sewing to hold the centre for loops. At no time do the pairs cross each other (see fig. 14b). Alternatively, some lacemakers prefer to have tighter crossings at all joins. This is achieved by working in a clockwise direction, always crossing one plait over another at the joins and

even at the join before the pairs return to their original places. Although the joins are closer together, the overall filling will also be drawn closer together (see fig. 14c).

15 Plaits can be used in many ways to fill a space between sections of work by using the edge- and worker pairs.

They can be worked in a clockwise or anti-clockwise direction (see fig. 15a). Irregular shapes can also be filled by using the two pairs from the work. At some points of the filling a plait is needed; there is no follow on point where this plait moves on to.

At this part of the filling a false plait has to be worked to fill this space. Work the plait to the last pin. Placing the pin between the plait pairs, take the outside pair from the plait and twist the pairs sufficiently to reach the edge-pin hole. Make a sewing into the pin hole and, on the return passage, twist the pair twice and make a sewing over the bar made on the outward passage.

Twist twice and make another sewing over the bar. For each two twists on the outward passage two twists and a sewing over the bar are needed for the return passage. End with two twists and continue plaiting with the pair left from the original plait. The false plait will be barely discernible from the real plait (see fig. 15b and also see section III, 11a and b).

The two pairs from the work can also be used to

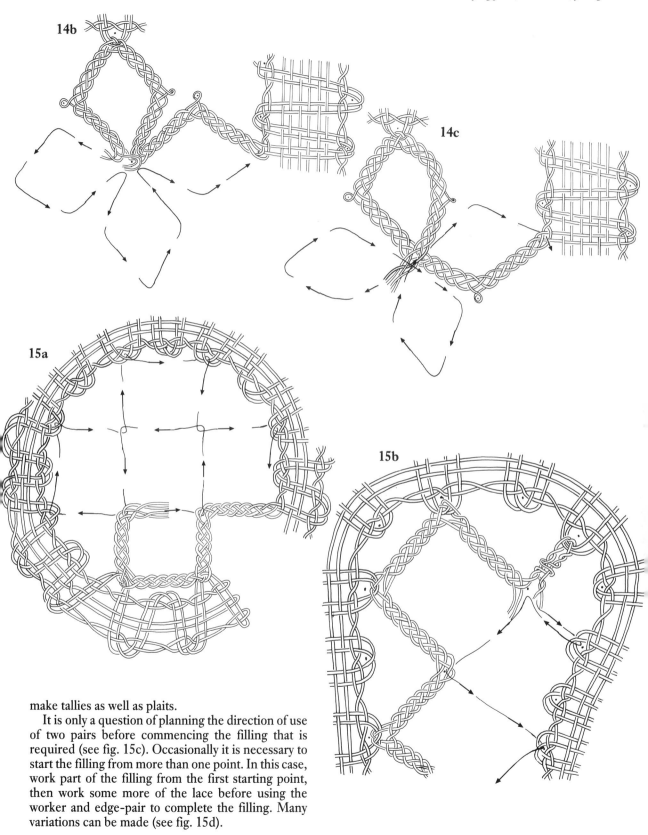

make tallies as well as plaits.

It is only a question of planning the direction of use of two pairs before commencing the filling that is required (see fig. 15c). Occasionally it is necessary to start the filling from more than one point. In this case, work part of the filling from the first starting point, then work some more of the lace before using the worker and edge-pair to complete the filling. Many variations can be made (see fig. 15d).

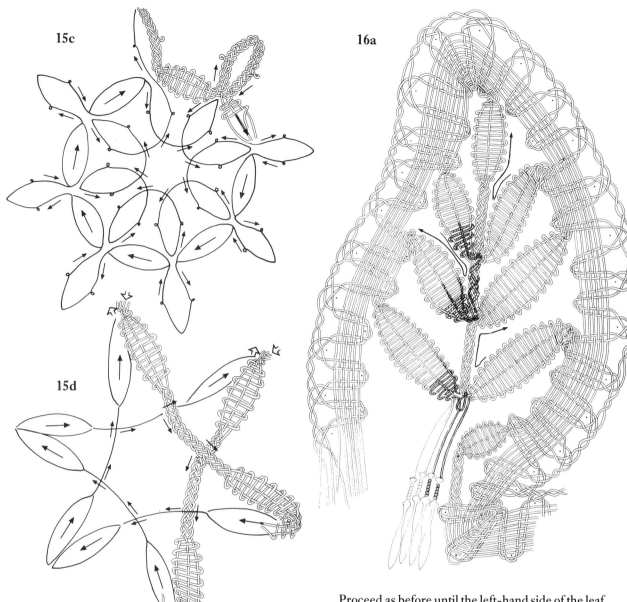

15c

15d

16a

16 A tally filling.

To fill in the centre of a braid leaf with plaits and tallies, so that the filling is worked at the same time as the leaf, two pairs are taken out of the braid at the bottom of the leaf and are worked in a plait to the base of the first tally (see fig. 16a).

Work the tally to where the tip of the tally touches the braid. The pairs are then incorporated into the braid again, until the top of the next tally. Leave out the two pairs here to make the tally. The tally is then worked downwards towards the centre of the leaf and a pin placed between the pairs before plaiting up the centre again to the base of the next tally. Tally to the edge of the braid again and incorporate these pairs.

Proceed as before until the left-hand side of the leaf is reached. Here the pairs will be let out to make a tally and the sewing will also be made at the base of the previous tally on the other side. Plait down the centre to the base of the next tally. Make another sewing and continue. In this way the leaf and its filling are worked at the same time, leaving no untidy ends (see fig. 16a).

17 To carry the pairs temporarily with the minimum bulk, thus causing less overall distortion.

Work the worker pair to the pin hole at which the two pairs are to be incorporated. Work a whole stitch with these new pairs, using the new pairs together as one thread. Twist and return the worker and then continue to use them as double threads until they are released (see fig. 17a). This draws the threads closer to the work.

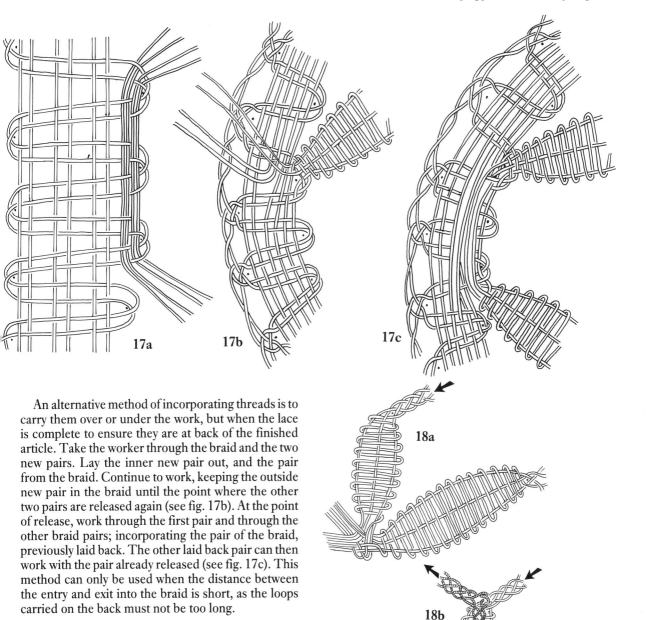

17a   **17b**   **17c**

18a

18b

An alternative method of incorporating threads is to carry them over or under the work, but when the lace is complete to ensure they are at back of the finished article. Take the worker through the braid and the two new pairs. Lay the inner new pair out, and the pair from the braid. Continue to work, keeping the outside new pair in the braid until the point where the other two pairs are released again (see fig. 17b). At the point of release, work through the first pair and through the other braid pairs; incorporating the pair of the braid, previously laid back. The other laid back pair can then work with the pair already released (see fig. 17c). This method can only be used when the distance between the entry and exit into the braid is short, as the loops carried on the back must not be too long.

18 It is sometimes necessary to carry pairs over the back of the work, for example when making a leaf at right angles to the work (see fig. 18a).

On a continuous piece of lace, two pairs can be used to make a leaf at right angles to the lace, joined with an edge or other part of the lace and taken back over itself to continue in its original work.

To do this, work the design to the point where the leaf is to be made. Pin between the pairs and make the leaf. Then, using each pair as a single thread, construct a half stitch with the two pairs from the connecting section. Pin in the centre of the pairs, twist the left-hand pair once and whole stitch through the first pair.

Cross the next two pairs (see fig. 18a). The two left-hand pairs then plait over the leaf made to their original pin hole, where a sewing is made with the outside pair to connect the overlaid plait to the leaf. The two pairs can now be worked in the lace and the design continued (see fig. 18b).

127

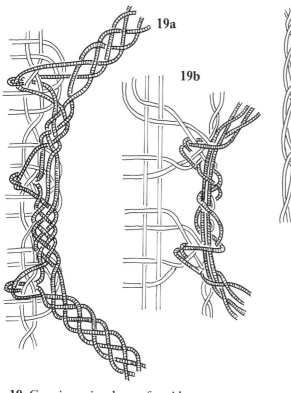

19a

19b

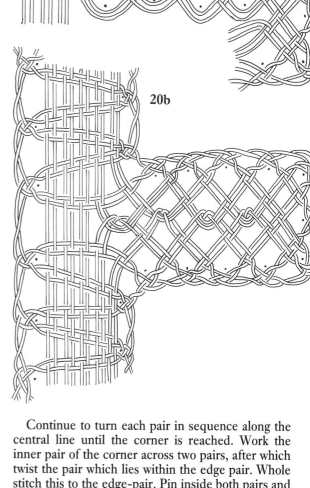

20a

20b

19 Carrying pairs along a footside.

Pairs can be carried along either a twisted footside or a straight footside. Take the pair nearest the footside and make a sewing into the edge. If the footside is twisted, the pairs to be carried are plaited between each pin hole before sewing into the footside at each pin hole (see fig. 19a).

When carrying pairs along a straight footside edge, the pairs can be sewn into the pin hole and also between each pin hole and the edge-pair. This produces a raised effect, outlining the work (see fig. 19b).

20 Using pairs from the braid and making a spur and returning them to the braid.

Work the braid to the point of the spur junction and then work across the braid to the non-spur side. Make up the edge.

Work back, making up the first edge-pin of the spur with this worker and edge-pair of the braid. Pin between them to support. Take the second passive pair from the pair on the right-hand side and turn this around the supporting pin, on a line with the centre of the spur. This pair works towards the right through the first passive and through the inner edge pair. It is then twisted, and the edge made up with the other edge pair. Pin between.

The first passive is then turned around the pin on the centre line of the spur and worked out to the edge in the same manner.

Continue to turn each pair in sequence along the central line until the corner is reached. Work the inner pair of the corner across two pairs, after which twist the pair which lies within the edge pair. Whole stitch this to the edge-pair. Pin inside both pairs and take the inner pair across the first pair. Repeat the sequence to make up the next corner pin hole.

Take the inner pair through the two pairs and make a sewing in the first central pin hole and leave (see fig. 20a). Take the second pair from the right, twist, and make up the edge. Pin on the inside of both pairs and take the inner pair through two pairs to a central pin, make the sewing and leave. Repeat this process until the last sewing has been completed. The inner edge-pair of the last pin hole of the spur then becomes

the worker and works right across the braid. The spur
is complete and the pairs are returned to their correct
sequence (see fig. 20b and photograph 20c).

21 Using pairs from a braid to make a curl tendril.
Work to the point of detachment and make up the
edge. Hang a new pair on the inner edge-pair before
whole stitching through the next passive. Hang on
another new pair. Twist this worker once and whole
stitch with the next passive.

These two pairs now become the footside pairs of
the tendril. Pin inside both pairs and whole stitch the
inner pair through three passives. Pass them over the
inside edge-pair. A pin may be placed as a temporary
support between the pairs before this pair passes
under the edge-pair and works through the three
passive pairs. The edge is then made up and this is
then repeated around the circle in an anti-clockwise
direction. The temporary pin must be removed
between each sequence (see fig. 21a). On completion
of the circle, to attach it to the braid again; the outer
edge-pair will return to become the second passive
pair on the right of the braid. The inner edge-pair
works across the tendril for the last time and whole
stitches across all pairs to make up the braid edge.
Two pairs are then laid out to be cut off later, and the
braid is continued (see fig. 21b).

22 Bar joins.
The worker pair may be taken out of one section of
lace to join with another in two ways.

Method A. Take the worker across the braid.
Support at the edge with a pin. Twist the worker to
where it is to be joined. Make a sewing at that join pin
hole. The worker is then twisted again to the next join;
it is joined with a sewing and twisted back to where it
left the braid. It works straight across the braid to

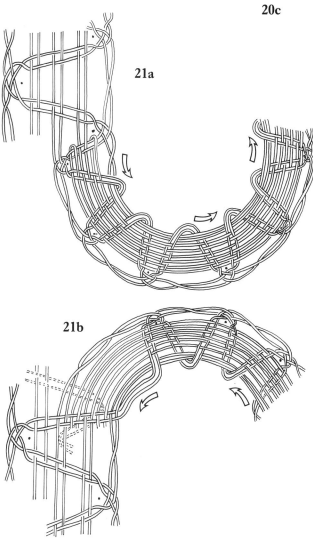

20c

21a

21b

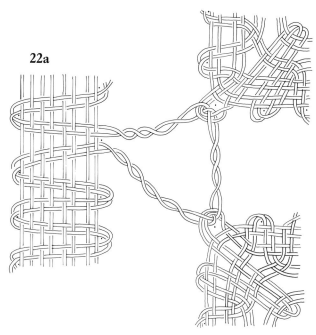

22a

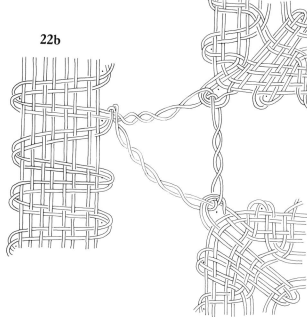

22b

where it commenced (see fig. 22a). It will be noted that this leaves a slight gap between the exit and entry of the worker to the braid.

Method B. This method is worked as for Method A, to the point where the worker is to re-enter the braid. But before doing so, make a sewing around the outgoing pair at the edge pin hole before continuing to work the braid (see fig. 22b). This method draws up the exit and entry points to give an appearance of the threads having just travelled around the edge pin.

23 A bar can also be made by using the outside passive pair to make the joins.

Take the worker to the opposite side of the braid where the joins are to be made and leave. Take the outside passive pair and twist to the first join. Join by sewing in a pin hole of the edge and twist to any other join; make sewing. Twist this pair back.

The pair is now taken in again to the braid as the outside pair (see fig. 23a).

A sewing can be made with the twisted pair before it is placed back into the work, in the apex of the pair where it left the braid, to draw the two pairs together. This is a matter of choice for the lacemaker.

24 'Rib', 'stem stitch' and 'ten stick' are all names given to a strip of lace with pins at only one side; usually used in raised work, and will have lace worked over them. Occasionally they are only used as stems of flowers and similar narrow edgings.

There are several methods of working these.

Method A. The simplest method is to work the rib, usually with about ten pairs. Two pairs make up the

23a

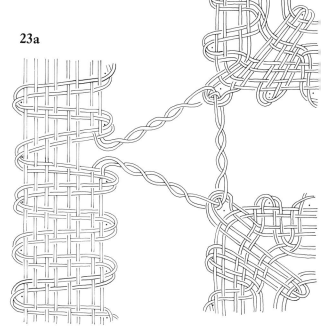

pin side of the lace and the rest of the pairs are passives. Whole stitch across the rib to the pin side, twist the workers and whole stitch with the edge-pairs. Twist both and pin on the inside of both pairs. Take the inner pair back across the rib.

On completion of the row the worker simply turns and reverses back. There is no pin or twist. Continue in this manner all the way down the rib. Care must be taken to keep the passives on the non-pin side in their

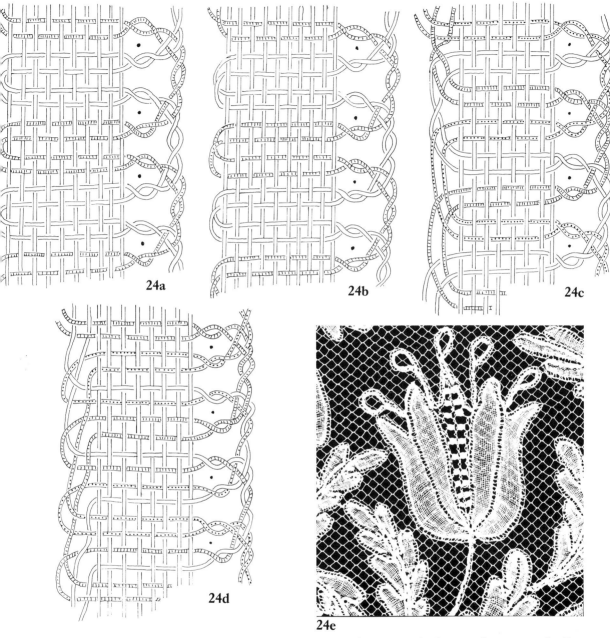

24a

24b

24c

24d

24e

correct position, in order to ensure that a good broad shaped rib is maintained (see fig. 24a).

Method B. A very similar rib is made by working as for Method A, except that before reversing back the worker pair is twisted once on the non-pin side. This produces a slight edge and is an available choice (see fig. 24b).

Method C. Make the footside edge as for Method A and B. Whole stitch to the non-pin side, twist the worker and leave. Take the inner pair of the last whole stitch worked back as the worker to the footside edge. This is repeated all the way down the rib, with the

pairs exchanging on both pin and non-pin side. Care must be taken to retain the shape of the rib, by keeping the last passive of the non-pin side in its correct place (see fig. 24c).

The next method is frequently used if the rib is to be curved around a small circle, as the pairs lie closer together on the non-pin side and thus sit neatly on the small inner circumference of a circle. When working with the non-pin side on the left, whole stitch to within the last passive pair. Cross the centre threads of the worker pair and the passive pair. Twist the left-hand two threads, then whole stitch the two pairs. The

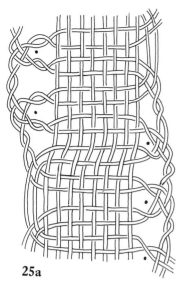

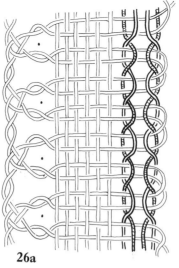

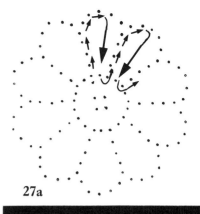

25a

26a

27a

inner pair then whole stitches across the rib to the footside edge.

This is repeated all the way down the rib. Care must be taken to control the shape of the rib by keeping the last straight passive on the non-pin side in its correct position (see fig. 24d). When the non-pin side is on the right-hand side, whole stitch the last two pairs. Then twist the outside two threads, leave the outside thread and cross the next two threads. Whole stitch back with the inner two threads. Illustrations of the uses of ribs, in stems up the petals of a flower and around the tendrils, are shown in fig. 24e.

25 Ribs can be made with the footside on either side; the pin side is capable of being reversed whilst under construction. At the exchange, take the worker to the opposite side, twist the worker and the pair that was the unpinned passive edge-pair. Whole stitch them together, pin on the inside of both pairs and then work the inner pair across the rib. The edge-pair from the old footside edge now hangs as the last passive of the rib on the non-pin side. Care must be taken to retain the shape of both sides of the rib, especially at the change-over point (see fig. 25a).

26 Rib with a decorative edge. An additional dimension can be given to a rib by using two pairs of gimp threads on the non-pin side, to raise the edge in a '3D' effect.

Hang on the pairs for the rib with two pairs of gimps on the non-pin edge. Take the worker pair over the first gimp thread, under the centre two gimp threads and then over the fourth gimp thread. The two central gimp threads are then placed one on either side of the

27b

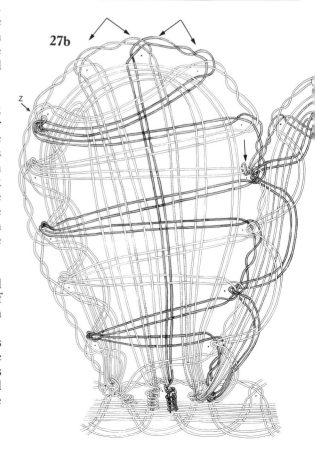

outside gimped threads, thus exchanging their positions.

Whole stitch the worker through the rib and make up the edge. Take the inner edge-pair back across the rib to the gimp threads. The worker pair is then lifted over the first gimp thread under the centre two and over the fourth.

The gimps then change position, with the two central threads being placed one on either side of the outside threads. Twist the worker and work back to the footside, first going over the edge gimp thread, under the central gimp threads and over the fourth gimp thread. The gimps change position again and the worker works across the rib.

This is repeated all the way down the rib. Care must be taken to keep the gimp threads on the non-pin side of the rib in their correct position and under tension, in order to ensure a good overall shape (see fig. 26a).

27 Raised work.

Illustrated is a flower where the work ribs up a petal and opens up; the pairs then working down the same petal over the rib and thus making a raised edge (see fig. 27a).

For the flower, work the central ring with a footside on the outer edge of the ring. Complete the ring and join up. The pairs from the central ring can be tied or cut off or alternatively carried, having been first tied to the commencement of the first petal.

Five pairs are needed to work the rib if the pairs are not to be carried. Join in five pairs on to the footside of the ring. Work the rib up to the sides, stopping at pin hole Z. At this pin hole, work the edge-pair from the rib to the non-pin side of the rib. Take the central pair from the rib and work that two pairs to the right. This pair will now hang as the first passive.

Add two new pairs above the edge. Whole stitch the left-hand pair with the edge-pair. Twist both and pin between them. Whole stitch the left-hand pair through three pairs and then the right-hand one through three pairs. Add another two new pairs on the outer edge and repeat.

Whole stitch the right-hand pair of the last whole stitch made to the right, through two pairs. Twist and make up the edge, with the edge-pair hanging on the support pin. Pin on the inside of both pairs. The inner pair becomes the worker and works across the petal to the rib edge, where a sewing is made.

Work back and forth, working a footside on the right-hand side and sewings on the left, until the last pin has been worked on the right-hand side. work one more row across the petal to the ring rib edge, where the worker pair is sewn and tied off. On the next ring pin hole, two pairs are tied off on either side of the hole. The other four pairs are sewn on the next ring pin hole and carried up to make a rib for the next petal.

This rib must be sewn into the edge of the first petal, usually a side sewing, as the bars of the first petal will be used for the sewings of the second petal.

Work the rib to the point where the petals separate. A new pair must be sewn on to the first petal to give a footside pair for the second petal. Then work the second petal as the first (see fig. 27b).

Proceed until the last petal, which is worked up and around its top until the petal meets the first petal, where the edge-pair is no longer required, and is tied off. Continue working the petal, making sewings on both sides until the petal is complete. Tie off all pairs on the ring edge-pin holes.

28 Carrying pairs from a central circle to the outer petals of a flower (see fig. 28a).

Work the central ring with a footside on either side; a cordonnet may be added on either side. On the completion of the ring, join each pair into its starting loop with a sewing (see fig. 28b).

Starting in the centre, tie the two threads with a single knot. Lay this knotted pair between the next sewn pair and tie the sewn pair with a single knot around them. The cordonnet, if used, is included. Lay these threads between the next sewn pair and tie a single knot around them. The inner cordonnet can now be laid back to be cut off later.

Continue to lay the pairs across the ring between the sewn pairs, tying a single knot around them before working to the edge-pin hole. At the edge-pin hole, lay all pairs from the ring, plus the cordonnet, between the last sewn pair. Tie a reef knot to secure. This has made a neat roll across the ring. At this stage pull all the threads up to the correct tension (see fig. 28c).

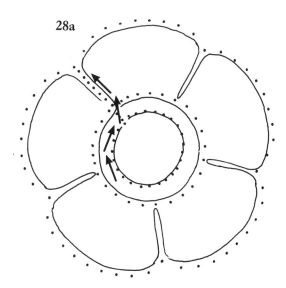

28a

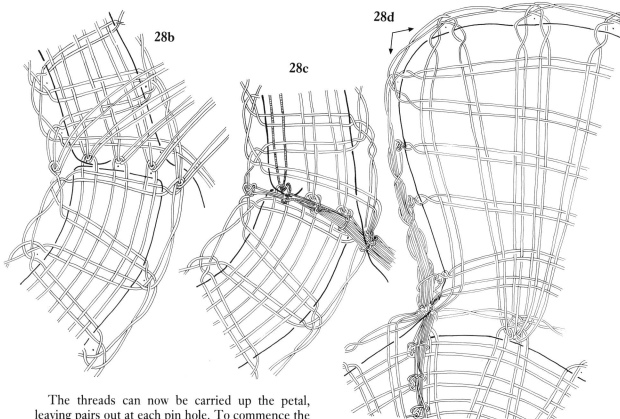

28b

28c

28d

The threads can now be carried up the petal, leaving pairs out at each pin hole. To commence the two threads that made the reef knot are taken under the group, crossed and brought to the top. Leave out four threads as two pairs, one to be the inner pair and the worker of the petal. Tie the crossed-over threads in a single knot. Pin between them.

This pair is now to be used as the second petal pair. Take two outside threads of the group under and cross them over the group. Tie these at the next pin hole and leave them out. Continue in this manner until only one pair remains. Hang two new pairs on a support pin on the curve of the petal. Whole stitch the left-hand pair with the single pair. Pin between them both. These pairs are then taken into the petal. The cordonnet left at the base can now be passed through all the pairs except the last edge-pair.

Starting at the base of the petal, work the first pair left, out through all the pairs to the top and through the cordonnet. Make up the edge with the new pair waiting on the support pin. Work the petal in and out, making sewings on the inner ring. Two sewings may-be required at each pin hole (see fig. 28d).

The cordonnet may be taken down between each petal and the pairs. Twist twice all pairs to give separation before it is taken out and used for the next petal.

Complete the flower and tie off around the starting roll.

29 Alternative carrying method from the central ring to a petal.

Complete the central ring. With the worker on the outer side of the ring, make a sewing with the inner edge-pair of the ring into its starting loop. Wrap this pair over the cordonnet and make a sewing into the next starting loop. Wrap a thread from this sewing over the first passive and make another sewing with the wrapping pair into the next starting loop.

Wrap this pair around the bunch, including the next passive pair, and continue across the ring, making sewings into starting loops and wrapping until the edge is reached. Make a sewing into the edge loops, open up the wrapping pair and lay all the pairs, including the cordonnet, between them and tie a single knot to secure them (see fig. 29a).

Fan the pairs out and lay the cordonnet between the fanned-out pairs and the knotted pair. The knotted pair becomes the edge-pair of the first petal. Take the second pair in from the cordonnet and work this out through one pair and the cordonnet, making up the footside edge. Pin between them. Take the inner pair back through the cordonnet and one pair; this pair now becomes a passive pair. Take the third pair in from the fanned group and work this through two pairs out to the edge. Make up the edge and pin

29a

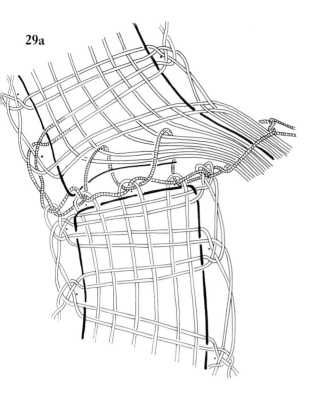

29b

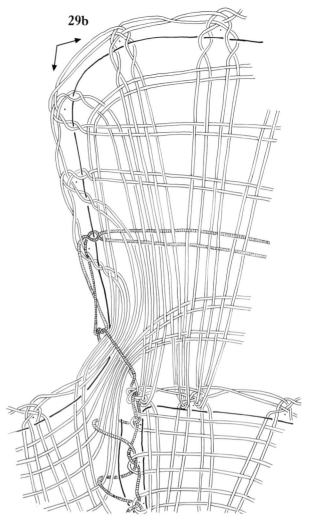

between, and take the inner pair back to become a passive. Add two new pairs on a support pin at the top of the petal.

Whole stitch the left-hand pair with the edge pair pin between. Take the left-hand pair through the cordonnet and one pair. Leave as passive and take the right-hand pair as the worker to work the petal.

Work to the base of the petal and make sewings into the edge of the central ring. Two sewings may be required in each pin hole. When the flower is complete, tie off into these first edge-pin holes (see fig. 29b). To separate the petals one from another, the cordonnet passes between each pair of the petals to the central ring. The pairs are then twisted twice before the cordonnet returns to the outer edge.

30 Carrying pairs from a petal to a petal along a central ring (see fig. 30a).

Work the central ring, complete and tie off. Hang new pairs on to the ring footside, sufficient in quantity to work a full half side of the first petal. Work around the top and down the second half. Variations of the construction of the tops of the petals can be seen at Section VII, figs. 12-18 inclusive.

Take the worker pair from the outer right-hand edge to the centre of the petal. Make a sewing into the ring footside.

This pair is now used to wrap around the first two passive pairs on the inside of the petal. Make a sewing with the wrapped-around pair and add it to the two wrapped passives. Take the fourth pair of the petal and wrap this pair around the bunch of three pairs and the next pair to its left (four pairs).

Make a sewing with the new wrapping pair to secure the bunch to the footside. Wrap around the bunch, including the next pair on the right, and lay this wrapped bunch and cordonnet and the last sewn pair between the edge-pair. This pair then makes a sewing into the edge of the ring, in order to secure the bunch at the base of the two petals.

Wrap the sewn threads once more around the bunch. Leave out three pairs and make a sewing in the ring pin hole in the first pin hole of the next petal. It is at this point that a pair is cut off from the bunch. It is no longer needed, as this half of the petal has no footside pair. Wrap the sewn pair around the

135

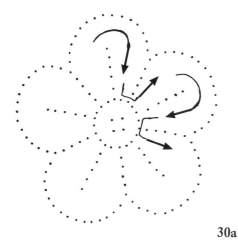

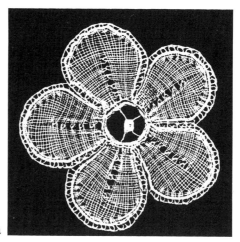

30a

30b

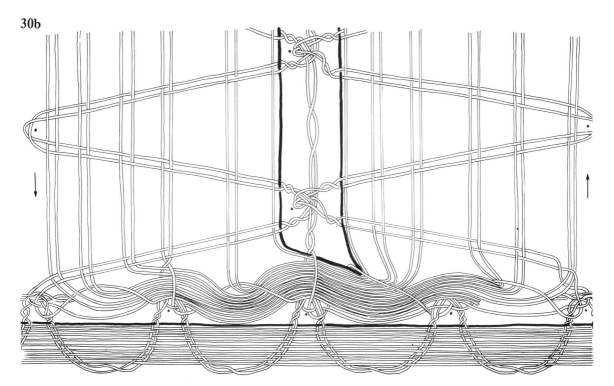

remaining bunch. Leave out all pairs and make a sewing with the wrapping pair into the ring edge-pin hole, level with the centre of the petal. This pair is now the worker for the first half of the second petal. It works back and forth, making sewings into the footside edge of the previous petal and travelling around the central pins of the petal (see fig. 30b).

After the separation of the petals, a new pair is added to work the footside of the second petal. Repeat for as many petals as are required. Tie off all pairs on completion.

31 An alternative to Method 30.

Work the petal as for Method 30 until the second half of the petal is completed. Take the edge-pair from the right to the centre and make a sewing with this pair into the centre pin hole of the ring. This pair is now the wrapping pair, used throughout the process of carrying the pairs from one petal to the next. Wrap this pair around the first two pairs and then wrap again to include the next pair. Make a sewing in the next ring edge-pin hole. Wrap the bunch and include the next pair.

31a

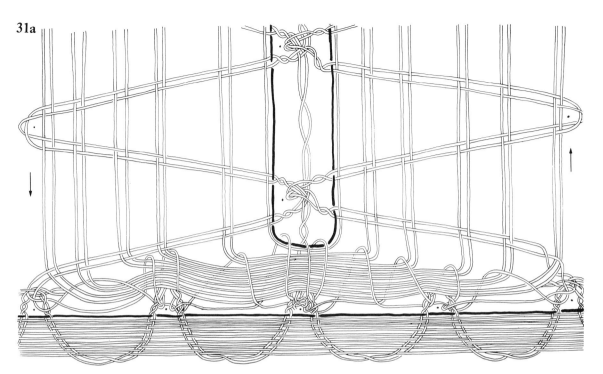

Make a second sewing in the ring pin hole. Continue wrapping the group and one pair at a time, until all the pairs are included. Make a sewing with the wrapping pair in the left-hand bar of the next ring pin hole. Leave while the edge-pair of the petal wraps around the bundle, sews and ties off at the same pin hole. This pair will be cut off later.

The waiting wrapping pair is wrapped once more around the bunch and makes a sewing into the right-hand side bar. The wrapping pair continues to wrap around the bunch. A pair in sequence is left out, make sewings in the ring edge, until the centre of the petal is reached. Make a last sewing in the ring. This pair now becomes the worker (see fig. 31a). The rest of the flower petals are worked as for Method 30.

32 Roll and tie.

A roll is a method of carrying pairs alongside a piece of work to the position where they are needed for continuing the work. An example would be a segmented leaf (see pricking at fig. 32a).

Work the first segment of the leaf with a rib. Open the rib at the top and add four pairs to work over the rib and back to the first segment. At the narrowing of the segment, throw out four pairs. The original number of pairs will then be turned and carried up in a roll beside the first leaf. To work this, take the inner edge-pair at the last pin hole on the footside edge across the segment and make a sewing. Work it back through the pairs, including the other edge-pair, omitting the twist between them.

Separate the now inner edge-pair and lay all the other pairs between them, except the outer edge-pair. Make a sewing in the first rib, one pin hole below the turning point. Leave this pair for later use.

The bunch is now twisted as many times as there are pin holes for it to travel along. The first edge-pair that lies with the bunches wraps around this bunch as many times as the bunch was twisted. A sewing is made at the pin hole on the first segment, where the top of the next segment separates from it. Return to the pair left for later use and with this pair make a sewing over the edge of the first segment pin hole and under the roll. Twist the pair once, make another sewing, and twist between in each pin hole until the top is reached. This secures the roll to the first segment.

The pair that made the last sewing now becomes the edge footside pair and the pair that wrapped the roll and made a sewing at the top works from the inside through all the pairs and makes up the outer edge. A pin is placed between these pairs and the inner pair is worked back through all these pairs, to lie as the first passive.

The inner pair from the group now works out to the edge. Make up the edge. The inner pair then comes back through and becomes the next passive. Two new pairs are now added on a support pin.

Whole stitch the right-hand pair through the edge-pair and pin between them. Work the right-hand pair through the group. This now becomes a passive. The left-hand pair from the pin now becomes the worker

32a

and works across all the pairs, to make a sewing on the first segment – as high as possible – usually where the other two sewings have already been made (see fig. 32b). Photo shows this method in use (see fig. 32c).

33 A high raised relief cord can be worked by making the raised relief cord first, then working over it; as in raised rib work.

Three pairs are needed to start, two for the side plait and one for the footside edge. The cord is thickened by using thicker threads or threads and wadding; these are held together by being wrapped over with one of the worker threads. Hang a cordonnet on a pin slightly above and to the left of the three pairs.

Whole stitch the three pairs together on a starting pin. The two left-hand pairs are half stitched together; the outside thread of the half stitch travels over then under the cordonnet thread. Cross it with the outside thread of the plait, half stitch with the plait pairs and repeat, taking the outside left-hand thread over and under the cordonnet thread, before making another plait stitch. Repeat this movement three or four times before reaching the point of the edge-pin hole (see fig. 33a).

The right-hand pair from the plait is then given an extra twist and joined with the edge-pair. Pin on the inside of both pairs. The inner pair is twisted twice and half stitched with the waiting plait pair, before wrapping procedure continues. The footside pair is twisted three times and is left until needed again.

To increase the height of the raised cord, more cordonnets or wadding may be added to form a bunch; add these one at a time on the inside of the cordonnet so the increase will remain smooth. The cordonnets can also be released one at a time to reduce the height of the cord. The rest of the piece can then be worked over the cord, and when the completed lace is reversed to its correct side, a '3D' effect will have been achieved (see fig. 33b).

32c

32b

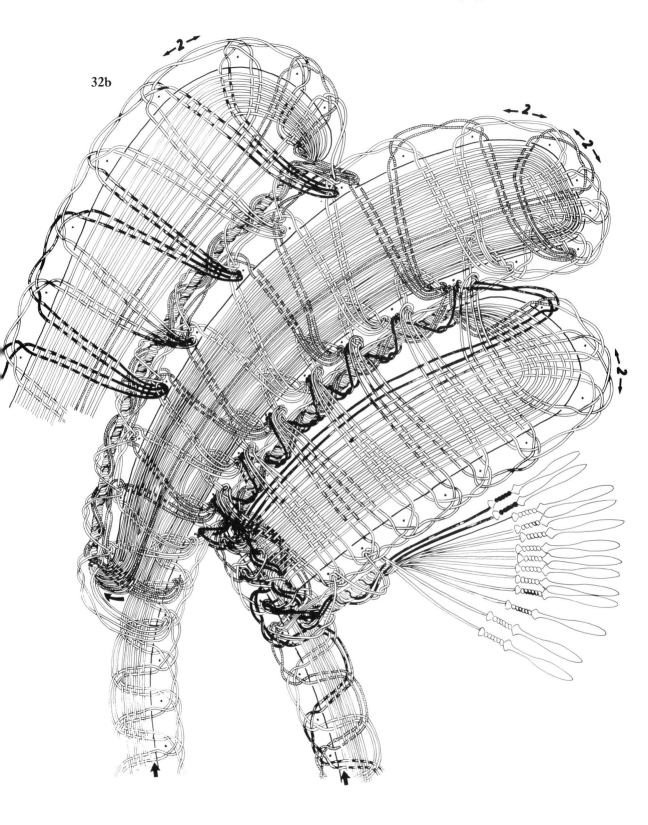

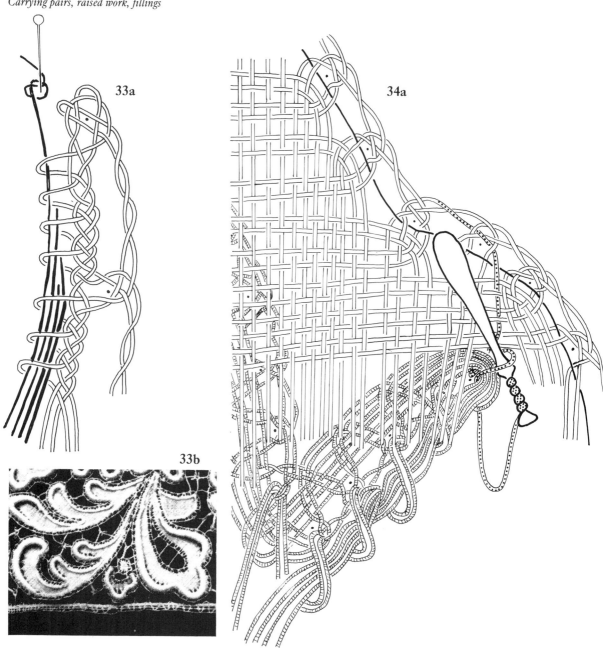

33a

34a

33b

34 Where a rib and roll vein has been worked prior to working the leaf the following method is used to connect the two together.

At the point where the leaf connects with the vein, arrange the passive pairs across the work evenly and, taking the bobbin that lies directly over the pin hole to be joined, make a self-sewing with this single thread;

i.e. pull the loop through the pin hole of the vein, and pass the bobbin through its own loop. This avoids distortion at the point of sewing. The bobbin now returns to its passive position; this method can be used wherever a connecting sewing needs to be made. The pin in the vein is left in until the sewing is completed to control its position better (see fig. 34a).

INDENTATION, CORNERS, CURVES AND HOLES

TURNING STITCHES

There are three ways to make a turning stitch.

1 Work the worker through the pair in whole stitch. Cross the centre two threads and continue working with the two right-hand threads. It will be noted the pairs have become divided (see fig. 1a).

An alternative method is to work the edge in whole stitch and then immediately work a half stitch with the same two pairs. Proceed back with the right-hand pair. It will be noted that in this method the outside thread remains constant (see fig. 1b).

Another method of achieving a turning stitch has to be used when working in half stitch. Work two consecutive half stitches at the edge. Again it will be noted that the edge-thread remains constant, thus retaining the line of the edge (see fig. 1c).

Any one of these three methods may also be used within a braid, in order to gain on a pin if the braid is curved.

2 A method of maintaining the even line of a zig-zag half stitch trail.

Work to the point of the turn of the zig-zag trail and

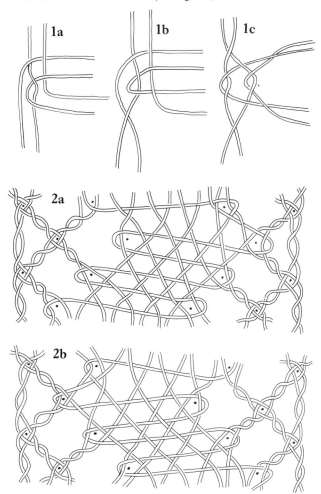

2c

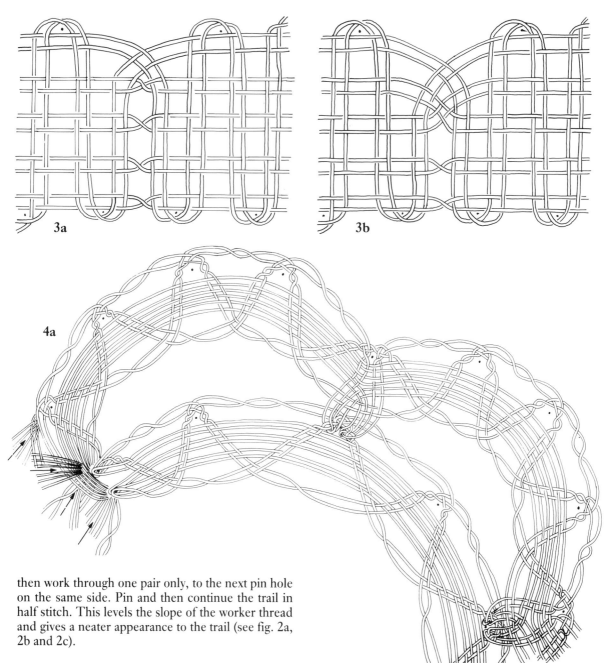

3a

3b

4a

then work through one pair only, to the next pin hole on the same side. Pin and then continue the trail in half stitch. This levels the slope of the worker thread and gives a neater appearance to the trail (see fig. 2a, 2b and 2c).

3 An indentation in a braid can be simply made by working across the braid. After the last whole stitch has been made, leave the worker as the passive and work the pair that was the outside passive pair back across the work, as the worker.

This makes a small indentation between one section of the tape and another. To make a stronger definition, each of the passive pairs can be twisted between the exchange of the workers (see fig. 3a).

A slightly deeper indentation can be made by working as fig. 3a but, instead of twisting all the passives between the exchange of the workers, the two passive pairs nearest to the exchange are whole stitched together. This draws the passives closer together and therefore also pulls the exchange whole stitches lower. This increases the depth of the indentation (see fig. 3b).

4 An indentation in a rib which is to be joined with sewings on to a footside edge.

At the point of the sewing, the rib is narrowed to make a neater join. Work the rib to its pin hole, above the pin hole of the edge into which the sewing is to be made.

Twist the edge-pair once only and pin beside both pairs. Take the inner pair across the rib and make a sewing through the left-hand bar of the pin hole. Work out through two pairs and leave that pair as a passive. The pair that was last whole stitched is then worked through one pair and a sewing is made in the right-hand bar of the same pin hole. Whole stitch this pair through the rib, twist once and make up the edge. Do not pin, as the pin is already in place between the two edge-joins. The rib can be continued to the next join.

This indentation forms quite naturally as the workers exchange, so drawing in the rib (see fig. 4a).

5 Turning a right-angled corner in a braid.
At the start of the turn, whole stitch the worker to the outside edge. Make up the edge. Take the inner edge-pair across the braid. This pair will become the inner passive of the braid.

Take the central passive pair through to the edge and make up the edge. Take the inner pair from this and pin back through one pair. This will become the outside passive pair of the braid. The edge-pair is twisted and turned around the corner pin. Turn the pillow. The edge-pin is then worked with the two pairs of the bobbins on the right (one edge-pair and one previous edge passive pair). The inner pair from this pin whole stitches back through one pair and becomes the central passive again of the braid. On the inner point of return, the pair that was previously the inner passive now becomes the worker and works out to the edge in order to continue the braid (see fig. 5a).

A right-angled braid turn with footsides on either side
At the start of the turn, whole stitch the worker to the outer edge. Make up the edge and work the inner pair back through the braid, excluding the edge pair. Take the other pair of this last stitch as the worker to the outer edge pin hole. Make up the edge. Take the inner pair back through one pair only. Turn the edge-pair around the corner pin. Turn the pillow.

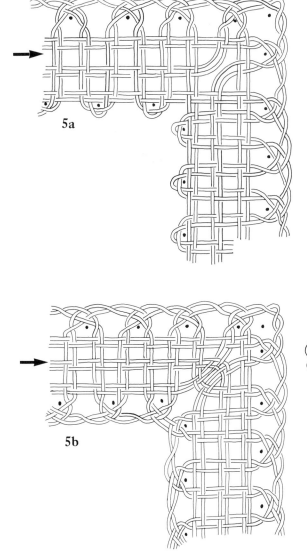

5a

5b

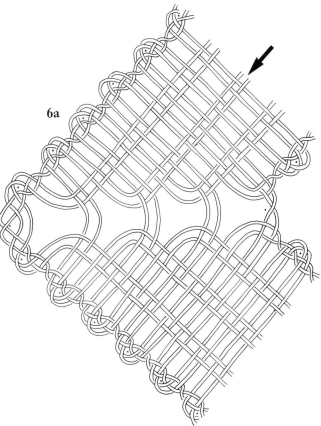

6a

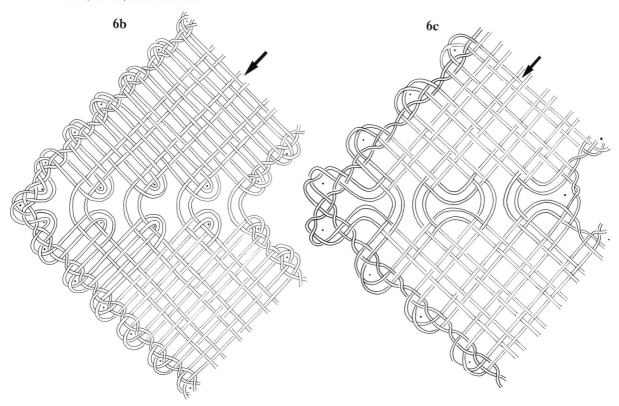

6b

6c

The edge-pin is then worked with the two pairs of the bobbins on the right (one edge-pair and one previous edge passive pair). The inner pair from this pin whole stitches across the work to within the inner edge-pair and becomes the inner passive pair again.

Whole stitch the last pair worked to the outer edge and make up the edge. This now becomes the worker for the turned braid (see fig. 5b).

6 Turning a wider braid through a right angle

At the point of the turn, whole stitch the worker to the inner edge-pair and support the worker only with the central pin.

Whole stitch the inner edge-pair across the work. Make up the edge and whole stitch back to the centre, where it is left. The last pair worked becomes the new worker. Repeat as many times as is necessary to complete the corner. The edge-pair is twisted and turned around the corner at the corner pin. The process is reversed in order to continue the braid.

To do this the next edge-pin hole is worked with the two edge pairs, the inner pair becoming a passive pair. Taking the first pair, previously left from the braid, as the new worker, work to the edge. Make up the edge, and pin. Work through one passive pair. The next worker will be taken from the previous braid and works in turn until all the pairs have been included (see fig. 6a).

Alternative method

Work to the inner point of the turn. Make up the edge and work to the outer edge, making up that edge. Work to the first diagonal pin hole. Do not include the inner edge-pair. Pin and turn around the pin and work back to the outer edge. At each diagonal pin hole the worker passes through one pair less.

Continue in this manner until the corner has been reached. The edge-pair is twisted and turned around the corner pin. The next edge-pin is worked with these two pairs. The worker continues around the diagonal pins, collecting a pair at each pin hole, until all the pairs are back in the braid (see fig. 6b).

A firmer alternative variation

The worker is left out on the inside edge-pin of the corner. The first inside passive is taken to the outer edge of the worker. The edge is made up and is worked through the braid, excluding the inner passive and edge-pair. The last passive pair worked now becomes the worker and is taken to the outer edge-pins and back, excluding the last worker pair and the adjacent passive pair on its left. The last passive pair worked then progresses to the outer edge and turns, to become the outer edge-pair of the turned braid. The other edge-pair turns around the next pin and works through the edge-pair and lays as the edge passive pair.

6d

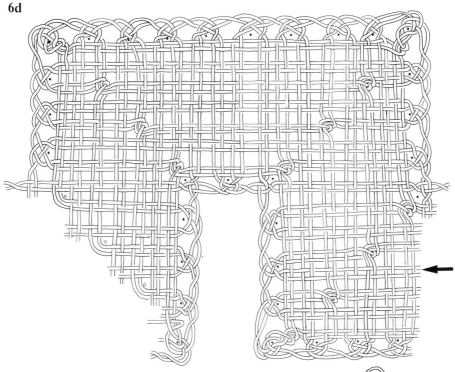

The next pair of bobbins to the right then becomes the worker; taken to the outer edge it makes up the edge-pin. It works back in sequence, including the next two pairs previously excluded from the braid. From the last whole stitch worked, take the left-hand pair as the new worker to make up the outer edge. Work back through all the pairs, including the inner edge-pair which then works across as the worker for the turned braid (see fig. 6c).

Another alternative variation

Take the worker to the inner corner pin. Make up the edge, pin between the pairs and leave both pairs. Turn the inner passive around the first diagonal pin.

This pair becomes the worker and progresses to the outer edge. Make up the outer edge. Take the inner edge-pair and work through the passives and leave. The last pair it works through is also left out. Place a pin to the right of the next pair on the left and use it as the worker. Work to the outer edge and make up the edge-pin. Work to the inner diagonal pin hole. Leave this worker and the pair it has just worked through.

Place a pin to the right of the next pair on the right and, using it as a worker, progress to the outer edge, making up the edge-pin. Take the inner edge-pair across to the diagonal pin hole and leave with the pair it has just worked through.

Take the last passive and make up the corner pin.

7a

7b

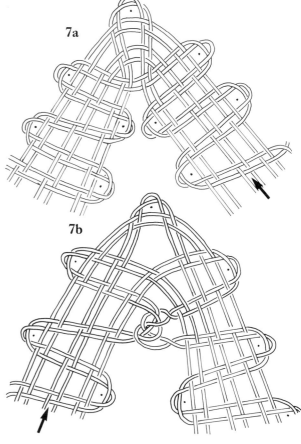

7c

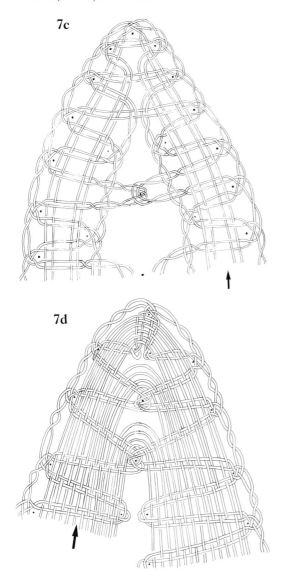

7d

Turn the work, take the inner pair and make a sewing beneath this corner pin hole. This pair now becomes the outer edge passive. * The passive pair left out to the right of the next diagonal pin hole now becomes the worker. It works to the outer edge and makes up the edge-pin hole and returns to make a sewing at the diagonal pin hole. The same pair now becomes a passive.* Repeat steps from * to * until the corner is turned. When the inner edge-pair becomes the worker, the corner is turned (see fig. 6d).

7 Turning braids

A sharp bend in a braid can be worked to the inside of the bend with the worker, leaving that pair and taking the last passive pair just worked through as the worker, out to the point of the bend. Take the pair around the pin in the point and return to the inside

edge, where it again exchanges with the old worker. The old worker now works the braid and the pair which worked the point is replaced as the inside passive (see fig. 7a).

A less acute bend can be worked by taking the worker to the inside pin hole of the bend, working around the pin; out to the outside edge and then back through all the pairs. Leave this pair to lie as a passive. Work the second pair from the outside edge out to make the point pin hole. Work it back through two pairs. This then returns to the inner passive position.

Work the second pair from the outside edge out to the edge. Make up the pin and work this pair back to the centre inside pin hole, where a sewing is made before that pair continues to work the braid (see fig. 7b).

A bend can be made in braid with footsides on either side. If the two halves of the braid are to lie close to each other after the bend is made, the braid will need to be connected by sewings in the centre. To achieve this the working pair on the first braid will at certain points need to travel further to the centre point than the original pin hole position in the footside. At this pint the worker pair whole stitches through the edge-pair and is twisted to cover and pass around a central pin, before it whole stitches through the edge-pair and back across the braid. The extended loop will be where the sewing will be made on the second braid.

At the turning point, whole stitch the worker across the braid through the inner edge-pair. Whole stitch the inner edge-pair out across the braid. Make up the edge and whole stitch this pair back to the centre.

Take the last passive pair whole stitched out to the edge and make up the edge-pin. Whole stitch the inner pair back and leave.

Take the last passive pair whole stitched through and make up the edge at the point. Pin on the inside of both pairs. Turn the pillow.

The process is repeated in reverse for the second braid (see fig. 7c).

A fuller braid turning

Proceed to the start of the turn. Whole stitch the workers from the central pin hole to the edge. Make up the edge stitch and work back to the next central pin hole, omitting the last two passive pairs. Whole stitch to the edge and return to the centre, omitting two more passive pairs. Work out the edge at the top point of the turn. Make up the edge. Stitch and work back through the same pairs to a second pin alongside, or, if preferred, a sewing may be made in the previous pin hole. Work to the outer edge and make up. Return through the braid, including the two pairs omitted at this pin hole. Make a sewing. Repeat this process at the next pin hole and then continue to work the braid with all the pairs included (see fig. 7d).

8 U-shaped bend.

Take the worker to the outside of the bend through to approximately two thirds of the braid's width. Pin and work to the outer edge. Turn around the pin and work back through approximately one third of the braid's width. Pin and work to the outer edge; work back through two thirds of the braid's width. Pin and work out to the outer edge. Work back through the complete width and the process can be repeated for a second bend (see fig. 8a).

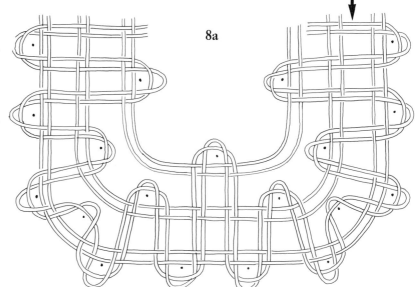

9 Even pin retention in a curve.

Take the worker to the inner-curve edge and leave. Take the passive pair last worked through as the worker to the outer edge. Make up the edge and work it back to the inner curve. Whole stitch with the pair left out previously.

Pin on the inside of the pairs and take the inner pair back as the worker. Make up the outer edge and work back to the inside curve, excluding the edge-pair. It now becomes the inner passive pair.

The inner edge-pair can now continue as the worker for the braid. It will be noted that less pins have been used on the inner curve than on the outer. This gives an even appearance to the braid (see fig. 9a).

An alternative method of using less pins on the inner curve can be achieved by taking the worker at the bend to the outside pin hole, then through two passives. The passive last worked through becomes the worker and continues the braid around the curve. Care must be taken to keep the tension even, or a slight hole may appear below the crossed pairs (see fig. 9b).

10 A more acute turn where there are more pins on the outside edge than on the inside.

Work to the last pin hole on the inside edge of the curve. Pin and work out to the outside edge. This pair then works right across the braid and becomes the inner passive.

Take the central passive and work this to the outer edge and back to the central position where it is left.

The last pair it worked through is now taken to the outer edge and is turned around the pin, in order to become the new worker and continue the braid (see fig. 10a).

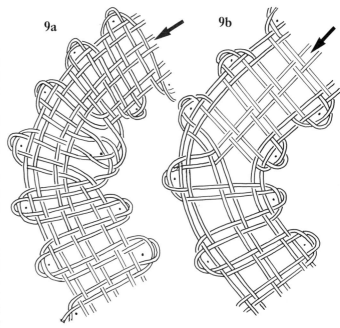

An alternative method of using less pins on an inner curve of a braid

Take the worker to the inner corner pin. Take it around that pin and out to the outer edge. Work back to the central passive pair and leave. The last passive pair worked through becomes the worker and is worked to the outer edge. Make up the edge and work back to the centre, excluding the inner passive pair. The worker passes over these and around the pin. It is then whole stitched through all the pairs.

The braid can then be continued. It will be noted that by not working the last passive pair on the inner curve, the pairs will lie closer together when the pin is removed (see fig. 10b).

147

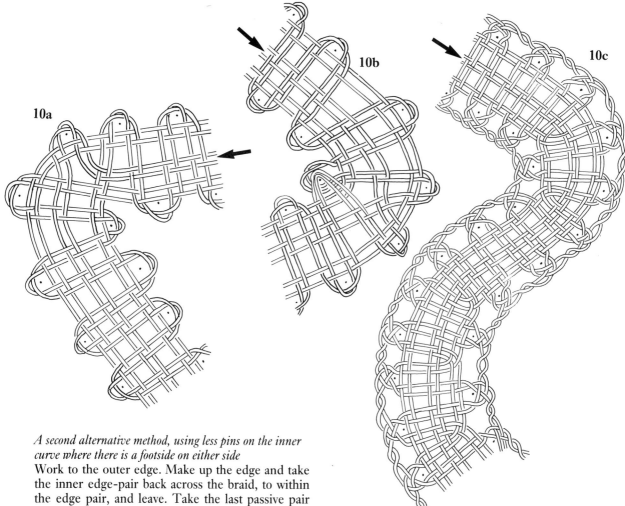

10a

10b

10c

*A second alternative method, using less pins on the inner
curve where there is a footside on either side*

Work to the outer edge. Make up the edge and take
the inner edge-pair back across the braid, to within
the edge pair, and leave. Take the last passive pair
worked through as the worker to the outer edge. Make
up the edge and work the left-hand pair across the
braid, including the inner edge-pair. Make up the
edge and take the right-hand pair of these across the
work to the outer edge. Make up the edge. Take the
left-hand pair back across all pairs, excluding the
foot-side pair. Leave.

This pair will become the inner passive pair. The
last pair worked through will now become the worker,
progressing to the outer edge. The braid can now be
continued. The method describes the first bend in
fig. 10c. If a more gradual curve is required the
method described here may be worked consecutively
(see lower curve bend at fig. 10c).

11 A curve can be worked by extending the pins on
the outer edge and compressing them on the inner
one. This method is not suitable for every occasion
(see fig. 11a).

There are alternative ways of maintaining the shape
of the braid during a curve.

First method

In fig. 11b the first method of gaining on the curve is
to work the worker across the braid, excluding the
inner passive pair. The worker turns and works out
again. This turn could be supported on the pin but it
is inclined to leave a loop which is undesirable.

Second method

This is to work right across the braid in making up the
edge of the first movement, returning to the outer
edge. On the second movement, only go to the inner
passive before returning to the outer edge. It will be
noted in fig. 11b that the central threads of the first
whole stitch made on the return journey are crossed
before the pair works inwards for a second time. This
crossing of the threads helps in securing the passives
in their correct position on the outer edge and thus
prevents them from being pulled away from the edge
of the curve.

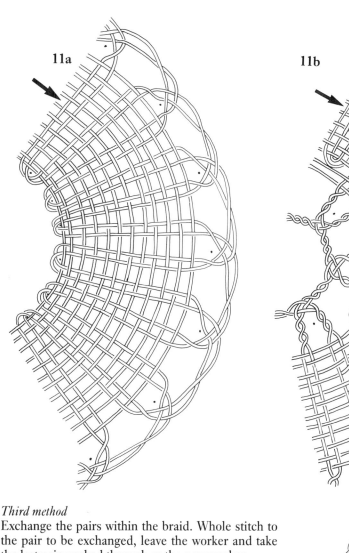

11a

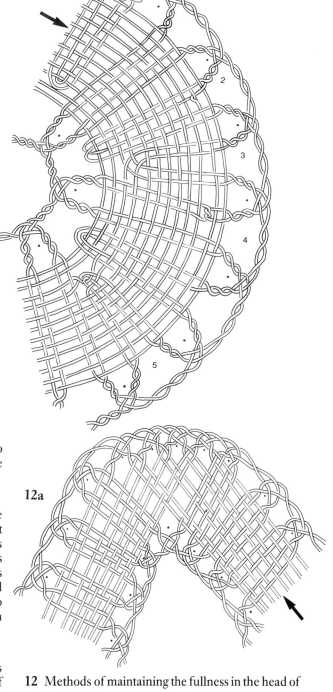

11b

Third method

Exchange the pairs within the braid. Whole stitch to the pair to be exchanged, leave the worker and take the last pair worked through as the new worker.

Fourth method

The worker works to the centre again but, before doing so, the worker pair has been tied in a single knot after working the first passive pair, which again retains the overall shape of the curve. The inner edge-pair is then made up and, after it is worked out again, is worked back across to within the last passive pair and passes under and over this pair, before returning to the outer edge. The inner passive pair must remain taut and in its correct position, or distortion occurs.

Fifth method

An exchange of pairs. Whole stitch the two pairs together that are to be exchanged, followed by a half stitch. The right-hand pair then becomes the worker. It will be noted that the inner thread of the passive pair remains constant and it is by the tension of this thread that the shape is retained (see fig. 11b).

12a

12 Methods of maintaining the fullness in the head of a turn.

When working around a turn, the pairs are often pulled towards the inner edge of the turn. To avoid this, work as follows.

Whole stitch the work across the braid to the inner edge. Make up the edge and pin on the inside of both pairs and leave both pairs. Work the outer passive pair to the outer edge and make up this edge. Whole stitch the inner pair across all the pairs to the inside, excluding the edge pairs. Work each passive outside pair in sequence to the outer footside edge. Make up the edge and work back across the work through the passives which have not yet been turned. The inside footside edge-pair can continue to work the braid when all the pairs have been turned (see fig. 12a).

This method is also used for a wider curve braid. It can also keep a constant footside pair (as illustrated in figs 12b, 12c and 12d).

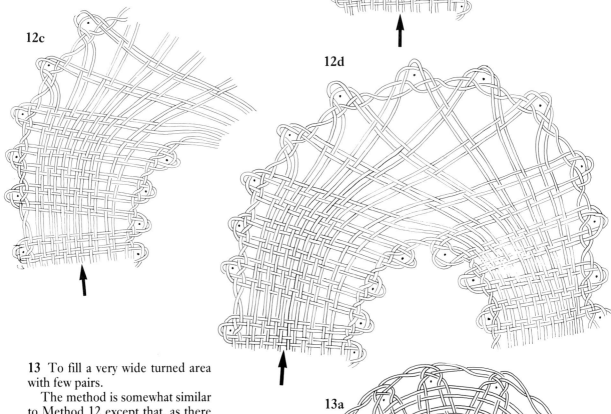

12b

12c

12d

13 To fill a very wide turned area with few pairs.

The method is somewhat similar to Method 12 except that, as there are fewer pairs filling a larger area, the pairs are whole stitched and twisted at each stitch. They also work across the work several times.

Work to where the shape is to be increased. Leave two passive pairs constant around the edge for the shape.

Take the workers to the outer edge and make up the edge, pin and leave both pairs. Whole stitch the third passive from the outer edge through all the pairs towards the

13a

centre, excluding the inner passive pair.

Place a temporary pin on the inside of that passive and pass the worker over the pin and passive pair and then under the pair. Twist this pair and leave both.

From the outside edge, whole stitch the inner pair through the constant two pairs and twist. Whole stitch and twist each passive pair in turn to the centre. Move the temporary pin along the curve a little and take the twisted worker over the pin and edge passives and then under the edge passive pair and leave both pairs.

Starting with the third passive pair from the outside edge, repeat the process in sequence, with each passive working out to the outer edge and then taking the inner pair into the shape. Whole stitch through the two constant passives, twist and work to the centre in whole stitch and twist until all the pin holes on the outer curve have been worked. To complete this shape, whole stitch across all the pairs from the outside edge, including the inner pair from the curve. Remove the last temporary pin. The braid can then be continued (see fig. 13a).

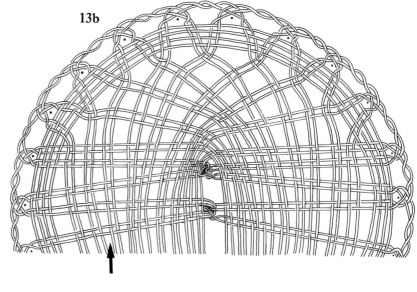

13b

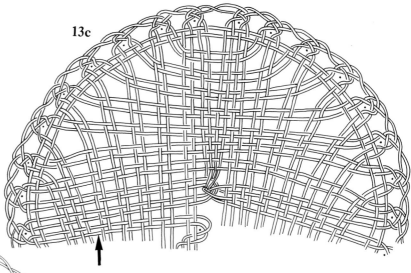

13c

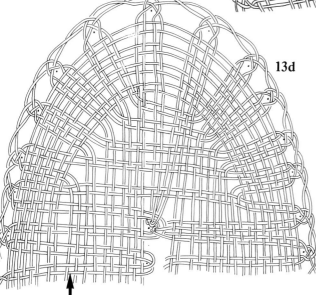

13d

The same method may be used at the top of a petal, either with or without twists between the stitches. If there are sufficient pairs (one for each pin) around the top circumference of the shape, then, by always working the third pair outwards first, the shape can be filled without repeating the sequence (see fig. 13b).

Alternatively, the sequences may be repeated after half the circumference has been completed, by working to the centre of the shape. Make a sewing into the last pin hole in the centre and work out to the outside edge, from where the sequence can be repeated a second time (see fig. 13c).

Variations can be made using these methods. The constant number of pairs can be increased and the crossover section worked only in the centre of the shape.

151

14a

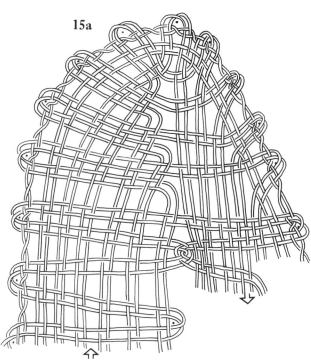

15a

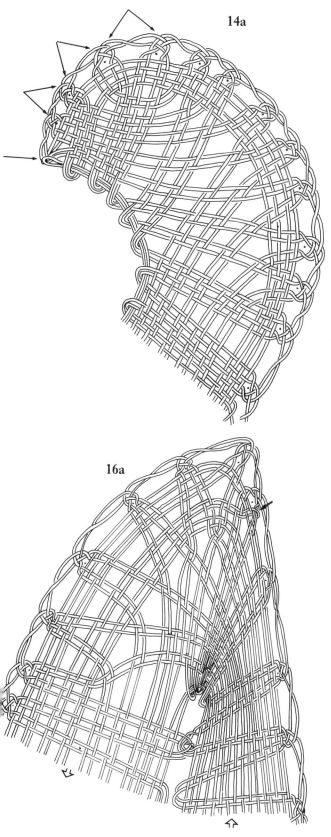

16a

With this method the edge has a firm appearance and remains close to the outer edge pins, by the inner space being filled with the crossed-over work. In fig. 13d there are four constant outer passives, and it is the fifth pair from the edge that always works outwards (see fig. 13d).

14 Method of maintaining a fullness in a widening crescent shape.

This method can be used for any curved braid in which there are insuffcient pairs to fill the braid.

Start the pairs at the point and work one or two rows, adding pairs along the outer edge until the crescent shape begins to widen. Keep two constant pairs along the outer curve and then work the third passive from the outer footside through the two constant passive pairs. Make up the edge with the inner pair and whole stitch to the inner edge of the curve. The edge can be made up or, if the curve is a tight one with insufficient space for the pins, then the worker can be taken over a temporary pin and the inner edge-pair, and then under that pair.

In either case the pairs are then left on the inner curve and the process is repeated in sequence. Start with the third passive pair working out to the outside curve edge. When the point of reduction of the curve is reached, then the worker can revert to work straight across the braid (see fig. 14a).

15 For fullness in a braid which is turned at a point but is to be of uneven widths.

The two sides of the turn can be worked differently.

Work the braid from the last central pin hole to the outer edge. Make up the edge and work back across all pairs to the centre.

The last passive worked through is then turned and continues to the outer edge. The edge is made up and this pair is worked across the braid and then left. This sequence is repeated until the top of the tape is reached. As the second side is narrower than the first, the worker from the tip works through all the pairs and is left. A new sequence is started by always working the second pair from the footside out to the footside, and back through the pairs until the central pin hole is reached. At this point a sewing is made. The braid can then continue.

Using pairs from the centre to work outwards first produces a fuller filling than if the pair to be worked is taken from just inside the outer edge towards the outside before working (see fig. 15a).

16 Using a mixture of methods to fill and turn a braid of uneven width sides.

Work the narrow side to the point of the turn. Whole stitch to the central pin through all the pairs, excluding the innermost pair. Place a pin on the outside of that pair, in the central pin hole. Take the worker over the edge-pair and pin. Then continue under the edge-pair. The worker can proceed to work the braid to the outer edge.

This process may be repeated several times, working over and under the inner edge-pair, as in fig. 16a. Remove the central pin and gently pull all the pairs evenly.

It may be found that as the second side is to be much wider, a new pair needs to be added. This can be done on the outside edge, at the pin before the top pin. The new pair is then whole stitched through three pairs and left as a passive.

When the topmost pin is reached and the braid is to be widened, work from the edge-pin holes through one passive pair, and leave. This turn has a constant four pairs running along the outer edge of the braid. Take the fifth pair from the edge each time in sequence and work out to the edge.

Make up this edge and work the inner pair back through the constant pairs and leave. When the turn is completed, the worker from this braid can make a sewing in order to join it to the first side, or it can just continue (see fig. 16a).

17 Crossover method of working, to produce a full effect with fewer pairs. Fig. 17a shows a leaf shape.

Start with two pairs at the top. Whole stitch, pin and whole stitch the pairs together. Twist both pairs and add two pairs at each of the next two pins to the left. Whole stitch and twist each in turn through the left-hand pair of the top pairs. Repeat on the right-hand

side. Work the first pair on the right, top pin to the left through four pairs. Whole stitch and twist with the edge-pair, pin, whole stitch both again and twist the edge-pair; leave both. Repeat in sequence down the right-hand side, working each pair to the left and making up the edge before leaving. Whole stitch the edge pair on the right and the nearest pair to it together; twist, pin at the edge, whole stitch and twist both again. Twist the edge pair and the inner pair, then work across the leaf to the left-hand side. The edge is worked and both pairs are then left. This is repeated, always working from the right until the shape is completed.

This fills the shape fully, without drawing the threads away from the outer edges in the widest part of the leaf. The centre of the shape can be worked in halfstitch; otherwise whole stitch and twist at every crossing to increase the fullness, if required (see fig. 17a).

18 Multi use of a pin.

A pin may have to be used on the inside edge of a curve many times. Work the braid until the pin is reached. The worker pair works through all the pairs to this central pin, excluding the last pair. Pin on the outside of this pair and then take the worker pair over the edge-pair and pin. Then continue under the edge-pair (see fig. 18a). The workers can be twisted but if the pin is to be used many times the twists are not needed. Take the workers to the outside edge, make up the edge and work back. Take the worker over the pin and edge-pair, then under it.

It is preferable to release the loops formed around the pin every two or three repeats, in order to allow the loops to settle in a smooth formation over the controlling edge pair (see fig. 18b).

When the central pin has been used for the last time, work out to the edge and back. Before making up the next pin, stitch and remove the centre pin. Pull each pair up evenly and then continue with the lace (see fig. 18c). It will be noted that the overall effect of the completed lace is smooth.

The photograph at fig. 18d shows this method in use.

19 Turning a curve smoothly.

Fig. 19a shows the use of the multi-pin, as described in Method 18 but, in this case, over the footside pair.

After the turn has been completed, the footside returns to its original position. The worker pair which travelled over and under the edge-pair may be twisted between each over-and-under movement, in order to maintain the position of the passives (see fig. 19a).

An alternative method of turning smoothly is to exchange the passive pair with the worker pair, thus gaining on the inside pin hole.

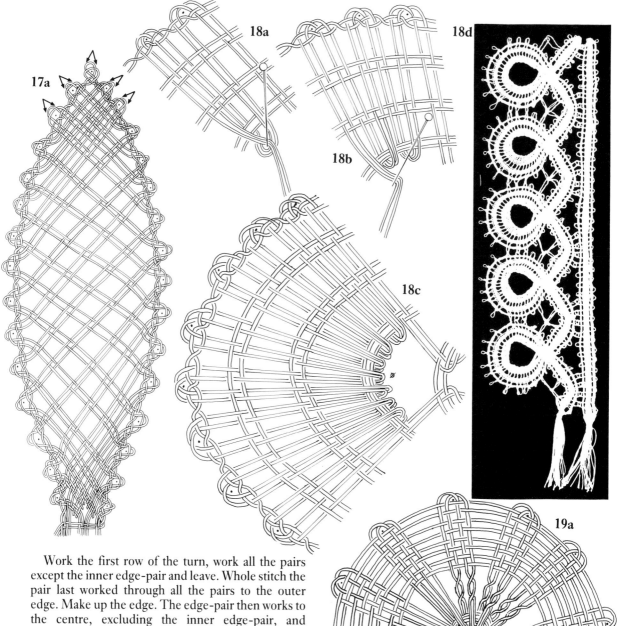

17a

18a

18d

18b

18c

19a

Work the first row of the turn, work all the pairs except the inner edge-pair and leave. Whole stitch the pair last worked through all the pairs to the outer edge. Make up the edge. The edge-pair then works to the centre, excluding the inner edge-pair, and exchanges with the last pair worked. This pair then whole stitches to the outer edge. Make up the edge and work to the first central pin. Work around that pin and then out to the outer edge.

Make up the edge and work back to the second central pin. This pair then works around that pin and out to the outer edge. *Make up the edge and work back through the braid, excluding the inner edge-pair. The last pair worked is then whole stitched out to the outer edge.* This movement is repeated from * to *. After the outer edge has been made up a second time the pairs work down the turned braid with a footside on either side (see fig. 19b). Pairs can be exchanged, as described in Method 19, right around

the turned curve. This leaves a slightly larger gap on the inner curve, but this is sometimes necessary (see fig. 19c).

A turning stitch is sometimes used to achieve the exchange of pairs. An advantage of using this stitch is that the constant inner thread remains in position at each exchange. This assists in preserving the smoothness of the curve, as it prevents the tendency to pull the pairs in an outward direction. To make the

154

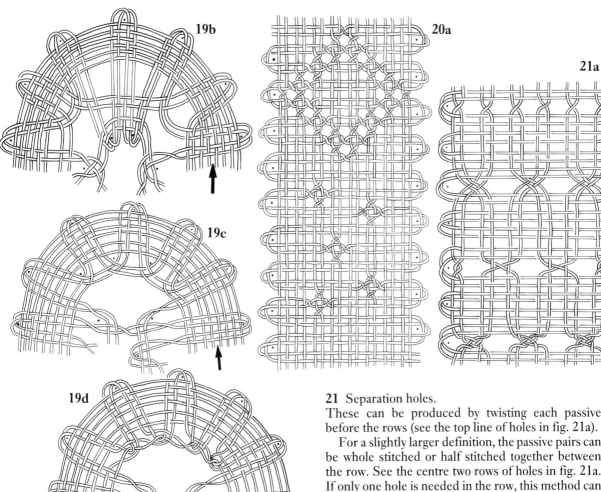

19b

20a

21a

19c

19d

turning stitch with the two pairs to be exchanged, whole stitch, then half stitch with the same two pairs (see fig. 19d).

20 Holes.
Small holes can be created within a whole stitched section of lace. To make a small simple hole, twist the worker pair on the row above the proposed position of the hole on the first row. Twist the passives on either side of this twist. On the return row, twist the worker below the top twist, and between the two twisted passives. These small holes can be worked singly or they can be grouped together to form a pattern within the whole stitched section of the lace, see the top half of fig. 20a.

A second way of producing a small decorative hole is achieved by twisting the worker and passive before and after they are whole stitched together (see the lower half of fig. 20a).

21 Separation holes.
These can be produced by twisting each passive before the rows (see the top line of holes in fig. 21a).

For a slightly larger definition, the passive pairs can be whole stitched or half stitched together between the row. See the centre two rows of holes in fig. 21a. If only one hole is needed in the row, this method can be worked with just four passive pairs.

The passives can have extra twists before and after they are whole stitched together, in order to achieve greater separation (see fig. 21a).

22 Diagonal holes.
These can be made by working the lace with two workers. Work side one to a diagonal pin. Turn the worker around the pin and work out to the outer edge. On the return to the centre of the braid, whole stitch to the next diagonal pin and, excluding one pair from the row above, continue, leaving one pair out after each turn until the edge is reached.

Starting on side two, work to the first diagonal pin and include the pair left out on side one. Continue in this manner until all the pairs have been added. Diagonal holes can be worked in either direction.

The excluded pairs can be twisted together in pairs; either whole stitched, and half stitched, or whole stitched, pinned and whole stitched; the combination of crossing the gap between the two sections is endless (see fig. 22a). A variation on this method can be achieved by the two sides pinning beside each other

155

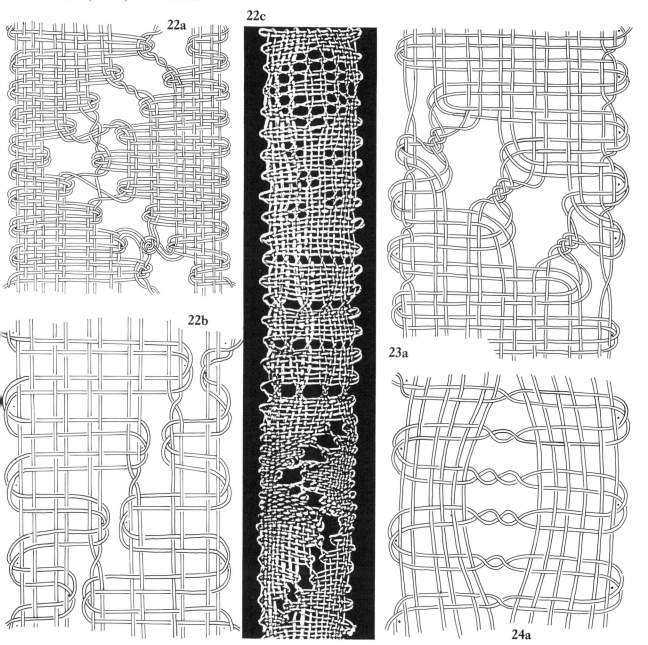

22a

22c

22b

23a

24a

instead of diagonally. This produces diagonally straight long holes (see fig. 22a).

A sample worked with Methods 20-22 is shown in fig. 22b.

23 Diagonal holes by exchanging pairs without the use of pins within the lace.

Work across the lace to the left-hand side to within the edge-pair. Leave the worker. Whole stitch the last pair worked through to the right-hand side, and make up the edge. Work back to the left side, excluding the pair to the right of the worker on the previous row.

The worker is then left out and the last pair is worked through; whole stitch to the right-hand footside edge. Continue in this way until all the pairs are left out. The pairs excluded can be twisted across the diagonal holes or whole stitched together in pairs. This depends on the decorative effect the lacemaker wishes to achieve.

Starting on the left-hand side with the inner pair to the edge, whole stitch out to the edge. Make the edge up and return through one pair. From the last whole stitch made, work the left-hand pair to the left-hand footside. Make up the edge and whole stitch across

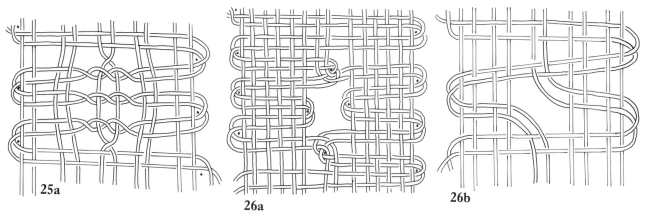

25a   26a   26b

the work, taking in sequence the two pairs previously left out. The left-hand pair of the last stitch worked then repeats the movement, working out to the left-hand side first. Continue until all pairs are in their correct position for the braid.

Care must be taken not to pull any of the threads too tightly, as this will produce unsightly holes where none were intended (see fig. 23a).

24 Twisted vein. Holes can be made down a braid by twisting the workers under each other on every row.

On the first row, twist the workers once only between the two passives. On the second row, twist the worker twice between the same two passives. Increase the number of twists on each subsequent row until the width of the vein is reached. Three twists with the worker is about average. When the vein is no longer required, the twists are reduced, one less on each row, until the braid returns to its original shape (see fig. 24a).

A small separation at the top of the two divided pairs can be prevented by half stitching these before the first row of twists is made. At the end of the vein, the pairs are twisted and the central threads crossed before being worked through on the straight row (as in fig. 29b in Section VII).

25 Decorative vein.
Whole stitch the worker to the central passive, twist the passive and the worker pair. Take the right-hand thread of the passive pair over the first worker thread, then under the second worker thread. Twist the worker pair and repeat with the second passive thread. Twist the worker and whole stitch to the end of the row. On the return, twist the worker and take the left-hand passive thread through the worker pair. Twist the worker pair and repeat with the right-hand thread.

Continue until the vein is no longer required. Twist the passive pair once before it returns to the braid (see fig. 25a).

26 Small hole.
Small decorative holes can be made within any braid. Four pins are needed. Work to the top of the hole. Pin between the last stitch made. The worker then whole stitches and returns to the edge. The edge is made up and the worker whole stitches to the inside pin. Twist around that pin and work out to the same edge.

Make up the edge, whole stitch to the lower pin hole of the hole, and leave. Return to the passive on the inside of the top pin hole stitch. Use this as the worker. Whole stitch the other side of the hole working out to the edge.

Make up the edge, and work back to the side pin hole of the hole. Whole stitch out to the same edge and back to meet the worker from the first side. Whole stitch the two together, pin and whole stitch.

The original worker is now left as a passive and the pair that started as a passive is the new worker for the braid. In this way the pins on the two edges remain evenly spaced (see fig. 26a).

An alternative small hole can be made without pins in the centre of the braid. Whole stitch the worker from the left-hand side to the centre and leave. The centre passive pair becomes the worker and whole stitches to the right. This new worker remains as the worker for the remainder of the braid. The hole formed will be smooth and neat (see fig. 26b).

27 Angular holes.
An angular hole can be made without pins by whole stitching the worker across a group of passives in the braid, as illustrated in fig. 27a through two pairs.

Twist, whole stitch and twist the next two passives to the right. The next pair to the right of those pairs is then twisted, taken as the worker and whole stitched across the braid to the outer edge. The edge is made up and the worker whole stitches right across the braid, to the other side. The entire process can then be repeated (see fig. 27a).

28 Medium hole.

Whole stitch the worker to the left, through two pairs, and leave. Pin between the next two passives and whole stitch the right-hand pair from this whole stitch to the right, through all pairs. Make up the edge and whole stitch back to the centre and leave.

Whole stitch the left-hand pair from the central pin from the left. Make up the edge and whole stitch back to the centre. Whole stitch the two centre pairs and pin between them. These two pairs return as the central passives of the braid. Whole stitch the left-hand pairs of the last whole stitch to the left. This pair now works the braid (see fig. 28a).

29 Hole with decorative centre.

Whole stitch the worker through two passives and leave.

The next passive to the left works to the left edge. Make up the edge and work to the right, through two pairs. Twist and leave. The centre two pairs are twisted, pinned, whole stitched and twisted. The left-hand pair whole stitches and twists with the pair already twisted. Pin to the left of the pairs. The left-hand pair then whole stitches through two pairs to the edge and is left.

The central right-hand pair whole stitches and twists with the twisted pair on the right. Pin on the inside of both pairs.

Whole stitch and twist the central pairs and pin between them. The twisted pair from the right-hand pair works to the edge, back across the two central twisted pairs, and is left as a passive. Lastly, the pair from the left-hand edge is the new worker for the braid (see fig. 29a).

A variation with a less twisted centre

Whole stitch the workers to the right-hand side, twist and leave. Half stitch the two central passive pairs to prevent the small separation of the top, before dividing them. The passive to the left of the half stitched pairs is taken to the left.

Make up the edge and whole stitch through all the pairs, including the left-hand divided pair. The worker on the right whole stitches to the centre. Twist both workers, whole stitch and twist. The left-hand worker whole stitches to the left, makes up the edge and whole stitches back to the centre.

Whole stitch the twisted right-hand pair to the right and leave. Twist the two central pairs and then cross the centre two threads. The worker waiting on the right then whole stitches the braid (see fig. 29b).

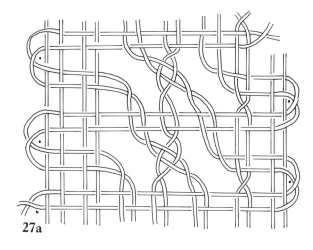

27a

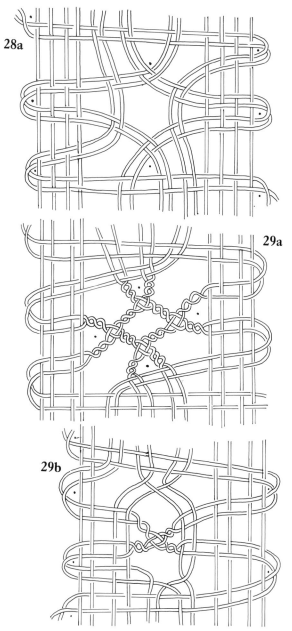

28a

29a

29b

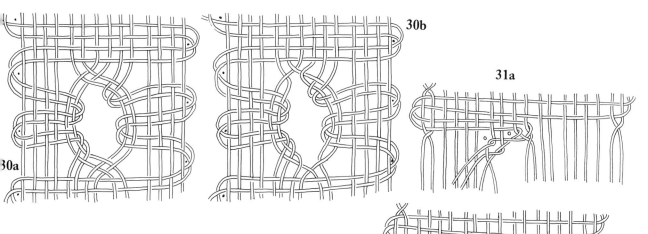

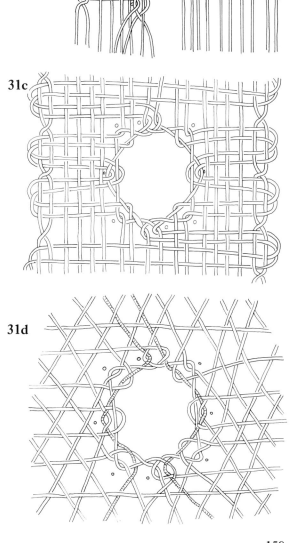

30 A round hole.

Leave the worker on the left outside edge, whole stitch pairs 3 and 4 together, whole stitch the right-hand pair from the whole stitch with the next pair to its right, twist the left-hand pair from the whole stitch and whole stitch the pairs together again. From this whole stitch, the right-hand pair works to the right-side edge. Make up the edge and whole stitch and back through three pairs; twist the worker pair and whole stitch back out to the right-side edge; make up edge and leave.

For the left-hand side of the hole, work the worker previously left out to the centre through three pairs; twist the worker pair and whole stitch out to the edge. Make up edge and whole stitch back through three pairs; twist worker pair and work another whole stitch with the last pair just worked. The right-hand pair of this stitch is then whole stitched with the other central pair, the hole is complete. The worker pair left out on the right-hand side now works the braid. This hole can have pins placed in the turns, but for a smooth hole it is best to work without pins (see fig. 30a).

For an even rounder top and bottom of the hole, half stitch the passive together, instead of whole stitching at the start of the hole. At the closing of the hole, twist both central pairs, then cross the central two threads. This prevents any unevenness to the hole (see fig. 30b).

31 Large round hole.

Work to the centre, and half stitch the worker pair with the centre passive pair, twist both, pin on the inside of the left-hand pair. The left-hand pair and the next passive to the left then half stitches and twists; cross the centre two threads and pin on the left of this stitch (see fig. 31a). Whole stitch the left-hand pair to the edge.

Make up the edge, whole stitch back to the centre edge-pair; these two pairs make a turning stitch. Half stitch twist, then cross the centre threads and pin on

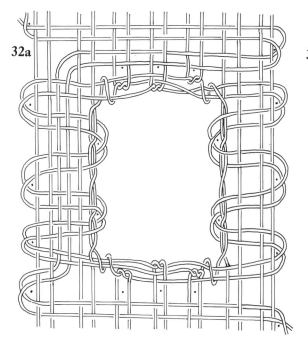

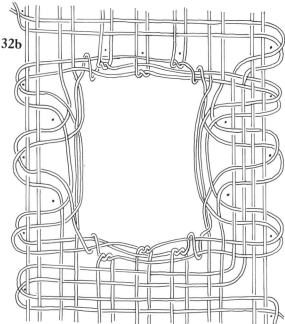

the inside of this stitch (see fig. 31b). Work to the left-hand edge.

Make up the edge and work back with the inner edge-pair; make another turning stitch, then leave both pairs. Repeat on the right-hand side, starting with the centre pair and the pair to its right. After the last turning stitch is made, remove all pins in the inner hole edge, pull all pairs gently, then make a turning stitch with the central two pairs. The pair on the right-hand side then becomes the worker pair, working first to the right-hand side. It will be noted that by using the turning stitch a constant thread supports the inner edge of the hole, so leaving a smooth large hole (see fig. 31c).

This method can also be used in half stitch for good effect. The turning stitch in half stitch is half stitch, twist, cross the centre threads and then twist; the last twist is added because a twist is needed on both pairs before continuing in half stitch (see fig. 31d).

32 Large square hole.

Work the worker to the inside of the last passive pair on the left-hand side and leave. The hole is made with five central pairs; number these from left to right. Make a single knot with pair 4, weave the left-hand thread of this knot through pairs 3 and 2, and tie pair 2 with a single knot, to enclose the spare thread.

The right-hand thread of this knot is placed between the threads of pair 3. Tie this pair with a single knot to enclose that thread. To work the left-hand side, wrap the thread from the knot of pair 2 around the threads from knots 4 and 3 to secure them.

These two secured threads become the workers for the left-hand side. The wrapped over thread is left to hang beside the outside thread of pair 1, and the two threads are used together as a single unit.

Whole stitch the workers to the edge, make up the edge and whole stitch back through all the pairs including pair 1, the pair with the double thread. Twist the workers and work out to the edge; this can then be repeated for the required length of the hole. At that point, whole stitch to the centre through all pairs, including pair 1, and leave. Work the right-hand side; the single thread from the knot of pair 4 is used to wrap around the threads from pairs 2 and 3. These two wrapped-around threads become the worker pair. Work as for the left-hand side, and at the point where the hole is to be closed, work the pair into the centre. Wrap the thread that has travelled with pair 5 around the right-hand workers, then wrap the thread which travelled with pair 1 around the workers on the left-hand side. The two top-wrapped threads then tie with a single knot in the centre, and these two threads become the passives of pair 3.

Weave the second wrapped-around thread from the left, through pair 3, and tie with the wrapped-around thread of the right-hand side; this is now passive pair 4. Weave the second wrapped-around thread from the right, through pairs 4 and 3 and tie with the wrapped-around thread; this pair is now passive pair 2.

All the knots can have temporary pins placed under them to help support the work while in progress, but they must be removed on completion of the hole.

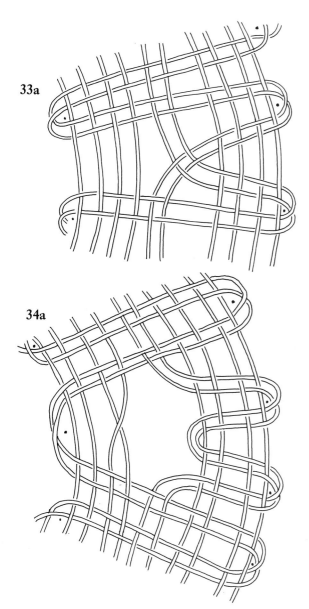

33a

34a

Pins may also be placed between each pair before the recommencement of the braid. These pins can be left in while the braid is made. The second pair from the left-hand side is worked out to the edge and becomes the worker for the braid (see fig. 32a).

A variation of this method can be made where the sides of the hole are pulled out, making the hole oval-shaped; work as for Method 32. On the inner edges, exchange the workers and inside passive pair each time. The spare thread just hangs down the centre edges or can be twisted over the passive pair before it is exchanged; depending on the degree of pull outwards required, pins may or need not be placed on the inside edge of both pairs on the exchange (see fig. 32b).

33 Holes worked on a curve.
A simple hole can be worked on a curve. Whole stitch from the outside of the curve to the centre of the braid, exchange the worker pair with the central passive pair, then whole stitch this new worker to the outside edge. Make up the edge. This pair now continues to work the braid; the stronger the tension on the old and new worker pairs, the larger the hole.

34 Medium hole worked on the curve.
Whole stitch the worker pair to the inner edge of the curve, pin and leave. Whole stitch the centre passive pair to outer curve edge. Make up the edge and whole stitch back to the centre. Turn the worker pair and whole stitch back to the edge. Make up the edge, work back to the centre and leave; this pair then returns to its centre passive position. Twist the passive pair to its left once, and leave.

Return to the worker pair previously left out on the inner edge, and continue the braid with this worker (see fig. 34a).

161

CORDONNET, GIMPS AND BEADS

A cordonnet/gimp can be used to give depth and added interest within a braid, or as an outline to a section of lace.

1 When passing a cordonnet through twisted pairs, to prevent the twist being undone it is necessary for the cordonnet to be passed through the pairs in a correct sequence.

Passing the cordonnet from the left-hand side through the pairs on the right-hand side the cordonnet passes over the first thread of the pair to be crossed, and under the second. When the cordonnet passes from the right-hand side through pairs to the left-hand side, the cordonnet must pass under the first thread of the pair and then over the second thread. In this way the twists are not undone (see fig. 1a and b).

2 Decorative single raised cordonnet.
This method has a correct viewing side. The diagram shows the side being worked as the correct side, on the completion of the lace.

Whole stitch across the lace and when the cordonnet is reached, place the cordonnet between the worker pair and continue to work across the lace. On the second row the cordonnet is passed over the worker pair. On the third row, the cordonnet is passed between the workers again; this is continued to the desired length. This makes a ridged appearance. If the work is to be reversed, then the cordonnet is passed under the workers instead of over as previously described (see fig. 2a).

3 A single cordonnet may be worked down the braid. This is worked by twisting the workers once, passing the cordonnet through the worker pair and twisting the workers again before continuing the braid. This is repeated at every row for the desired length.

This use of the cordonnet may also be made on the outside edges of the braid, or may be moved to different positions by one stitch on any row. This gives a diagonal or outlining effect (see fig. 3a).

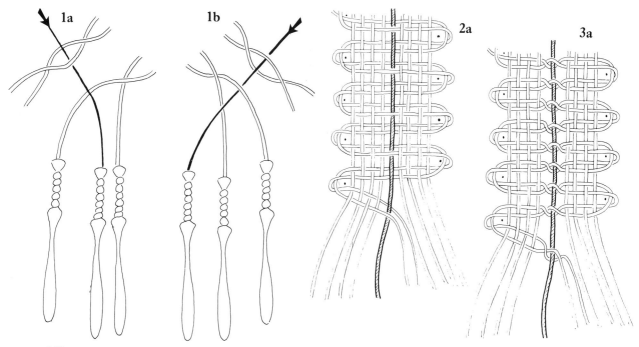

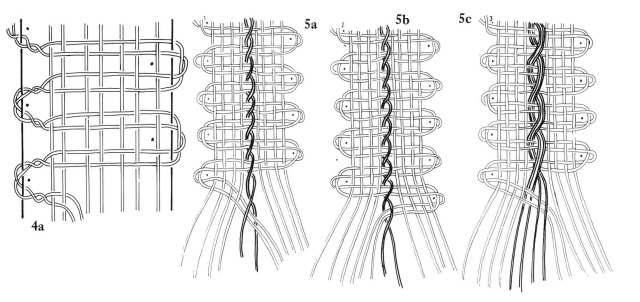

4a **5a** **5b** **5c**

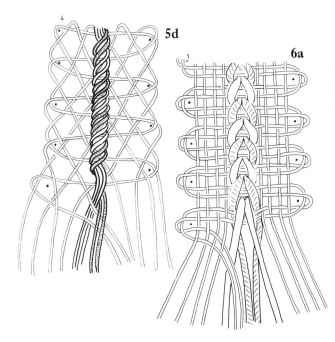

5d **6a**

4 A cordonnet can be used as a retaining thread, either separated from the lace or as an outline thread lying as part of the work.

Whole stitch the workers to the edge and twist. The greater the number of twists, the greater the distance that the cordonnet will lie from the main section of the lace.

Pass the cordonnet between the workers, twist the workers and pin on the inside of the cordonnet. Twist the workers to correspond to the number of twists on the outward passage. Whole stitch across the braid. The cordonnet must be kept under tension at all times in order to retain a good shape (see the left-hand side of fig. 4a).

The cordonnet can be used as one thread of a pair of threads and is whole stitched with the spare thread throughout the length of the lace. This outlines the lace without separation (see the right-hand side of fig. 4a).

5 Twisted cordonnet.

A pair of cordonnets is needed for this twisted construction.

The worker pair is passed between the cordonnet pair and the cordonnet pair is then twisted right-over-left (see fig. 5a). The workers whole stitch to the end of the row. On the second row the workers are passed between the cordonnets, then the cordonnets are again twisted right-over-left (see fig. 5b).

If a tighter twist is required the cordonnets are twisted between each thread of the worker. This can only be done if the weave is loose, because the twist will take up too much space in the centre.

This method can also be used with four cordonnet threads. The worker is passed over the two cordonnet

threads and then under two cordonnet threads. In the second row the workers pass under the two cordonnet threads and over the two cordonnet threads. The cordonnet threads are then twisted once in pairs. This is repeated down the length of the lace. It will be noted that in this double cordonnet method the position of the cordonnets are only exchanged every two rows (see fig. 5c).

This double twisted cordonnet also works well in half stitch. Two rows of half stitch are passed over and under, and under and over, before the cordonnet pairs are twisted (see fig. 5d).

163

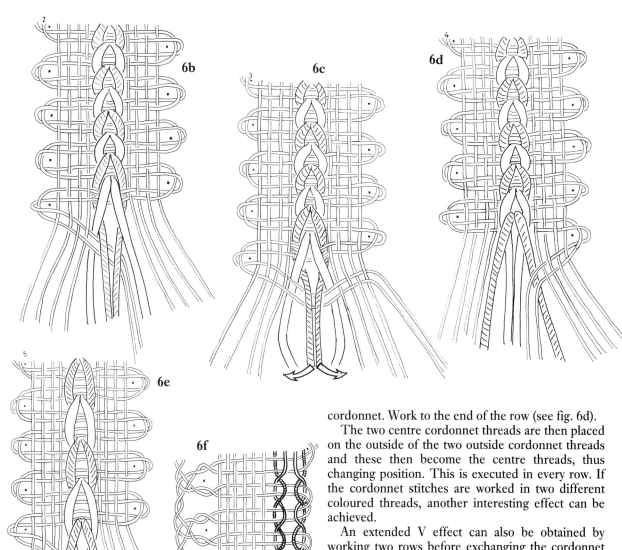

6b 6c 6d 6e 6f

6 Interlocking V's.

To produce an interesting V shape, two pairs of cordonnets are needed. The worker is passed over the first cordonnet (see fig. 6a). Under the centre pair (see fig. 6b) and over the outside thread (see fig. 6c). The worker is then worked to the end of the row.

The cordonnet threads that were in the centre are separated and passed, one to the left and one to the right of the former outside threads of the cordonnets (as also seen in fig. 6c).

Work the second row and pass the workers over the first cordonnet, under the centre pair and over the last

cordonnet. Work to the end of the row (see fig. 6d).

The two centre cordonnet threads are then placed on the outside of the two outside cordonnet threads and these then become the centre threads, thus changing position. This is executed in every row. If the cordonnet stitches are worked in two different coloured threads, another interesting effect can be achieved.

An extended V effect can also be obtained by working two rows before exchanging the cordonnet position (see fig. 6e). This may also be worked in half stitch or two colours for varied effects.

All these methods for cordonnets can be used at the edge of the work as well as in the middle, depending on the desired effect. When using the interlocking cordonnets on the edge it is optional whether a pin can be placed on the inside of the worker pair before it reverses back (see fig. 6f).

7 Spaced out central cordonnet pair.

Whole stitch to the cordonnet pair. Twist the workers and the cordonnet pair and pass the top thread of the worker pair over a first cordonnet thread. Then pass the other worker pair under the same cordonnet thread. Twist the workers and repeat, taking the first worker thread over the cordonnet thread and the second worker thread under it.

Twist the worker pair and whole stitch to the end of the row. This is repeated in either direction, twisting before, between and after passing the cordonnet

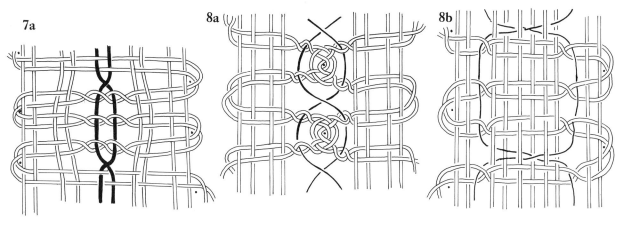

7a **8a** **8b**

threads, between the worker pair, for the required length of this spaced vein. Twist the cordonnet before returning it as the central passive of the braid (see fig. 7a).

8 The cordonnet can outline any combination of stitches.

In the example shown, the cordonnet outlines the simple exchange of two worker pairs.

Between the exchange the cordonnet threads are crossed to exchange the sides that they surround (see fig. 8a).

To outline a wider section of lace, the cordonnet can be passed between the passive pairs while they are exchanging. The cordonnets pass between the passive pairs in the same spacings so they sit as one during the exchange (see fig. 8b). The passive pairs can be twisted before and after, if the pattern so requires (see fig. 8c).

Although the cordonnets mostly cross each other within the same space, if a feature of the crossing is required the passives can be twisted between one cordonnet, exchanging with another. This will leave a separated section between the crossing.

9 To secure a cordonnet passing around a shape it is sometimes necessary to anchor the cordonnet at the corners, in order to prevent a more rounded shape being produced than is required.

Work the pattern as designed. The pair which the cordonnet passes through at the extreme corner can be twisted.

The cordonnet is then passed through the same pair again, before that pair works out of the cordonnet shape. In this way the corner is held at a good right angle (see fig. 9a).

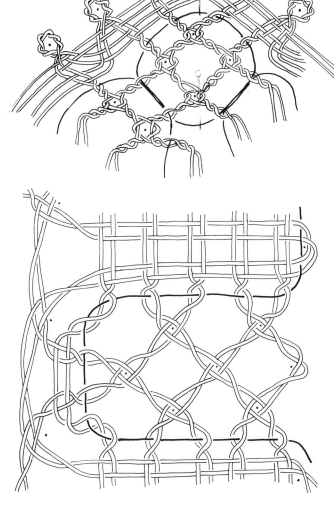

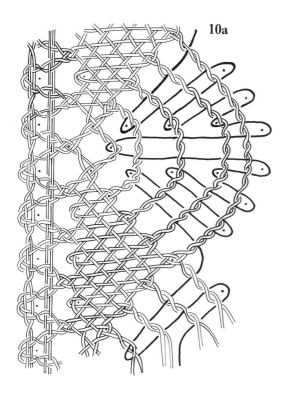

10a

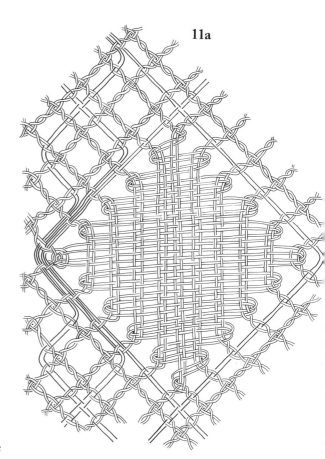

11a

10 A cordonnet can be woven through pairs to make a heavier outline for a shape.

In the example shown (fig. 10a) the cordonnet is passed between the twisted pairs into a fan shape.

The cordonnet needs to be somewhat thicker than the thread of the lace in order for it to be most effective.

11 Cordonnets can also be worked in pairs, as a pair, when passing across a pair of threads which are then treated as a normal pair. The two pairs may be whole stitched with each other.

In any part of the lace, if more cordonnet threads unite then the cordonnets can be divided into two groups and whole stitched with the crossing pair. Each group of cordonnet unit is treated as a pair (see fig. 11a).

12 Cordonnets can be carried across the lace surface to give a '3D' texture to the work.

Construct the lace in accordance with the pattern and, at the edge, centre or any other place where the cordonnet is to be anchored to the lace, lift a passive over the cordonnet. Continue the work. In this way the cordonnet will be trapped under a passive pair and both cordonnet and the lace can be continued (see fig. 12a).

12a

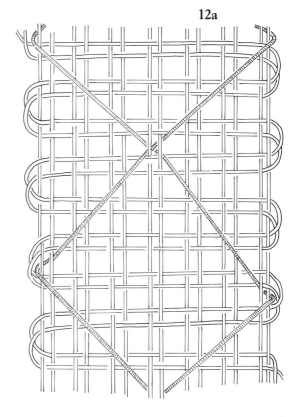

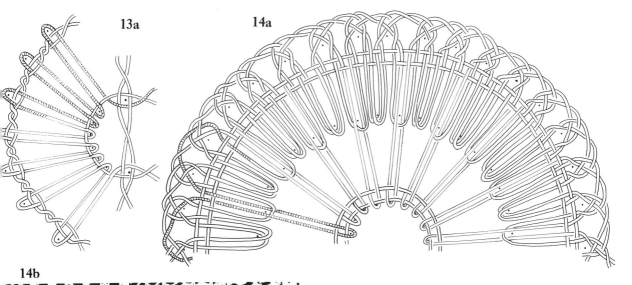

13a   **14a**

14b

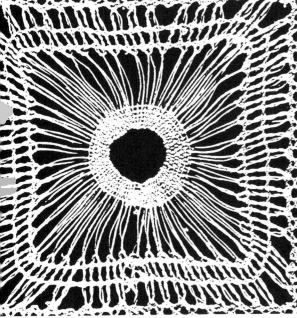

14 A thread from a split pair of bobbins can be used to fill a small central hole where two threads would be too thick.

Work the outer ring of the lace. On each alternate row use only one thread of a pair to weave in and out of the central pair. Return the thread to its partner and continue to the outer edge, and repeat until complete (see figs. 14a and 14b).

15 Beads in the lace.

Beads can be incorporated into the lace in many ways.

Small beads can be threaded on the thread of the worker bobbin. When the position of the bead is reached, just push the bead up the thread to a required position and continue (see fig. 15a).

16 Beads can be added to the lace on a passive pair. The left-hand passive bobbin thread is threaded with the small beads.

Push a bead up to its position. Separate the passive pair and pass the worker pair between them. Twist the passive pair twice.

Work to the edge on the return passage, separate the twisted passive pair and pass the workers through it. Work to the edge and repeat, pushing up a bead at each alternate row and twisting twice between the rows (see fig. 16a).

To obtain a bead in each row, both passive threads must be beaded. Push the left-hand threaded bead to its position and pass the worker pair through the separated bead pair. Twist the beaded pair and repeat on the return passage, pushing up the bead on the new left-hand thread. Separate and pass the workers between the beaded passive and then twist the passives. This is repeated for the desired length (see fig. 16b).

13 A pair of bobbins can be divided in some instances and only one thread used in order to fill a tight bend or to make a lighter part of the lace.

The example shown uses one thread only to make a small fan. Separate the pair on the inside and take one thread of the pair out to the outer edge. Weave it through an edge-pair, pin on the inside of the thread and weave back through the edge-pair.

The single thread can then be carried over its original partner thread and taken around the pin and then under that thread. This is repeated around a fan shape. On completion of the fan the two separated threads are twisted together and reintroduced into the lace (see fig. 13a).

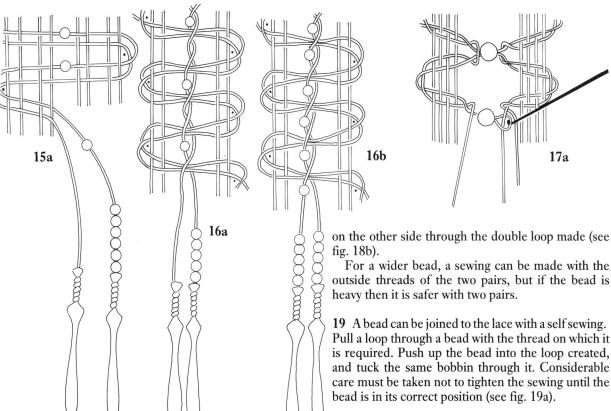

15a

16a

16b

17a

on the other side through the double loop made (see fig. 18b).

For a wider bead, a sewing can be made with the outside threads of the two pairs, but if the bead is heavy then it is safer with two pairs.

19 A bead can be joined to the lace with a self sewing. Pull a loop through a bead with the thread on which it is required. Push up the bead into the loop created, and tuck the same bobbin through it. Considerable care must be taken not to tighten the sewing until the bead is in its correct position (see fig. 19a).

17 Beads can be attached to the lace by means of a sewing.

If the lace has two workers, and the bead is required in the position of the two workers crossing, work both workers to this point. Place a hook down the bead, take a thread from one worker and pull a loop through the bead. Make a sewing with the thread from the other worker pair and pull up gently. Each worker can then continue with its own side until the next joining position, where the process is repeated (see fig. 17a).

18 Beads can be added on the passive pair with sewings.

When a bead is required to be included in the lace, make a sewing through the bead, pulling a loop through the bead and passing the second bobbin of the passive pair through this loop.

Pull up gently and replace the passive pair in its correct position. The worker can then work across the lace and the process can be repeated whenever a bead is required (see fig. 18a).

Larger oval or square beads can be joined to the lace. As they extend beyond the width of a pair of passives, the sewing can be a double one. This is carried out by taking a pair of bobbins and making a loop with them through the bead and passing the pair

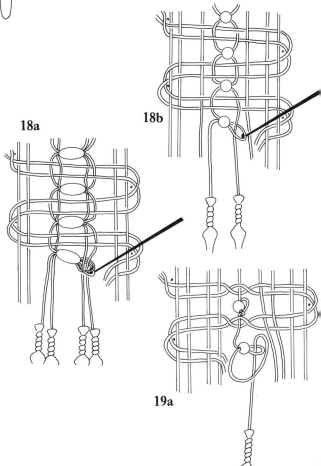

18a

18b

19a

COMPLETIONS, ENDINGS AND FINISHINGS

This section is concerned with endings and finishes. It will be appreciated that there are many methods of tying off at the end of an individual piece of lace and that each must be ended in some way. These endings should be invisible and yet they should be strong.

By selecting and using the most suitable ending it is possible to minimise the effect of the ending on the completed work. It is for the lacemaker to decide which method is the most suitable for the particular piece of lace. Factors involved in the consideration must include the use to which the lace will be put, the material used, and its construction.

The following section gives the lacemaker a wide and varied choice.

1 Having completed a strip of lace, the simplest method of finishing is to take each pair of bobbins in turn, twist them into a loop and thread the pair of bobbins through this double loop, making a knot with them.

Ensure that the knot is slipped up as close as possible to the end of the work. This will produce a fringe effect and the pairs of bobbins can then be cut off, leaving a fringe of even lengths (see fig. 1a).

2 This method involves ending a strip of lace with a selvage – for example, an insertion.

Continue the pattern to within one centimetre of the required length of lace. Before commencing the next line, twist all the pairs of bobbins once, work four rows of whole stitch and repeat this process twice

more. Remember to twist the pairs once more after each four rows of whole stitch are worked. Then take each pair and knot them tightly up against the base of the completed work.

Cut off all pairs just below the knots. Alternatively, just simply cut off each pair.

Fold either the knots or the raw edge together with the last four rows of whole stitch worked, the fold being on the last twisted row. Fold up again at the next twisted row. This will bring the edge of the fold up to a line level with the first twisted row. Then sew with a needle (in the same thread used to make the lace) into the first line of twisted pairs, thus securing a firm selvage.

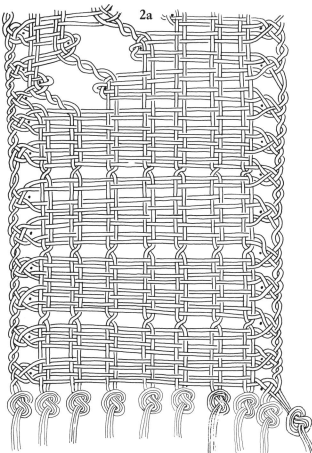

2a

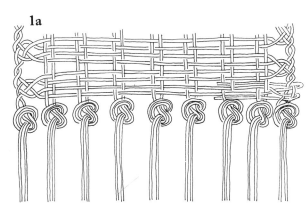

1a

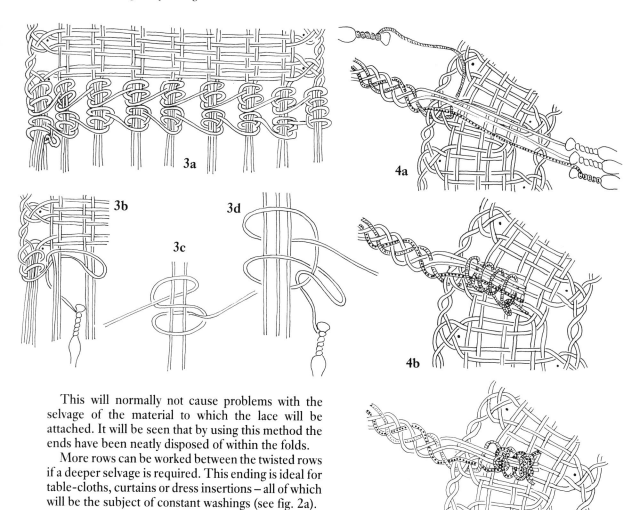

3a

3b

3d

3c

4a

4b

4c

This will normally not cause problems with the selvage of the material to which the lace will be attached. It will be seen that by using this method the ends have been neatly disposed of within the folds.

More rows can be worked between the twisted rows if a deeper selvage is required. This ending is ideal for table-cloths, curtains or dress insertions – all of which will be the subject of constant washings (see fig. 2a).

3 'Tails' can be made in order to achieve a firm end to a strip of lace.

Bunch one thread from the worker pair and the next pair together. Pass the single thread of the other worker pair under and back over the bunch. Then tuck the bobbin down through the loop that has been created.

Repeat this once more, passing the single thread under the bunch of three threads, back over the top and down into its own loop. Carry this single thread over the bunch and under the next pair on the right-hand side and repeat, making two knots around each pair (see fig. 3a and 3b).

Care must be taken that the thread passes under the new pair first before making the first knot. With the last pair, make four knots instead of two. It is interesting to note that because the single knotting thread is being pulled while worked, one pair after another, the two knots slip naturally one over the other, thus ensuring a tight, interlocking, compact knot (see fig. 3c).

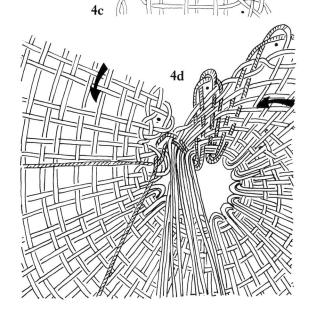

4d

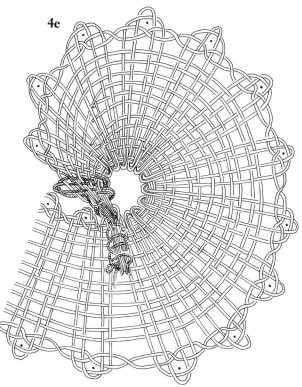

4e

Continue by working to the left-hand side again, and make sure that the knotting thread passes underneath the pair to be knotted first (see diagram 3b).

When the end knot is reached, but before pulling tight, insert the knotting bobbin down into the loop once more. This makes a double knot in order to effect an appropriate end (see fig. 3d).

On completion of the above, all the pairs can be cut off close to the work.

4 To tie out pairs on to a finished piece of lace it is possible to use the same knot – a half hitch – as explained in Method 3.

First make a sewing with one of the pairs to be tied out. To make the sewing, remove the pin in the edge of the finished piece of lace, insert a hook or needle pin into the hole located by the pin, and draw up a loop of one of the threads of the pair. Pass the other thread of that pair through this loop and pull both tight (see fig. 4a).

If only two or three pairs need to be tied out at the same spot then only one sewing is needed. Lay the other pairs down beside a single thread of the same pair. With the other thread of the sewn pair, work four half hitches around this bunch, making a double knot to end. Cut off all ends close to the work (see fig. 4b).

An alternative to fig. 4b is to create a sewing as in fig. 4a, then to lay all the pairs between the sewing pair. Wrap this pair over the bunch and tie a reef knot.

Then cross the reef-knotted pair both under the bunch and back over the top, knotting again before cutting all pairs off closely as before (see fig. 4c).

Method 4 is a useful and tidy method to use when there are several pairs such as in a scroll. For though many pairs can be laid back to reduce the number, there always remains a bunch at the completion of the bend. Make a sewing with the worker or workers (see fig. 4d).

Lay all pairs beside one of the worker threads and, with the other worker, make a small 'tail' with half hitches ending with a double knot. All threads can then be neatly cut off (see fig. 4e).

5 This ending is suitable for certain work, such as pictures, tableaux etc., where the strip of lace needs to be joined with its starting point.

The work can be started with single threads knotted together on pins, instead of the usual looped pair start. These threads must be left long in order to make the ending simpler (see fig. 5a).

To make the join, pass each bobbin over the start of the work and the corresponding thread to lie back beside it, over the end of the work. In this way the loose ends lay over the end of the work and the bobbin threads lay over the start (see fig. 5b).

These threads can then be knotted off, as in Method 3. For simplicity, work the bobbin threads side first and then repeat the method on the loose threads side. It is sometimes easier to do this side if the ends are temporarily tied to bobbins whilst being worked; the tension is then more readily maintained (see fig. 5c).

On completion all the ends can be closely cut off, leaving a neat and almost invisible join on the side to be shown (see fig. 5d).

5a

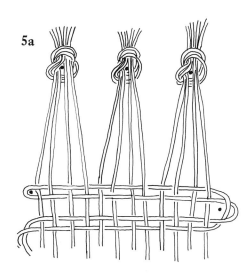

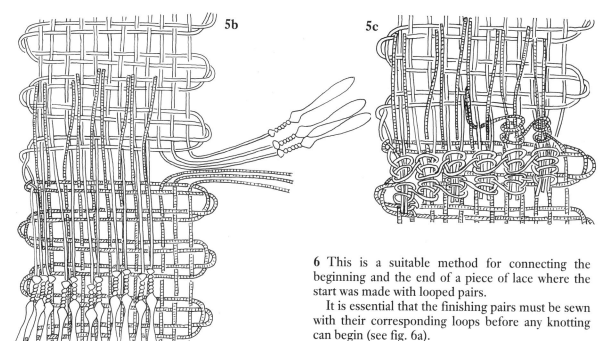

5b

5c

5d

6 This is a suitable method for connecting the beginning and the end of a piece of lace where the start was made with looped pairs.

It is essential that the finishing pairs must be sewn with their corresponding loops before any knotting can begin (see fig. 6a).

To make the sewing, place a hook or needle pin in the starting loop and pull one of the corresponding finishing bobbins up into this loop, placing the other thread of the pair through the loop and pulling both bobbins tight. These sewings join the work together (see fig. 6a).

The pairs can then be knotted off with little 'tails' as described in Method 3 (see fig. 6b).

7 This ending is suitable for a pattern which has a loose or uneven edge, but needs to have a strong finishing selvage.

Continue making the lace until it is 2 cm longer than needed. Cut off the bobbins close to the work and, on the wrong side, fold back over the work to the exact length required. Then fold back over the extra 1 cm so that a 'Z' shape is produced, the raw edge level with the fold which is its full length (see fig. 7a).

In the same thread used for the lace, construct a small whole stitch strip 2 cm wide and the exact width of the lace actually worked. Twist the worker pair down the centre of each row in order to make an easy fold-line when completed. Knot off each pair and then tuck the loose ends inside the fold (see fig. 7b).

Fold lengthwise down the twists and slip this folded piece under the raw edges, over the top fold of the lace (see fig. 7c).

Both the raw edge and the knots of the extra strip are now invisible inside an envelope created by the spare piece of lace.

Oversew around the perimeter of this entire selvage with the same thread used in making the lace (see fig. 7d).

6a

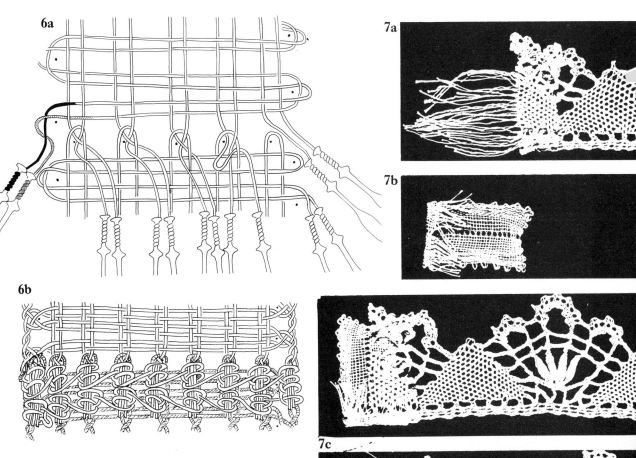

6b

7a

7b

When this is turned to the correct side of the work the pattern of the lace is shown neatly, yet there is a firm selvege as required (see fig. 7e).

8 This method illustrates how a border of lace can be terminated. It requires the completion of an entire extra pattern, following which all bobbins need to be cut off closely.

Using a finer thread than that used for the work, but of the same type and colour, whipstitch or oversew these two patterns together, tucking in any loose ends. This should be done off the pillow. The two patterns must overlap each other exactly and considerable care must be taken that they do not slip, as it would be unsightly seeing one through the other.

This is a very strong finish and is often used for handkerchiefs and other articles which are frequently laundered (see fig. 8a).

9 Oversewing join.
The lace can be commenced by knotting threads at the start (see fig. 9a). Work an extra pattern. Ensure that there is a good overlap, which will not distort when the lace is removed from the pillow.

Cut off the bobbins, leaving about 10 cm of thread.

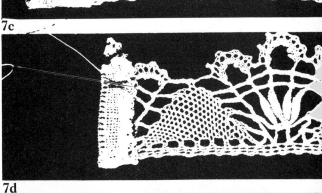

7c

7d

7e
Pin the two ends together, overlapping each other. Use a finer thread than the lace if possible, but of the same variety; e.g. cotton for cotton lace, linen for linen lace. Oversew with the finer thread in the whole stitch

areas, sew two diagonal stitches over each stitch and the weavers in sequence across the lace. In the half stitch or net grounds, oversew twice around each stitch. A double row of oversew stitches is safest.

When completed, cut off the spare lace and threads on either side, as closely as possible to the join. This leaves a good flat join which is very strong (see fig. 9b).

10 This method illustrates a suitable finish for a piece of lace that will have a correct side and a reverse side. This could be in a picture where many pairs are used in a solid block, with only a few needed in the background, or perhaps where a straight hole is to be created.

Work to the last pin of the lace and then place a pin between each pair of bobbins, except the workers. Turn each pair around the pin so that the pairs lie on top of the lace worked (see fig. 10a).

Turn the workers, as a pair, around the pin in the normal manner, work each pair in whole stitch over the lace to the other side and, with the workers, make a sewing into the last edge-pin hole of the under lace. Work back another row and again make a sewing on the first side; work back through two pairs and tie off all bobbins. A reef knot is suitable as it will lie quite flat.

If the pairs are lying too close together to tie individually, it is suggested that they could be tied in

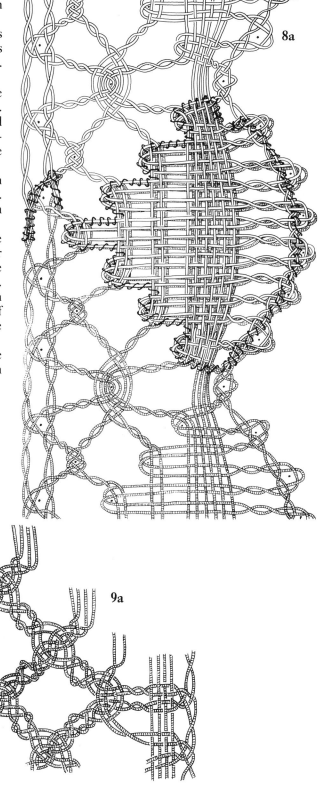

8a

9a

174

bunches. The bobbins can then be cut off. On the 'correct' side it will be seen that nothing will detract from the neat finish (see fig. 10b).

This method is also useful in order to obtain a clean join between two pieces of lace, especially if one of these is made in an open variety, such as half stitch. Join the whole stitch tape with sewings before it is folded back on itself. Work as Method 9 to finish off the whole stitch tape. On the 'correct' top side a clean neat edge is left on the half stitch piece; there will be no loose threads remaining to show on the reverse side (see figs 10c and 10d).

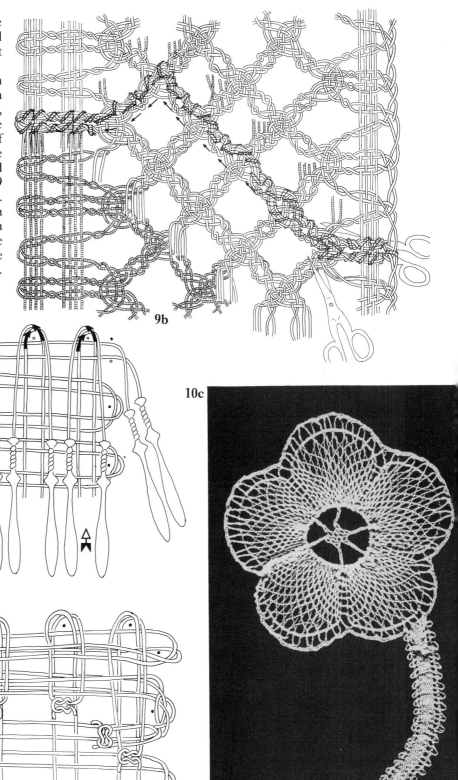

9b

10a

10b

10c

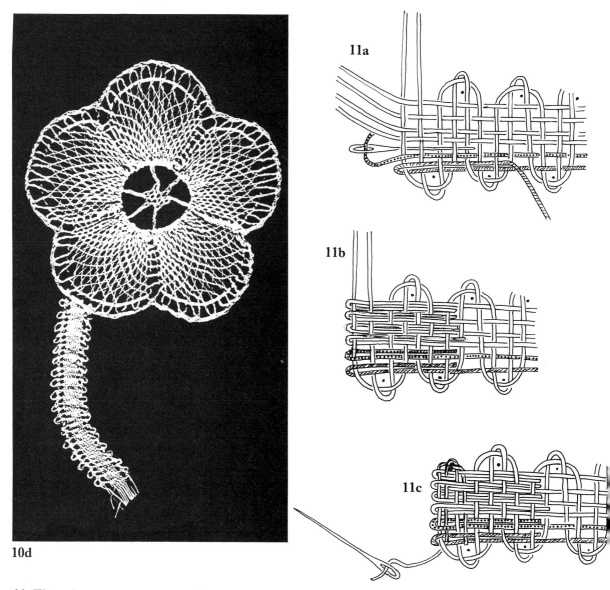

10d

11 This relates to turning up an edge of lace that is quite solid. The method can be used at the end of a picture, or strip of lace that needs to have a flat edge – such as a belt or insertion that has no direct light passing through the lace. This is because it makes a denser part, which would show if it is to be a 'see through' decoration; but if only strength is needed, this method is quite useful.

Having worked to the end of the pattern, leave the worker pair on one side and start at the other. Cut off each bobbin in turn, leaving 20 cm of thread. Thread individually into a needle, one by one, and weave back the threads up the work for two or three rows lying parallel and corresponding with itself (see fig. 11a and 11b).

Lastly, take the worker back across the entire work,

pull all the pairs uniformly taut and cut off close to the work (see fig. 11c).

12 This is a suitable method for joining the beginning to the end of a rectangular or circular piece of lace, such as a continuous handkerchief or table-cloth border.

Having completed the lace to be worked, each pair of bobbins should correspond to a loop at the start. Working each pair in order, either from right to left or from left to right, make lacemaker's sewings (described in Method 4) as shown at fig. 12a. Then knot each pair individually with 1½ reef knots (left-over-right, right-over-left, left-over-right). Each pair should then be cut off neatly, close up to the end of the completed work (see fig. 12b).

13 This is an alternative method to make a join at the completion of a rectangular or circular piece of lace, and is seen by some as a rather neater method of finishing.

Proceed as above (Method 11), up to the completion of the sewings. Then, starting at the left, take the first pair and make a single knot, right-over-left.

Take the right-hand thread over the left-hand thread and leave the right-hand thread. Make a single knot with the left-hand thread and the first thread of the next pair. Again, take the right-hand thread over the left-hand thread and leave. With the left-hand thread, make another knot with the next thread.

Continue in this way to the right-hand side of the work. With the last pair, on the extreme right, tie right-over-left, then left-over-right (see fig. 13a).

Leave the left-hand thread and take the right-hand thread over it, working to the left, tying a single knot, right-over-left; always leaving the left-hand thread under the right. Take the right-hand thread on to the next thread and knot each time across to the extreme left of the work, making a second knot with the last pair. Gently tighten all the threads individually at this point. The knots will then slip, one beside the other, making a tight roll.

The ends can then be cut off, neatly, close up to the end of the completed work (see fig. 13b).

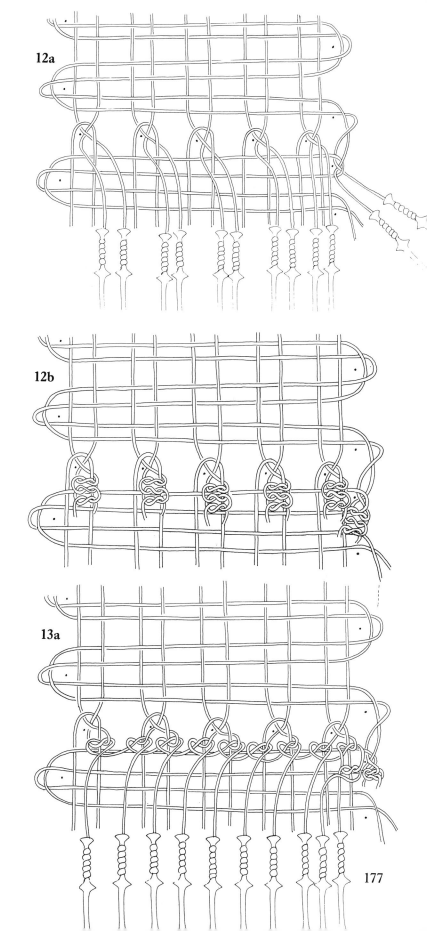

12a

12b

13a

177

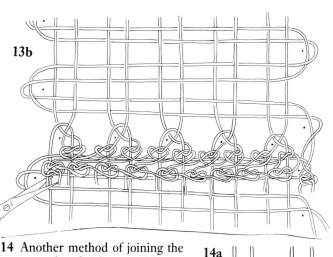

13b

14 Another method of joining the start to the finish, as with the previous two methods.

Work the last row of the pattern; make sewings into the loops of the starting loops with each correct corresponding finishing pair.

Lay the workers between the first pair and tie a single knot, right-over-left, with that pair (see fig. 14a).

Take one of the worker threads and make a half hitch around the other three threads. Make two more half stitches in the same gap (see fig. 14b); this should leave all the threads at the position of the next pair to be finished. Lay the three threads between the next pair to be finished, excluding the thread that made the half hitches. Tie that pair around the three threads and make a single knot, right-over-left, and lay that pair on the right of the other three threads.

With the half hitch thread, make a half hitch around the five threads and leave out a thread on the lower left-hand side. This will be the second original worker thread. Make another half hitch around the four threads and leave out another thread. Make one more half hitch, thus completing three half hitches between the gaps. Repeat by placing the three threads between the next pair to be finished and continue until the end is reached. At the extreme edge on the right all the pairs must be turned and, after each half hitch, one thread is left out (see fig. 14c).

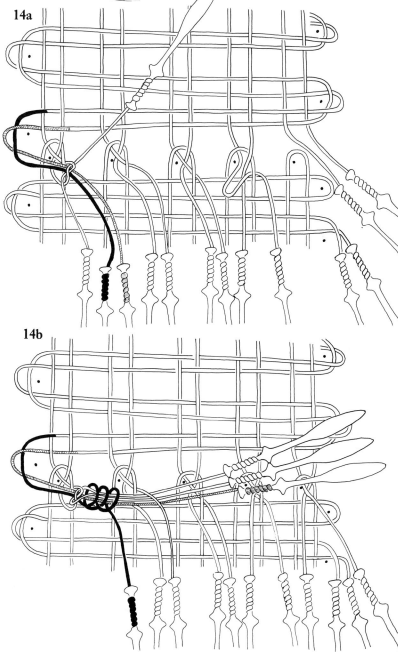

14a

14b

Make a sewing into the footside to hold the roll down the side, make one more half-hitch and sew the last two ends in with a needle or, at the last half-hitch, make a second sewing and a double-hitch to end.

All the other ends can be cut off close to the roll. This finish makes a very firm and neat end, which is capable of withstanding constant laundering and yet is quite unobtrusive (see fig. 14d for the wrong side of the work and fig. 14e for the correct side).

14c

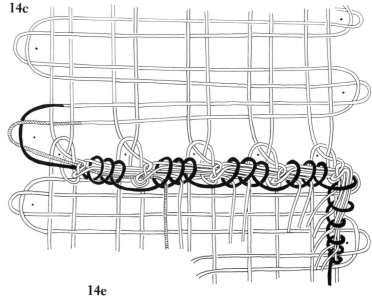

14d

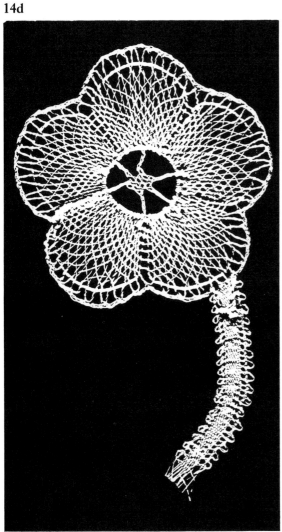

14e

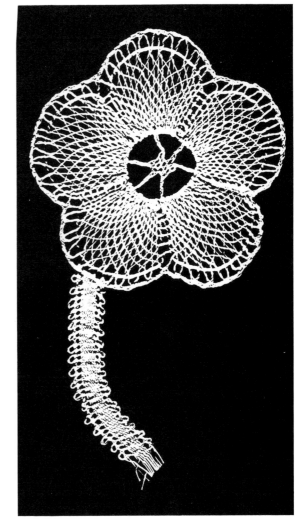

179

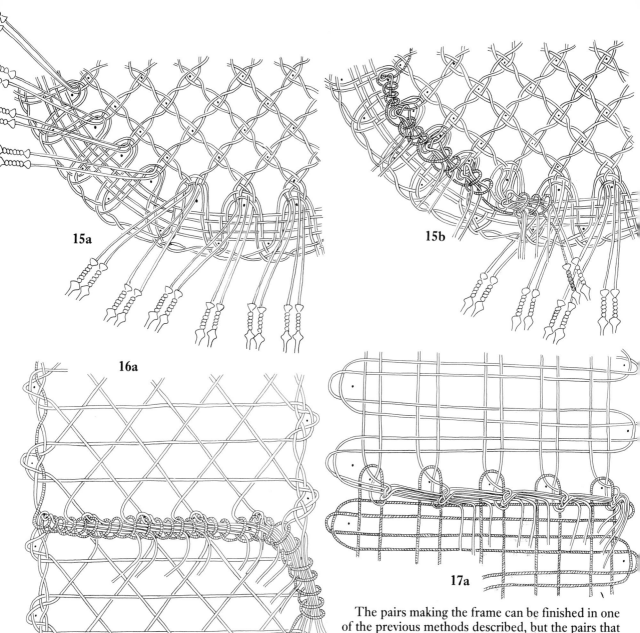

15a

15b

16a

17a

15 The half hitch roll.

This is an excellent method of finishing off pairs that are no longer required from a curved piece of lace where the edge is continuous. For example, a frame of a circle or the curve of a collar, where pairs are taken out of the piece but its edge continues.

Work to where the first pair is to be discarded, whole stitch that pair and lay it back over the work. Continue the edge and, when the next pair to be removed is met, whole stitch again and lay back the pair as before. Continue in this manner until the end is reached.

The pairs making the frame can be finished in one of the previous methods described, but the pairs that were laid back can now be half hitched and knotted as described in Method 14, starting with the first pair that was discarded.

This tight neat roll sits over the edge, so that from the correct side no ends or unsightly distortions of the edges of the piece are visible. It is also very strong for laundering (see fig. 15a and 15b).

16 To complete a circle, as in Method 14, but on this occasion in half stitch.

Make a sewing with the worker pair. Then take one of its threads and make three half hitches around the other thread. Take in the nearest crossed-over half stitch thread and make two more half hitches. Then take the second half stitch thread and make a self

180

sewing through the loop of the corresponding start.

Make two more half hitches and take in another crossed-over thread from the half stitch. A single thread can now be left out, and, after another half hitch, another one can be left out and after a further half hitch another can also be dropped.

Make another self sewing into the next loop and continue in this manner, letting out the threads until the end of the row. Then turn and work along the outer footside edge with half hitches and occasional sewings into the footside, letting out threads as the work proceeds. Sew in the last two ends, or make a double knot and then cut off all the other ends neatly (see fig. 16a).

17 An alternative to Method 14 for completing a circle, perhaps where the thread is somewhat thicker than normal.

Work the last row of the pattern and make sewings with the loops of the starts with each correct corresponding finishing pair (see fig. 12a).

Lay the workers between the first pair and tie a single knot, right-over-left, with that pair. Lay these two pairs between the next pair to be finished and tie a single knot. Leave out three threads and carry the other three remaining to the next pair to be finished. Tie a single knot. Leave out three threads and carry the other three threads to the next pair to be finished. Tie a knot, leave another two threads out, and continue in this way until the end of the row (see fig. 17a).

With a finer thread of the same colour and variety and with a threaded needle, oversew the completed work, leaving out one thread at each stage as it has been oversewn (see fig. 17b). This makes a considerably neater finish for coarser work, as the overall roll is finer than with the alternative method.

18 This is a method for joining loose net or grounds. Make sewings with the pairs that are completed with the corresponding start. Do *not* tie a knot. Take a finer thread of the same variety and colour. Oversew the sewings and the ends, leaving out single threads after they have been secured.

The lacemaker may find it rather easier to work this method off the pillow. All the threads can then be cut off finally close to the completed work when the roll has been finished (see fig. 18a).

19 This method is suitable for joining a rectangle or circle, starting both sides at the same time and working in opposite directions to meet at the centre of the base. The method could be used for a picture frame.

Take the workers in their final stitches inwards towards the centre and leave (see fig. 19a).

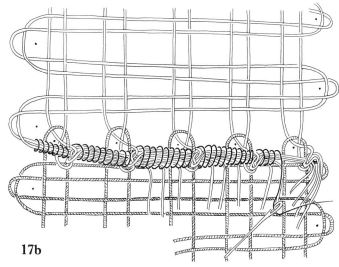

17b

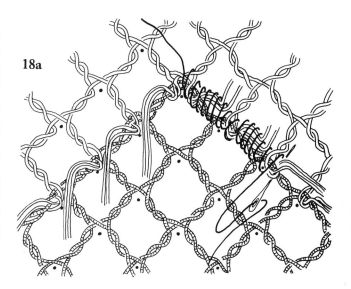

18a

Twist each thread with its opposite number and lay it back over the work on each side (see fig. 19b).

Whole stitch the two workers around the last pin to complete the frame and, working one side at a time, take one of these worker pairs right across the folded pairs (see fig. 19c).

Make a sewing into the edge with this working pair, whole stitch back across the work; make another sewing. Work halfway back across the row and tie off each pair. Cut off each pair close up to the work (see fig. 19d).

Now repeat on the other side in a similar way. When this work is reversed and the join made, all the ends will be virtually invisible.

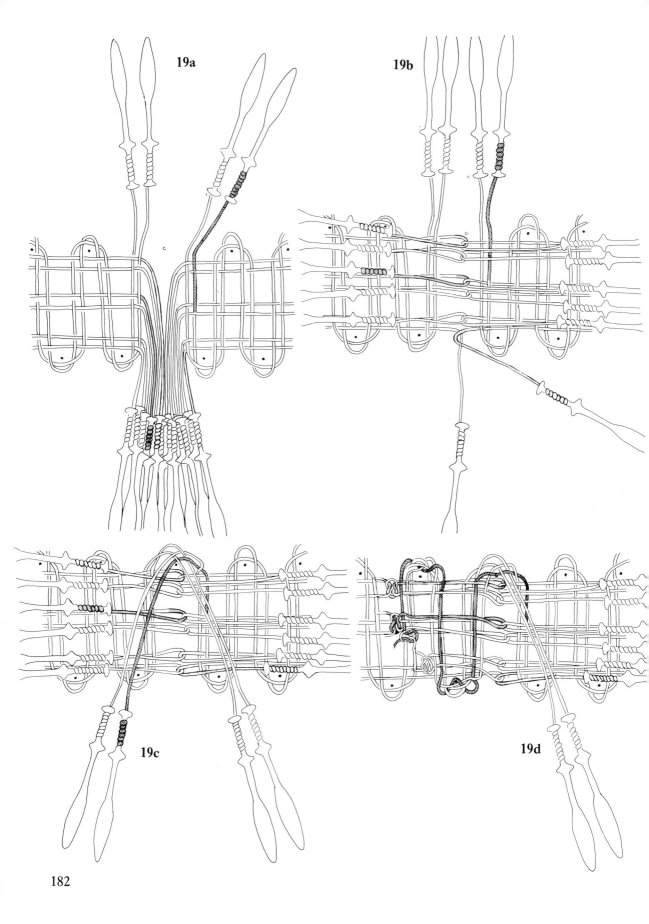

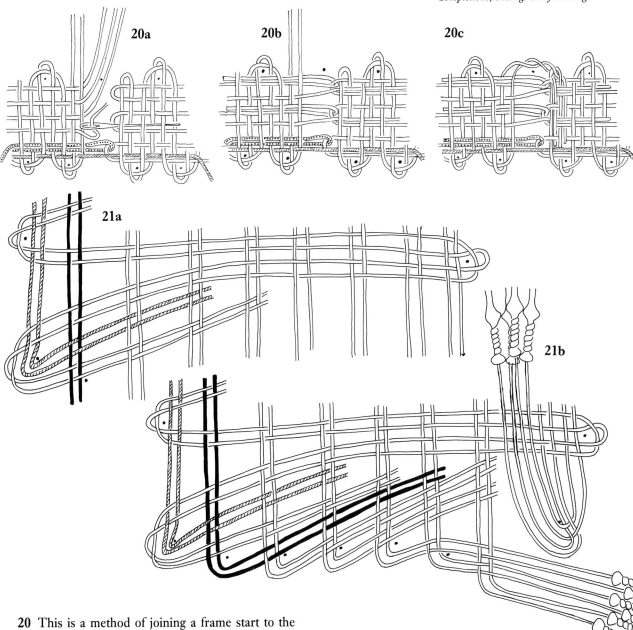

20a   **20b**   **20c**

21a

21b

20 This is a method of joining a frame start to the finish.

Work the last row of the pattern. Leave the worker pair on the inside edge. Starting at the side opposite to where the workers were left, leave about 20 cm of thread and cut the first pair of bobbins off. Thread each thread individually into a needle, one at a time, and weave one thread down into the beginning of the work whilst the other thread of the pair loops through the starting loop. This is then woven back through the work just completed (see fig. 20a).

The aim is for each of the woven threads to correspond with the existing thread lying side by side (see fig. 20b).

Continue right across the work and, lastly, take the worker pair across the work in a similar way (see fig. 20c).

Cut off all the ends close to the completed work. This method makes a slight thickening and is not so attractive when the lace is to be viewed without a background. This join may be more easily worked off the pillow than on.

21 This is to form an ending if it is immaterial how thick the base line is to be.

Turn the worker and the first passive pair around a temporary pin placed as close to the base line as possible. Then whole stitch these two pairs to the

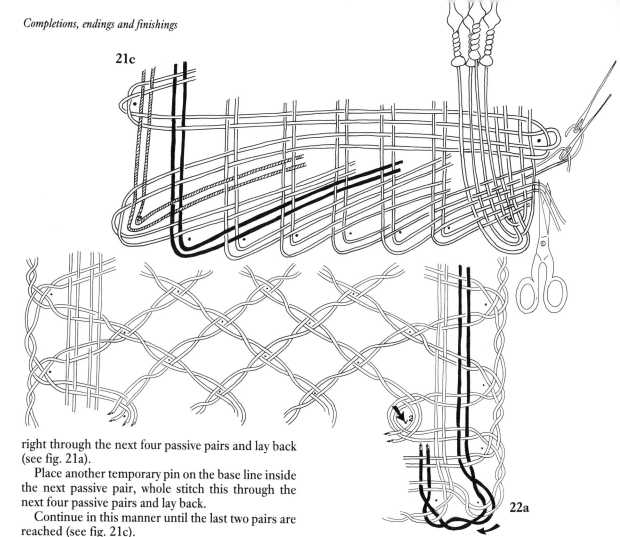

21c

22a

right through the next four passive pairs and lay back (see fig. 21a).

Place another temporary pin on the base line inside the next passive pair, whole stitch this through the next four passive pairs and lay back.

Continue in this manner until the last two pairs are reached (see fig. 21c).

Place another temporary pin at the extreme corner of the base line, turn the last two pairs in the opposite direction around this pin and lay back (see fig. 21c).

Cut off all the bobbins not yet secured, leaving a length of about 20 cm on each thread. Then weave with a needle all the threads individually through each other. This secures these loose ends.

Remove all the temporary pins and gently tighten before again cutting off all the threads close up to the completed work. This produces a fine roll at the end of the work, which is barely discernable.

22 This method finishes off a frame, where the pairs at the end of the work and the frame can be completed simultaneously.

Work to the bottom of the pattern and continue to the right-hand corner of the frame and around the actual corner. The last pin of the pattern is used twice (see fig. 22a).

Work the frame and, taking in pairs from the pattern, work through three whole stitches, after which they can be laid out (see fig. 22b). Then

continue working to the far corner. When this corner is reached, work the corner with the left-hand pairs. By careful manoeuvring, each pair can be whole stitched through the pairs coming from the right, so that every pair has been whole stitched three times. Pull all the pairs uniformly tight and cut off close up to the end of the work (see fig. 22c).

If the lace requires laundering it would be preferable to knot the ends prior to cutting off. But this is not normally necessary.

23 This is another method suitable for completing the frame and the base of a piece of work at the same time, as was Method 22.

Work to the bottom of the pattern, work the left-hand corner of the frame and continue just around this corner. Work one of the edge-pairs back up through the passives of the frame and lay out. Take one of the pattern pairs, work through the frame and make up the outer edge (see fig. 23a).

Leaving these for the moment, work a pair from the pattern through the frame pairs and lay out. Returning to the pairs at the edge, work one pair up through the passives and lay out (see fig. 23b).

Continue in this manner, taking one of the worker pairs and one of the pattern pairs out at each base. Pinhole until the bottom of the frame is completed.

The last four pairs are knotted with their counterparts to complete the frame (see fig. 23c).

This is an orderly and tidy method of ending.

24 This method is suitable for tying out pairs on to a frame when the work is completed.

Make a sewing with the pair to be tied out into the loop of the frame, keeping the shape of the work accurate. Cut off the ends, leaving 20 cm of thread and, with a needle, weave back up into its own thread: about four weavings should secure it. Complete all ends in a similar manner (see fig. 24a).

After the weavings have been completed, cut off the surplus threads.

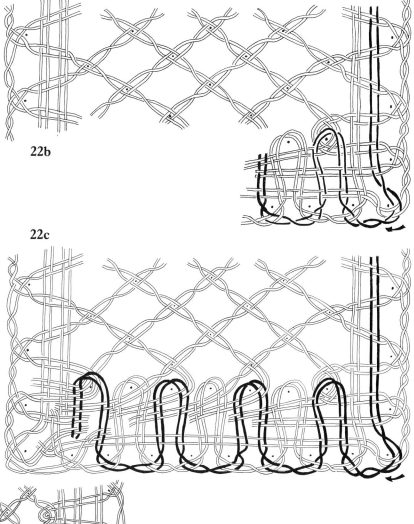

22b

22c

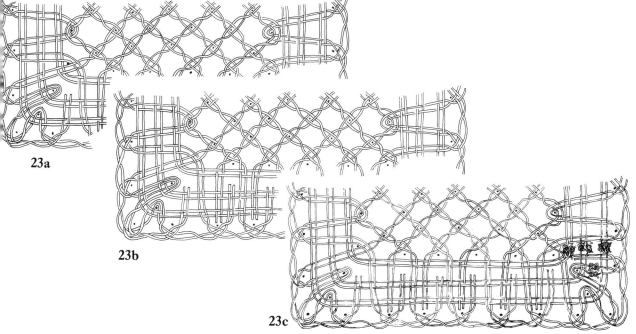

23a

23b

23c

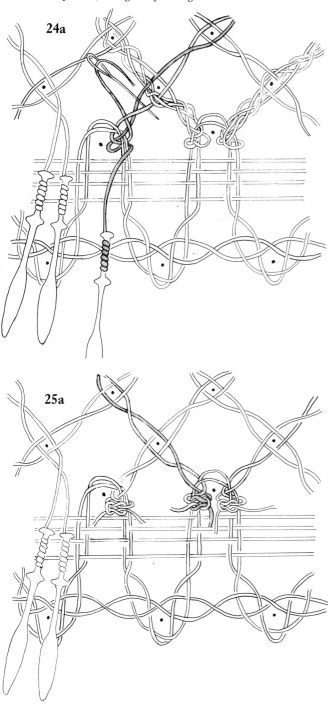

24a

25a

25 An alternative method for tying out pairs on to a frame.

Make a sewing with the pair to be tied out into the loop of the frame, keeping the shape of the work again accurate. Tie a reef knot (right-over-left, left-over-right). Cut off close to the end of the work (see fig. 25a).

Continue similarly for all the other ends.

26 A method suitable for tying out pairs on to a frame and completing the frame in the same manner.

Make sewings into the appropriate loop, keeping the pattern accurate. Take one thread and make a half hitch three or four times around the three threads. This can be tied down by making a sewing with this half hitch thread into the frame and another half hitch before cutting off. The edge of the frame can be completed by taking the pairs around the pin on the base line and half hitching and sewing into the frame, with an extra half hitch to complete. Cut off all loose threads (see fig. 26a).

27 A further method for tying out pairs on to a frame and for completing a frame in the same manner.

Make sewings into the appropriate loops, keeping the pattern again accurate.

Plait the four threads over the frame and then make a knot around the plait with one of the threads. This can then be cut off. Alternatively, make a sewing into one thread of the frame. Make another knot before cutting off close up to the end of the work.

The frame can be finished by taking the pairs around the pin on the base line and plaiting back over itself, finishing with a knot or with another sewing and knot to secure it (see fig. 27a).

28 A method of reducing the number of threads on a pillow if working in whole stitch.

Place the bobbin pair not required to the rear of the pillow. Continue with the work for a few rows and then cut off the threads close to this work. Take care to discard only one pair on each row. Failing this, a hole appears within the work (see fig. 28a).

An alternative method of reducing the number of threads, which many lacemakers find preferable to the previous one.

Take the left-hand thread of a passive pair and leave its partner. Take the left-hand thread of the next pair, laying it underneath the right-hand thread of the first pair. Lay this thread back with the other left-hand thread. This is the pair that will be cut off after the next few rows. The effect will be to prevent a large stepping-stone hole from appearing in the work, as the threads have the effect of drawing the work together.

Continue with the work for a few more rows and, after these rows have been completed, the threads laid back can be cut off (see fig. 28b).

29 To remove a pair from a whole stitch section of lace, which has to be frequently laundered, the lacemaker may prefer the tie method.

Make a single knot with the pair to be tied out, and weave the left-hand thread to the left and the right-hand thread to the right, so that they lie close and

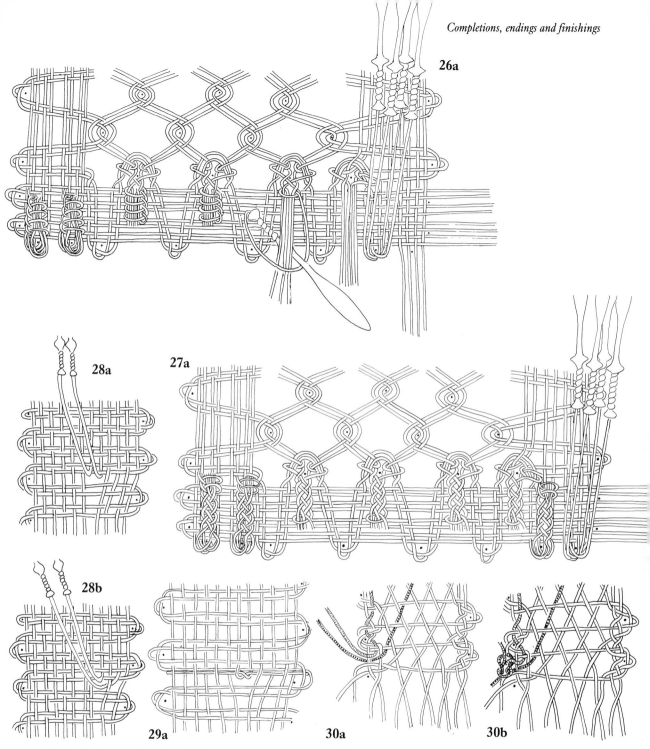

26a

28a

27a

28b

29a

30a

30b

parallel to the last worker thread. Care must be taken that they are woven through the passive pairs to correspond with the movement of the worker thread.

When these two threads reach the edge of the work they are laid back and cut off later (see fig. 29a).

30 It is almost impossible to take out pairs in half stitch unobtrusively in the centre of any piece of work,

and it is therefore usual to try and discard at the edge.

Whole stitch the edge-pair and whole stitch the next pair to it (see fig. 30a).

The pair that was in half stitch will now be lying on the outer edge. After completing some more half stitch this particular pair can be tied off in a reef knot and secured prior to cutting off close to the end of the work (see fig. 30b).

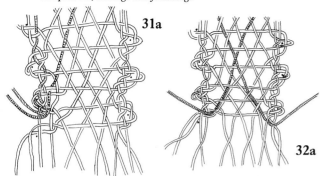

31a

32a

31 This is another method for discarding a pair at the edge in half stitch.

Whole stitch the edge-pair and work across to the other side. On the return, whole stitch the pair before the edge-pair and then the edge-pair as well. Make up the edge.

Work back two whole stitches and then half stitch across the work. The two centre threads of the two adjacent whole stitches can then be laid back. These can be cut off after some more work has been completed as they will have been whole stitched twice and therefore are secure. The hesitant lacemaker may still tie a knot, if worried (see fig. 31a).

32 Although it is preferable never to discard a pair when working half stitch in the centre of the work,

nevertheless it is sometimes required; the best of the methods available is given.

The two centre pairs are held together so that each two threads are treated, in the future, as just one thread. The half stitch is worked in the normal manner, back and forth, but keeping these two threads lying adjacent to each other until the outer edge is reached. For a closer fit, these two threads can be twisted together, but whichever method is used there will be an undoubted thickening throughout the work, which is visually undesirable (see fig. 32a).

33 This method is for working to a point and discarding the pairs, in order to reach this desired goal with footsides.

Work down to the point, leaving out a pair of passives at each line until the point is actually reached. Whole stitch the two footside pairs around the pin (see fig. 33a).

Lay those two pairs between the worker of the footside and tie a reef knot (right-over-left, left-over-right) around them. Divide the threads, three on either side (see fig. 33b).

Lay the three threads on the left-hand side between the first pair that has been left out. Tie a reef knot around them (see fig. 33c).

Cut the two threads which have now been knotted twice and lay the next three up to the next pair left out. Repeat by tying a reef knot around these threads and cut a pair off. Place the next three threads between the next pair (see fig. 33d).

Continue on in a similar manner until the last passive to be tied out is reached. Then tie 1½ reef knots. Cut all the ends off neatly (see fig. 33e).

Repeat on the other side. When the lace is turned over it will be seen that none of the ends will be visible.

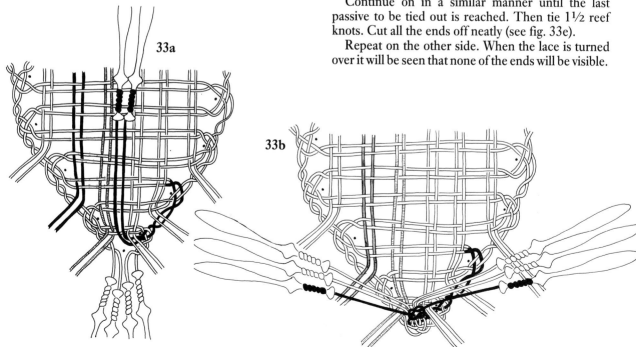

33a

33b

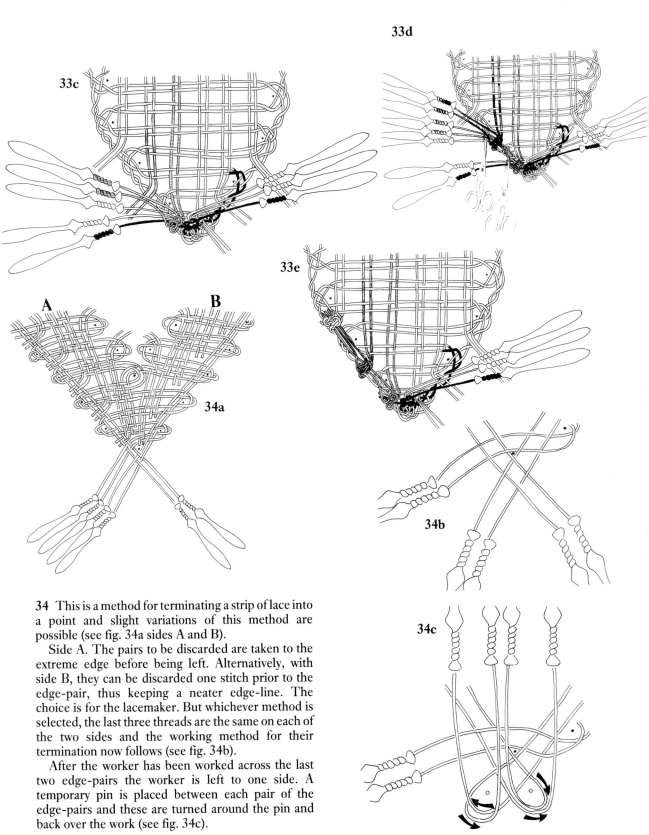

33c

33d

A   **B**

33e

34a

34b

34 This is a method for terminating a strip of lace into a point and slight variations of this method are possible (see fig. 34a sides A and B).

Side A. The pairs to be discarded are taken to the extreme edge before being left. Alternatively, with side B, they can be discarded one stitch prior to the edge-pair, thus keeping a neater edge-line. The choice is for the lacemaker. But whichever method is selected, the last three threads are the same on each of the two sides and the working method for their termination now follows (see fig. 34b).

After the worker has been worked across the last two edge-pairs the worker is left to one side. A temporary pin is placed between each pair of the edge-pairs and these are turned around the pin and back over the work (see fig. 34c).

34c

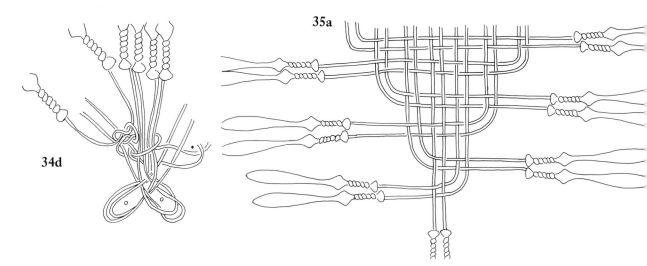

The worker is then wrapped around these two pairs and either a reef knot or a half-hitch may be worked around this bunch, in order to render secure. Remove temporary pins and pull the work tight (see fig. 34d).

Cut off all ends neatly and on the correct front-side a neat, tidy finish will be seen.

35 An additional method of completing a piece of lace that has no footsides, bringing it to a point.

Work the pattern until the start of the point of shaping is reached. Leave the worker on the right-hand side. Using the outside passive pair nearest to where the worker was left, work across to the left-hand side and leave this pair (see fig. 35a).

Take the next passive on the left and again work it across to the right and leave. Continue until all pairs are left out. Weave the threads individually across the work, using a threaded needle (see fig. 35b). This creates the point. Then cut off all the loose ends.

36 This method should be used when working a piece of lace to a point with picots on the outer edge.

A passive is left out on the inside edge as soon as the first point of reduction is reached (see fig. 36a).

Continue to the ultimate point, always working the pair for the reduction through the passive pairs. A picot is then made, that pair is worked back and a previous pair is then omitted (see fig. 36b).

At the ultimate tip, both sides having been worked, a false picot has to be constructed. This is created by working a whole stitch, twisting one pair around the pin and whole stitching back. The false picot has thus been created. These two pairs are then worked through the three pairs on either side back up to the work.

The three pairs on either side that then meet each other in the centre are knotted, thread by thread, one from either side, finishing in six knots (see fig. 36c).

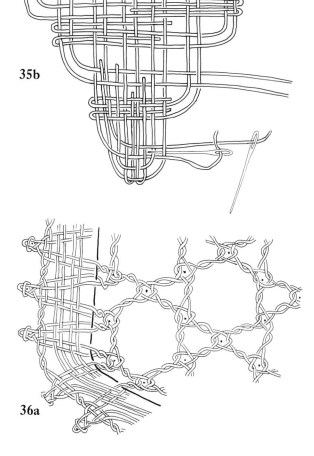

Every other pair that has been left out can now be pulled evenly and cut. On the correct side, when the lace is turned over, a neat and complete edge will be visible.

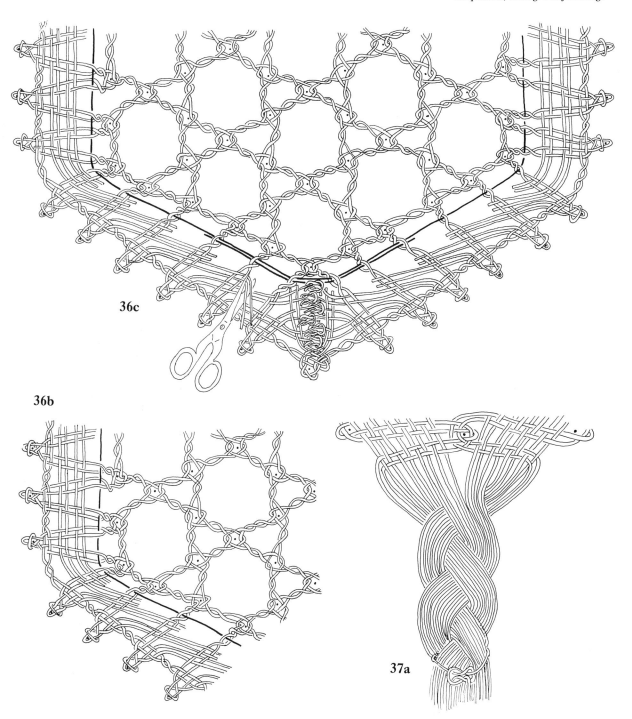

36c

36b

37a

37 This method is the first of several for ending a strip of lace, such as a bookmark, where many pairs need to be taken out at the same place. The method can also be used at the bottom of a large piece of lace, such as a curtain where the pairs can be grouped together. The ending will be found to have a decorative effect.

By far the simplest of the various methods is to divide the pairs into three groups and to braid the pairs together, so making a flat tassel. When the length of braid required is reached, take an outside thread from either side of the braid, cross them over and then wrap them under the braid and secure on top with a reef knot. All ends can then be cut off at an appropriate length as desired (see fig. 37a).

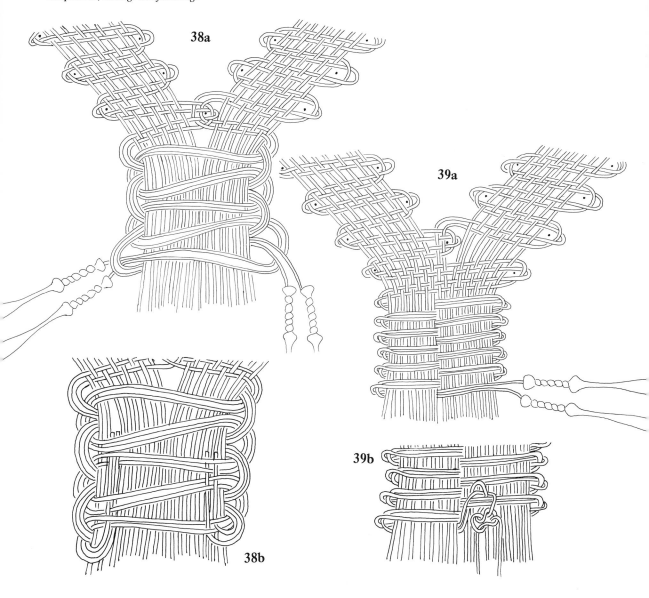

38 As for 37, but using a flat knot. A pair of threads on either side are used to make the flat knot. All the threads are laid carefully down the centre of these two pairs. The pair from the left is then taken under the bunch and over the right-hand pair. Then the right-hand pair is taken over the bunch and the bobbins are tucked down into the loop made by the left-hand pair on the edge of the bunch. The right-hand pair and the left-hand pair are then taken over the work, tucked into the loop made by the pair that travelled underneath (see fig. 38a).

Continue in this way, making sure that the pair that travelled under always remains the under pair and the top pair remains as the top pair.

When the correct length of braid is reached, sew the two pairs up the work, then pull tight. The fringe can be cut off, giving the required length. This gives an interesting scalloped effect down the side of the tassel (see fig. 38b).

39 As for 37 and 38: another method of finishing. Divide the groups of bobbins into two bunches, excluding one pair. Take this pair under the left-hand bunch, over the right-hand bunch, under the right-hand bunch and over the left-hand bunch. Then proceed again under the left-hand bunch and over the right-hand, weaving in this way until a good, flat tally-type tassel is produced (see fig. 39a).

To finish, make a sewing over one of the bunch of threads and a reef knot to tie off (see fig. 39b). All pairs can then be cut off, leaving the appropriate length of tassel.

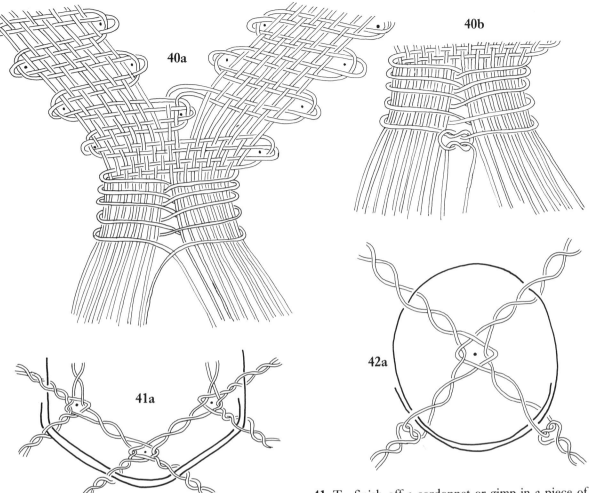

40a

40b

42a

41a

40 Similar to Method 39, with minor variations. Divide the bunch again into two groups and take a thread from either bunch's outside edge. Cross these threads over each bunch, cross them in the centre and take them separately, one to the left and one to the right, under and over the restricted bunches. Cross the threads in the centre again and continue taking them one to the left and one to the right, wrapping them round bunches with the relevant crossings in the middle. Continue until a long tally is produced (see fig. 40a).

To complete, simply tie the two threads into a reef knot in the centre and cut off all threads at the appropriate length (see fig. 40b).

Throughout this section conventional endings have been used. But with some modern threads – man-made and natural – the natural springiness of the fibres may need to receive some degree of glueing in order to prevent fraying. A thinned-down transparent wood glue is quite effective.

41 To finish off a cordonnet or gimp in a piece of work.

Complete the pattern within the cordonnet/gimp. Cross the two cordonnets/gimps over and pass the left-hand cordonnet through two pairs to lie on top of the cordonnet already in place. Repeat this on the right-hand side, ensuring that the two cordonnets lie alongside each other. Then these should be laid back and cut off, after some further work has been completed (see fig. 41a).

42 Another method of finishing off a cordonnet or gimp in a piece of work.

Sometimes the cordonnet will end at a point and after the two cordonnets cross there will only be one pair on either side that the cordonnets can overlap and pass through. If this is the case, after the cordonnets have passed through the single pair on either side, tie a single knot right-over-left with these pairs and this will then secure the ends of the cordonnet. Lay back the cordonnets back and cut off when further work has been completed (see fig. 42a).

43 To remove the surplus pairs at the base of a cordonnet surrounded pattern.

Work the pattern within the cordonnet as normal. At the end of the pattern, cross the cordonnets. Overlap as in Method 41.

The pairs to be taken out are then tied with a single knot, right-over-left around the cordonnet, thus making it easier to pass one thread to the right and one to the left. These are then threaded with the cordonnets. They can be laid back with the cordonnets and cut off when some further work has been completed (see fig. 43a).

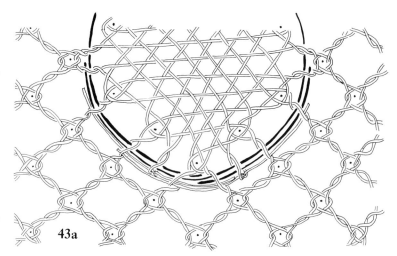

43a

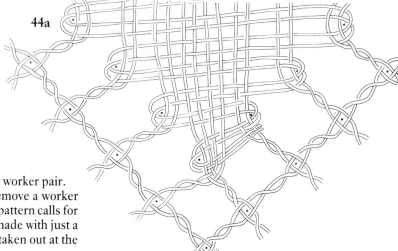

44a

44 This is a method for removing the worker pair.

Although it is unusual to need to remove a worker pair it is sometimes unavoidable if the pattern calls for a thickening infill. This is sometimes made with just a worker pair which therefore has to be taken out at the end of this infill.

Work the infill to its extreme point. Whole stitch the worker back through at least two pairs. Lay back. Continue with the net pattern and, after the completion of some additional work, the pair can then be cut off safely (see fig. 44a).

45 To join and end a piece of lace at an angle on to a completed piece of work.

When the two pieces meet, the worker is sewn and then worked back and, as the joining piece becomes narrower, pairs are laid back. The number laid back varies according to the angle of the join.

Continue with the workers, making sewings at the appropriate places where they touch the completed piece. Continue until all the pairs except the worker pair and the edge pair have been laid back. These two last pairs can then be sewn and knotted into the completed piece and finally tied off. All pairs can then be cut off (see fig. 45a).

46 Similar to Method 45; tying off a piece at an angle on to a completed piece.

The worker is taken across and is sewn into a pin-hole of the completed piece where the two meet. This pair is then tied off in a reef knot. The nearest passive to the edge is then taken across as the worker.

If the angle is acute, the next passive pair to the completed piece is tied off with a sewing and a reef knot on to the completed piece.

If the angle is not so acute, this pair need not be tied out at this point.

The pair that became the worker crosses the work and goes back to the join. A sewing is then made and it is similarly tied off with a reef knot. The next passive becomes the worker and works across the work.

Continue in the same manner until all pairs are tied off, including the final two worker- and edge-pairs (see fig. 46a).

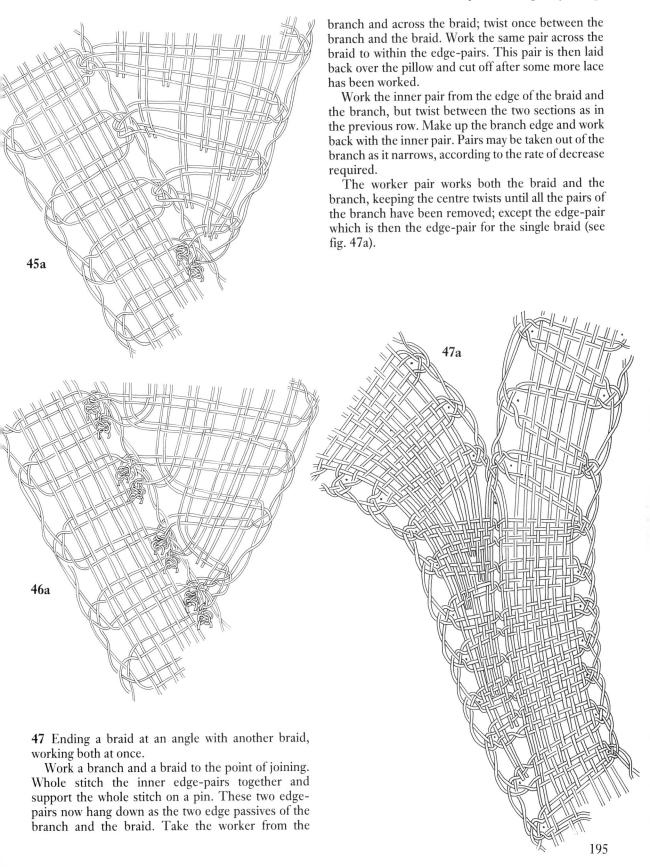

45a

46a

47a

branch and across the braid; twist once between the branch and the braid. Work the same pair across the braid to within the edge-pairs. This pair is then laid back over the pillow and cut off after some more lace has been worked.

Work the inner pair from the edge of the braid and the branch, but twist between the two sections as in the previous row. Make up the branch edge and work back with the inner pair. Pairs may be taken out of the branch as it narrows, according to the rate of decrease required.

The worker pair works both the braid and the branch, keeping the centre twists until all the pairs of the branch have been removed; except the edge-pair which is then the edge-pair for the single braid (see fig. 47a).

47 Ending a braid at an angle with another braid, working both at once.

Work a branch and a braid to the point of joining. Whole stitch the inner edge-pairs together and support the whole stitch on a pin. These two edge-pairs now hang down as the two edge passives of the branch and the braid. Take the worker from the

195

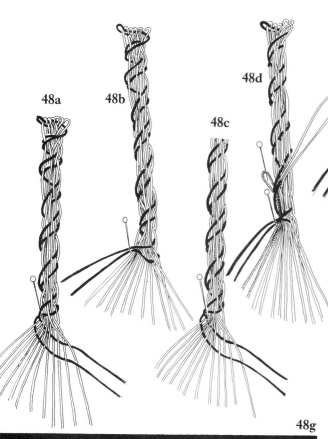

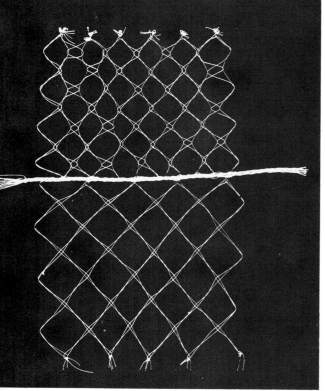

48g

48 To complete a tubular roll finish.

A tubular roll can be formed, into which pairs may be both discarded or added. The tubular roll is a very useful method of removing surplus pairs of bobbins between two different sections of lace, as well as being capable of use as an outside edge, into which pairs may be removed.

To make the roll at least six or seven pairs are needed; the seventh pair being the worker. Whole stitch from the left through all six pairs (see fig. 48a).

When the right-hand side is reached, the worker is laid over the six pairs and a temporary support pin is put under them (see fig. 48b).

It is imperative that the pairs are retained in their correct order. The worker is then taken through again to the right (see fig. 48c).

The worker is then taken back over the roll and the temporary support pin is moved down one stage. After each crossing the pairs must all be gently tightened in order to keep an even roll.

The pairs being removed from the work on the left of the roll are simply incorporated into the roll and, if they are of no further use, then one of the existing pairs can be laid back (not the pairs just taken in) and cut off later – thus keeping the number in the roll fairly constant (see fig. 48d).

It may sometimes be necessary to take two pairs in at the same time. This is possible, but it is preferable to discard at staggered intervals (see fig. 48e).

Similarly, pairs may be taken into the roll on the right-hand side and here again simply worked through them; so incorporating them into the roll without any additional problems. Again, they must be kept in order, so that the tube remains firm and even (see fig. 48f).

The completed roll (see fig. 38g) can be seen to be a neat, yet efficient, method of ending pairs without having to knot them out, as the whole stitch holds the ends firmly and almost invisibly.

MOVING UP AND MOUNTING

Sometimes it is necessary to move the lace up during its construction. The overall pattern may be larger than the pillow. The pillow may also be needed temporarily, thus entailing the move of the lace from one pillow to another.

1 Lay all the bobbins on a cover cloth (see fig. 1a). Fold the sides in of this cover cloth (see fig. 1b). Then fold the bottom over and pin, in order to secure the bobbins in their correct position within this created envelope (see fig. 1c).

Release the tension on the threads by pushing the envelope forward (see fig. 1d). Remove all the pins from the pricking.

Care must be taken that the weight of the envelope does not pull against the lace. The lace and the bobbin-encased envelope can then be lifted quite safely off the first pillow (see fig. 1e).

Prepare the next pillow with the same pricking (see fig. 1f). Place the completed lace and its bobbin envelope on the new pillow, matching up the lace to the pricking underneath (see fig. 1g).

Taking care to place no tension on the threads, insert the pins into the lace and the pricking for about 2 cm up to where the lace was last worked (see fig. 1h). Slowly lower the envelope with bobbins and unfasten the package.

Spread out the bobbins into their correct sequence and the lace is then ready to be continued in its new position (see fig. 1i).

1b

1c

1a

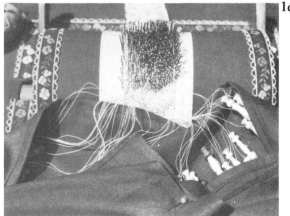

1d

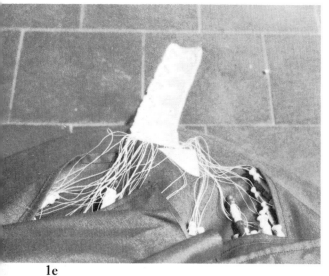

1e

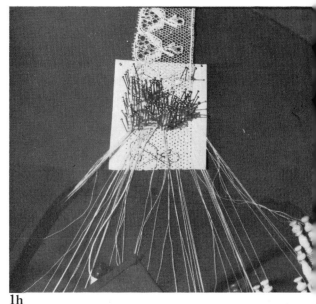

1h

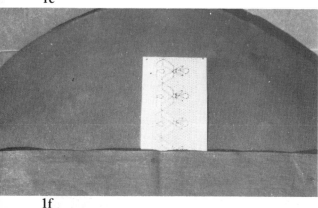

1f

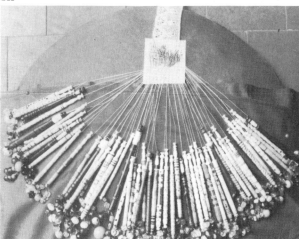

1i

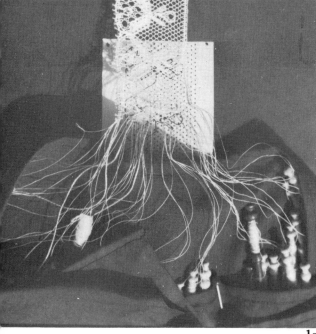

1g

2 A somewhat lazy but easy way of moving the lace up can be achieved by working on to a wedge.

This wedge can be made of several layers of felt or cut from a strip of high density polystyrene foam – the type that does not crumble (see fig. 2a).

Place the wedge under the lace and the pattern to be moved about 3 cm before the moving point is reached (see figs 2b and c).

Work the pattern so that after the 3 cm of lace have been worked the pins for a good 2 cm length are pressed into the wedge only and not the pillow (see fig. 2d).

Fold the envelope around the bobbins and the threads, as for Method 1. This envelope and the completed lace, pins, pricking and wedge can then all be lifted off the pillow (see fig. 2e).

Prepare the new pillow and place the wedge pattern to line up with the pattern in the new position on the pillow; pin in position (see fig. 1f).

Spread the bobbins out and continue working down the wedge on to the new pillow, until the lace has been worked about 2 cm beyond the wedge.

At this stage the wedge can be removed. This does save moving the pins and replacing them (see fig. 2g).

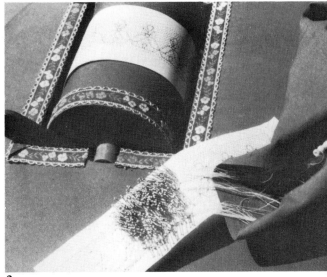

2e

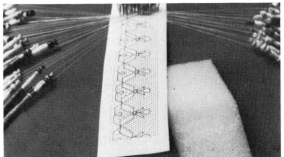

2a

2b

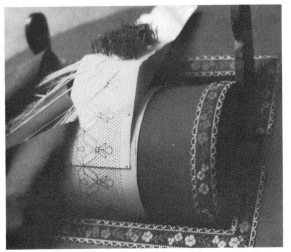

2f

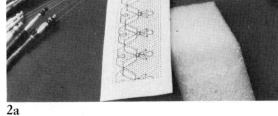

2c   2d

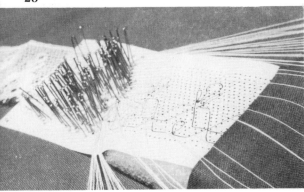

2g

Mounting the lace

When mounting lace, the most important matter to consider is the necessity to match the lace with the right weight of fabric. The lace must grace the fabric it is to be attached to and not lost on a fabric which is too heavy or appears to be unrelated to it. Both fabric and lace should blend, in order to give an overall aesthetic balance to the beauty of both.

The lace can be mounted in two main ways.

1 The material can be prepared so that it is the exact size in order to fit the lace.

2 Alternatively, the edge of the fabric and the lace can be worked simultaneously. There are several methods of preparing the fabric.

3 A hem can be made to the shape and size of the lace.

Many books on sewing and embroidery give several decorative variations of hem stitching. For a plain hem, pull a thread to mark a straight line along the fabric. Turn the material over twice so that the raw edge is along the inner fold. Tack the hem into position and press. The stitches are worked from the right to the left on the wrong side.

Only one or two threads of the fold of the hem should be taken into the needle. The stitch should slant (as in fig. 3a). They should be small and evenly spaced. The corners will need to be mitred.

4 If using a very fine fabric then the edge can be prepared before the lace is attached. Alternatively, in one process, the lace can be attached whilst the edge is being worked.

Roll up a fine roll of the edge between the thumb and index finger and, working on the wrong side, whip under the roll over and back under. On completion, the seam should be smoothed out.

If the lace is to be attached at the same time, the needle passes under the roll and into the edge of the lace, then back over the roll. (See figs 4a and 4b, showing the wrong and the right sides of the lace attached in this way.)

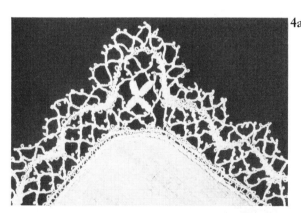

4a

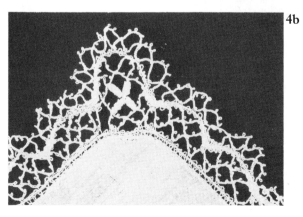

4b

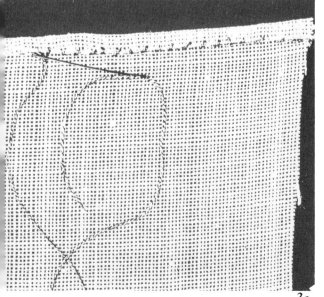

3a

5 For coarser fabrics the material can be prepared before the lace is attached.

With a fine crochet hook and the thread used for the lace, crochet a row of double crochet stitches along the edge. The raw edge can be worked on (see fig. 5a) or the edge can be folded over and a row of double crochet stitches worked on the fold (see fig. 5b). These stitches must be neat and each must be made close up to the next and not more than three or four threads of the fabric deep.

On completion of the crochet edge the excess material can be cut away close to the base of the stitches (see fig. 5c). The lace can then be attached to the top of the crochet stitches with an oversew stitch. This allows the lace to stand above the fabric; the crochet stitches make a good oversewn hem (see fig. 5d).

6 The fabric can also be oversewn, in order to produce a very neat edge before the lace is attached.

Pull off the excess threads, leaving about 1 cm of upright threads showing. Starting on the left side, fold down the first few threads to lie along the top of the fabric.

Oversew along this edge, working over the threads which have been laid down to a depth of about three threads. The tiny threads which have been laid down prevent the edge then pulling away from the fabric (see fig. 6a and 6b).

If an uneven shape or circle of fabric is to be prepared, it is best to machine a single row around the edge, before cutting the material to about 2 cm larger

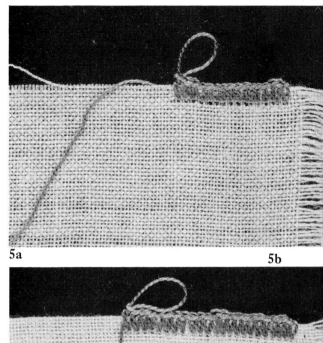

5a

5b

5c

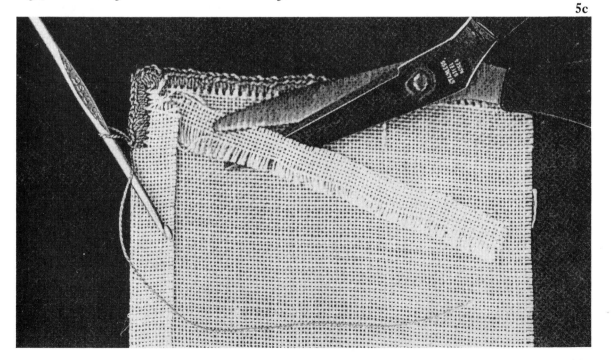

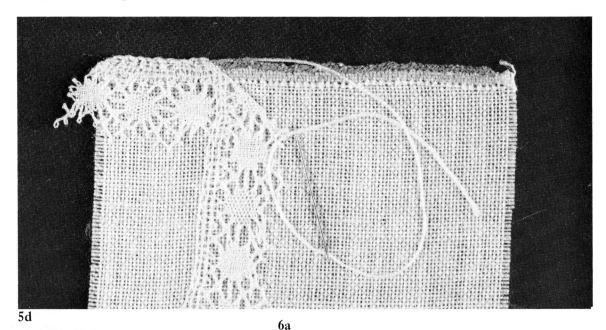

5d

6a

6b

than that required. Work slowly, cutting only about 3 cm at a time, down to 1 cm above the edge.

Pull the excess threads off the edge. The machine line of stitches will be the guide line. Hold the upright threads down and oversew the folded-down threads over the row of machine stitches, to a depth of about three threads. These will be a different three threads as the circle progresses.

7 Three-sided punch stitch.
Lace can be mounted at the same time as the edge is worked. Pull a thread of fabric as a guide line for a straight edge. The fabric can be folded on this line to give a double thickness to the hem, or it can be left standing up under the lace. In either case the excess fabric will be cut off at a later stage.

Pin the lace to the fabric, leaving about 2 cm of excess material all the way round. Tack the lace in place. The three-hole punch stitch is one of several suitable stitches for working the material and lace together.

Use a fairly coarse needle, as this parts the threads of the fabric and thus makes a feature of the stitch. Work on the correct side (see fig. 7a) for the positions A, B, C and D, and also for the repeat position B/A B D/C and D. Place the needle in at A and out at B, then in at A and out at B again. Then in at C and out at B, in at C and out at D, repeat in at C and out at D. Place needle in at B and out at D. Place needle in at B, now remarked A.

The sequence is then repeated with all the lettering having moved one place to the left, so that the place which was B is now A and so on (see fig. 7b).

All the excess fabric can then be cut away.

202

8 Four-sided stitch. This is an alternative method of working over the folded or unfolded edge and the lace.

Prepare the fabric and the lace by marking out and tacking the lace to the fabric. This stitch can be worked on either side, but is usually worked on the correct side (see fig. 8a) For the position of the lettering and the instructions see fig. 8a.

From position A, place needle in at B and out at A. Place needle in at B and out at C. Place needle in at A and out at C. Place needle in at A and out at D. Place needle in at B and out at D. Place the needle in at B and out at C. Move the lettering along to the left one space and repeat the sequence. The needle at C is now the new A (see fig. 8a).

If each stitch is pulled fairly tightly, a decorative edge is formed with a square pattern on the right side and a neat X over the pattern on the reverse.

This is a strong, successful and decorative method of joining lace to all materials.

9 A crossover stitch can also be used.
Prepare the fabric and lace as for Method 8, working on the correct side, from left to right. For the position of the lettering and the instructions see fig. 9a. Place the needle in at C and out at B (understitch). Repeat. Place the needle in at E and out at D (understitch). Repeat.

Move all the lettering along to the right one place and repeat the sequence. Always catch only two or three threads in the needle between B C and D E. The stitches can be pulled firmly. This adds to the overall decorative effect of the stitch (see fig. 9a).

10 Oversewing. The edge of the fabric can be neatened at the same time as attaching the lace.

Lay the lace and the fabric with the reverse sides together so that the edge of the lace is just below the raw edge of the fabric. Pin, then tack into position.

The fabric may be turned into a fold. This fold lies between the lace and the fabric. Oversew with small stitches. One oversew stitch is needed for each thread of the fabric, about three threads deep.

The edge of the lace will be caught in the oversewn stitch at the deepest point, so that only the very edge of the lace is caught within the stitch (see fig. 10a).

On completion, fold up the lace and press. If the fabric has been turned in then cut off any surplus fabric close to the row of stitches (see fig. 10b).

On the correct side, after pressing, a small neat roll of stitches will be arranged along the edge of the fabric and the lace attached will stand up quite free and clear (see fig. 10c).

11 The oversew stitch at Method 10 can also be used on any irregular shaped lace.

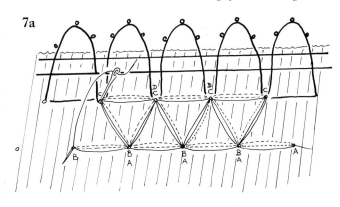

7a

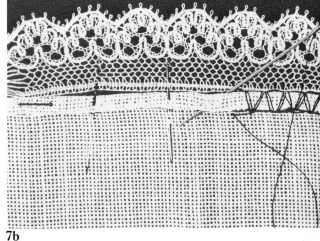

7b

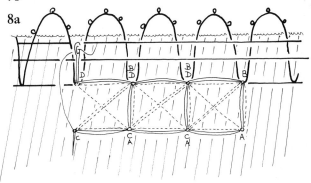

8a

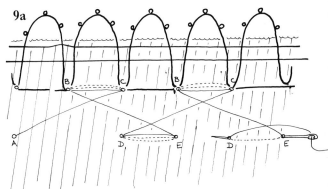

9a

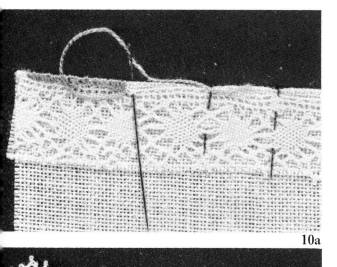

Place the lace in the position required and tack down. The fabric will not be able to be turned under, so it is necessary to work in neat oversew stitches to a depth of at least three threads. Between each thread of the fabric, catch the outside footside threads of the lace only. On completion, trim all the spare fabric close to the stitches (see fig. 11a).

12 An alternative stitch to the oversew stitch is a small button hole stitch, which can be made over the lace and the fabric.

The stitches should be small, evenly spaced and placed as close together as possible. Fold the material with the lace tacked thereon upwards when working. Start on the left-hand side and work to the right. Place the needle in the material, about three threads lower than the edge of the lace. Bring the needle up through the material and the footside of the lace.

Hold the thread down with the left thumb and make a loop. Place the needle into the material close to the last entry. Bring the needle up under the material and the edge of the lace and over the small loop formed by the temporarily held part of the thread.

This stitch is then repeated all around the work. On the completion the spare material is cut away (see figs 12a and 12b for the photograph of the correct and reverse sides of the button hole stitch).

13 If the lacemaker has insufficient time to attach the lace with hand sewing, it may be joined with the zig-zag stitch on a sewing machine.

If worked neatly this can give the appearance of hand oversewing.

10a

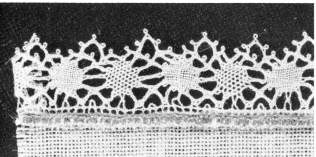

10b

10c

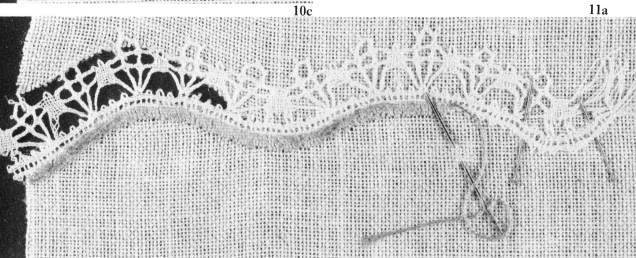

11a

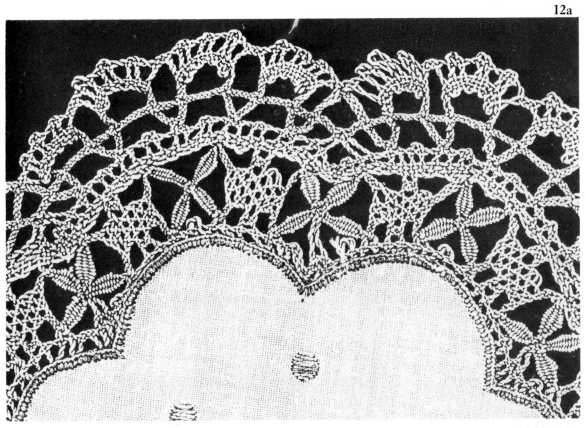

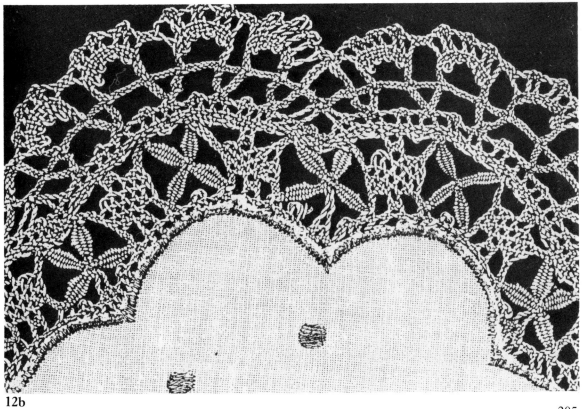

12b

LACE SUPPLIERS

United Kingdom

Christien Bobbins
26 Cedar Drive
Kingsclere
Newbury
Bucks RG15 8TD

Frank Hemming & Sons
27 High West Street
Dorchester
Dorset DT1 1UP

D.J. Hornsby
149 High Street
Burton Latimer
Kettering
Northants NN15 5RL

All branches of John Lewis

Lambourn Valley Cottage
  Industries
Lambourn
Berks RG16 7XS

Mace and Nairn
89 Crane Street
Salisbury
Wiltshire SP1 2PY

Dorothy Pearce
5 Fulshaw Avenue
Wilmslow
Cheshire SK9 5JA

Bryn Phillips
'Pantglas'
Cellan
Lampeter
Dyfed SA48 8JD

Silk threads
Jack Piper
'Silverlea'
Flax Lane
Glensford
Suffolk CO10 7RS

J.S. Sear
Lacecraft Supplies
8 Hill View
Sherington
Bucks MK16 9NJ

Sebalace
Waterloo Mill
Howden Road
Silsden
West Yorks BD20 0HA

A. Sells
49 Pedley Lane
Clifton
Shefford
Bedfordshire

D.H. Shaw
47 Zamor Crescent
Thurcroft
Rotherham
S Yorks S66 9QD

S.M.P.
4 Garners Close
Chalfont St Peter
Bucks SL9 0HB

Christine and David Springett
21 Hillmorton Road
Rugby
Warwickshire CV22 5DF

George White
Delaheys Cottage
Thistle Hill
Knaresborough
North Yorks

United States of America

Robin and Russ Handweavers
533 North Adams Street
McMinnvills
Oregon 97128

Robin's Bobbins
RTL Box 1736
Mineral Bluff
Georgia 30559

Lacis
2150 Stuart Street
Berkely
California 94703

Frivolité
15526 Densmore N
Seattle
Washington 98113

Van Scriver Bobbin Lace
130 Cascadilla Park
Ithaca
New York 14850

Belgium

Kancentrum
Balstraat 14
8000 Brugge

Manufacture Belge de Dentelle
6 Galerie de la Reine
Galeries Royales St Hubert
1000 Bruxelles

West Germany

Der Fensten Laden
Berliner Str 8
D6483 Bad Soden
Salmünster

P.P. Hempel
Ortolanweg 34
1000 Berlin 47

Heikina De Ruijter
Kloeppelgrosshandel
Langer Steinweg 38
D4933 Blomberg

Bobbin makers

T. Brown
Temple Lane Cottage
Littledean
Cinderford
Gloucestershire

T. Parker
124 Carhampton Road
Boscombe East
Bournemouth BH6 5NZ

Sources of information

The Lace Guild
The Hollies
53 Audnam
Stourbridge
West Midlands DY8 4AE

The Lace Society
Linwood
Stratford Road
Oversley
Alcester
Warwickshire BY9 6PG

The British College of Lace
21 Hillmorton Road
Rugby
Warwickshire CV2 5DF

The English Lace School
Honiton Court
Rockbeare
Nr Exeter
Devon

English Director: International Old Lacers
Mrs Susan Hirst
4 Dollius Road
London N3 1RG

INDEX